DeskJet Unlimited

2nd edition

Steve Cummings

PEACHPIT PRESS

DESKJET UNLIMITED
2nd Edition
Steve Cummings

Peachpit Press, Inc.
2414 Sixth Street
Berkeley, CA 94710
415/548-4393

Copyright © 1991 by Steve Cummings and Peachpit Press, Inc.

Trademarks:
Many of the designations used by manufacturers and sellers to distinguish their products are claimed as trademarks. Rather than printing a trademark symbol with every occurrence of a trademarked product name throughout this book, we state that we are using the names only in an editorial fashion and to the benefit of the trademark owner, with no intention of infringement of the trademark.

Notice of Liability:
The information in this book is distributed on an "As Is" basis, without warranty. Neither the author nor Peachpit Press shall have any liability to any person or entity with respect to any liability, loss, or damage casued or alleged to be caused directly or indirectly by the instructions contained in this book or by the computer software and hardware products described herein.

0 9 8 7 6 5 4 3 2 1
Printed and bound in the United States of America
ISBN 0-938151-11-8

Introduction

✦

This second edition of *DeskJet Unlimited* testifies to the worldwide popularity of Hewlett-Packard's marvel of economical, high-quality desktop printing, the DeskJet. Since I wrote the first edition of this book almost two years ago, the DeskJet's skyrocketing sales have made it one of the standard personal computer printers. These days, nearly every up-to-date software program comes ready to work with the DeskJet. That makes it much easier to take advantage of all the DeskJet's capabilities than it was when I first wrote this book.

But there's still a lot to know about your printer if you want to get the best possible printouts from every software program you use. *DeskJet Unlimited* has the information you need to get the most from your printer. Whether you're looking for the simplest way to print attractive documents or for advanced details on DeskJet programming, whether you're interested in printing fancy illustrated newsletters or staid business correspondence, this book will show you how to get the job done. This second edition has beenbrought fully up to date with all the major software versions current at publication time, including WordPerfect 5.1, Microsoft Word 5.5, Lotus 1-2-3 Release 2.3, and Microsoft Windows 3.0.

Between these two covers you'll find a wealth of practical advice and how-to-do-it procedures on everything from basic maintenance through specific software programs to full-scale DeskJet programming. There's a great deal of material you won't find in the *Owner's Manual*. For example, I've included background details on how the DeskJet's ink cartridges work in Chapter 1, and I've devoted three full chapters to an extended discussion of what fonts are and how they should be used in Section II. For completeness, I've included most of the information from the DeskJet *Owner's Manual*, although the discussions of many important topics are considerably enlarged. In many places in the book, I've highlighted important concepts or procedures by printing them as supplementary tips, cautions, and notes. Whenever possible, I've pointed you toward other resources for further information.

One important point should be made clear at the outset: *DeskJet Unlimited* is primarily a book about using the DeskJet with MS-DOS computers, the millions of IBM PC-compatibles now in use worldwide. Section III on application software is devoted exclusively to MS-DOS programs, and the utilities and special-purpose programs described in Chapters 4 and 18 through 20 are all DOS-based products. Nevertheless, if you're using the DeskJet with another computer or operating system, you'll still find much useful information in the first two sections on DeskJet basics and fonts, and in the extensive chapter on DeskJet programming in Section IV.

Chapter-by-chapter summary

Here's a summary of the contents of *DeskJet Unlimited*:

Section I, Fundamentals, introduces the DeskJet and how it works.

Chapter 1, Meet the DeskJet, provides an overview of the DeskJet's capabilities and its few limitations. You'll learn about the technology under your printer's hood, with special emphasis on the unique inkjet system designed specially for the DeskJet.

Chapter 2, DeskJet Hardware, focuses on the mechanical aspects of operating your printer: how to connect the DeskJet to your computer, how to use the function switches, how to operate the keypad buttons and lights, how to load paper, and how to perform basic maintenance.

Chapter 3, The Brain in the Machine, explains what's involved in getting the DeskJet to print what you want it to. You'll learn how your computer and the DeskJet communicate, and how the DeskJet's built-in computer translates the data it receives into printed text and graphics.

In Chapter 4, DeskJet Utilities, you'll see how a variety of inexpensive software programs that can make printing easier and more efficient by setting up the DeskJet for you, and by minimizing the time you spend waiting for your printer to finish.

Section II, Fonts, explores the rudiments of typography in theory and in practice with the DeskJet.

Chapter 5, Typographic Fundamentals, explains the differences between typefaces and fonts and offers definitions of many other basic typographic terms as well. You'll also learn tips on how to use type effectively to produce attractive documents that communicate well.

In Chapter 6, DeskJet Fonts, you'll get an overview of the kinds of fonts available for use with the DeskJet and how to access them in your documents. A short section is devoted to cartridge fonts.

Chapter 7, Using Soft Fonts and Scalable Type, is devoted to a detailed exploration of the types of fonts that offer the greatest variety and flexibility: soft fonts, the kind you can buy on floppy disks, and scalable type faces, which can be printed at any size. You'll learn how to prepare your printer for soft fonts, how to install them on your computer's hard disk, and how to use them in your letters and reports. The chapter also covers a variety of font-oriented utilities that simplify soft font management and give you more font choices.

Section III, Application Software, contains a compendium of techniques for getting the most out of your DeskJet with your favorite programs.

Chapter 8, Working with Applications, outlines a general approach you can take with any program to ensure you're using the DeskJet to its top potential.

Chapter 9, Controlling the DeskJet from DOS, shows you how to send printer commands and print plain text files directly from DOS.

In Chapter 10, Microsoft Windows, you'll find an outline of Windows' capabilities and limitations when it comes to the DeskJet. I then run through the procedures for installing Windows for the DeskJet and for adding DeskJet support to an existing Windows system. The chapter closes with a discussion of how to print from any Windows program.

Chapter 11, Word Processing, is devoted to the most popular PC application of all. DeskJet-specific techniques are detailed for top-sellers WordPerfect and Microsoft Word, and you'll also find information on many other popular word processors as well.

Chapter 12, Desktop Publishing, opens with an overview of desktop publishing and the DeskJet's capabilities in this area. I then discuss the most popular PC desktop publishing software from heavyweights Ventura Publisher and PageMaker to inexpensive but capable packages such as Publish-It!.

Chapter 13, Graphics Software, describes the basic types of graphics programs (paint, draw, and illustration) and includes capsule studies of the some of the top programs from each class.

In Chapter 14, Charting Software, you'll learn about the programs that let you communicate data visually via pie charts, bar graphs, and the like.

Chapter 15, Spreadsheets, describes the basic techniques you can use to control the DeskJet from any spreadsheet program. It then goes on to cover DeskJet-related specifics on 1-2-3, Quattro Pro, and Excel, and SuperCalc, which together account for the vast majority of spreadsheet sales.

In Chapter 16, Database Software, you'll discover that although the DeskJet isn't the right printer for high-volume database printing, it can be ideal for the summary reports for which many people use their databases. dBase and Paradox receive specific attention here.

Chapter 17, Forms, Labels, and Faxes, offers some basics on using the DeskJet for these everyday business printing chores.

Section IV, Special Topics, covers a variety of miscellaneous ways to use your DeskJet.

Chapter 18, Printing Envelopes, shows you how to load envelopes into your printer and how to print them conveniently from DOS or your word processor. An excellent envelope printing utility for the DeskJet is also profiled.

In Chapter 19, Printing Screenshots, you'll learn why and how to print out images captured from your PC's screen on the DeskJet. A variety of screen capture utilities are discussed, and there's a special section on capturing screens from Windows.

Chapter 20, Pretty in PostScript, introduces the special software that can turn your DeskJet into an excellent imitation of a true PostScript printer.

Chapter 21, Printing with the Macintosh, shows you how to hook up your DeskJet to a Mac and print successfully. You wouldn't buy a DeskJet as a Macintosh printer, but if you have a DeskJet and want to use it with a Mac, this chapter has the instructions you'll need.

Chapter 22, DeskJet Programming, provides extensive coverage of all the commands you can issue from your computer to control the DeskJet. For each command, I've provided a quick reference summary as well as an extended explanation.

Chapter 23, Troubleshooting, offers advice on how to deal with just about anything that can go wrong with your printer.

Appendix A provides samples of many of the DeskJet's built-in character sets. Appendix B contains a brief list of sources for up-to-date information on the DeskJet. Completing the book is a comprehensive index. I've worked hard to make the index complete and consistent, so you should be able to find the topic you're interested in quickly.

The inevitable disclaimer

Although I've tried my best to make this book accurate, the number, variety, and complexity of the concepts and products I've covered make occasional errors almost unavoidable. Please be sure to test the procedures I recommend with sample data before relying on them for vital files or documents. Although I believe my judgements and recommendations regarding specific software products are fair and well-informed, you should use them to complement, not replace, your own investigations. Keep in mind that most software is revised or upgraded every few months, so that some details that were up-to-date when I wrote the text will already be incorrect by the time the book is published.

Conventions

Tips, notes, and cautions are printed in italic type for emphasis. As in most computer books, keys you're to press are printed in boldface. Special keys that don't correspond to printed characters are indicated by ovals containing the abbreviations or symbols that appear on most keyboards, for example (ALT), (ESC), and (F2). The Enter or Return key is represented by the symbol (↵). When you're supposed to press two keys at the same time they are printed side by side, like this: (CTRL)C.

Any suggestions?

If there's anything you've learned about the DeskJet that you'd like to share with a wider audience, feel free to send me your tips and tricks in care of Peachpit. I'll see to it that they get into the second edition. Likewise, if there are any additional topics you'd like to see covered, or if you have any other suggestions about how to improve the book, please let me know.

—Steve Cummings

Acknowledgements

These acknowledgements are brief, but my debt is great and my gratitude profound. Thanks first to my publisher, Ted Nace, for his generosity in proposing the book, his trust and help as the project took shape, and his patience during the delays before its completion. Thanks also to my editors, proofreaders, and parents, Selden and Celia Cummings. Both teachers, they found and helped me correct many glaring errors and stylistic lapses in my manuscript drafts; those that remain are my own fault. Thanks are due as well to Greg Wallace and Cathy Hiemstra at Hewlett-Packard who got me started with the DeskJet at the beginning and helped me get the facts straight at the end; to Skene Moody and Gary Elfring, who willingly provided their hard-earned DeskJet secrets; and to Bob Cowart for my career as a writer. Finally, deep and contrite obeisances to my wife Diana and my daughters Amy and Laura.

Production notes

DeskJet Unlimited was produced in my home office using PC-Write with Mouse on Fire for word processing, and Ventura Publisher for layout. Prinicipal fonts are Adobe's ITC Garamond Light, Avante Garde, and Sonata. Paperback Software's Keycap Fonts provides the keyboard symbols. I threw together an admittedly rough PostScript font of my own for a few stray symbols (such as the escape character, ◄) with ZSoft's Publisher's Type Foundry. HiJaak, Hotshot Grab, GrafPlus, Collage Plus, Tiffany Plus, and Scrapbook+ were all used to capture the screen illustrations.

This time around, I used a Dell 320N notebook PC for revisions and writing, and a "Hi-Tech USA" desktop with an Imtec full-screen monitor for layout and printing of the book itself. Final text pages were printed on a LaserJet III equipped with an HP PostScript cartridge. The full-page sample DeskJet printouts (for example, the font sampler in Chapter 7 and the PostScript page in Chapter 20) were actually printed by a DeskJet Plus. The character set tables in Appendix A were also printed on the DeskJet. All pages were reduced photographically by 18 percent to the final 7 x 9" trim size. The book was printed conventionally.

Contents

SECTION I—Fundamentals

SECTION II—Fonts

Chapter 7: Using Soft Fonts and Scalable Type   **73**

SECTION III—Application Software

SECTION IV—Special Topics

Fundamentals

1

Meet the DeskJet

❧

Before February 1988, the revolution in document quality begun by laser printers had yet to show up in most people's day-to-day letters and reports. Despite the laser printer's awesome ability to produce documents that look professionally typeset, laser machines were just too expensive for many personal computer users, and too big to fit on their desks.

All that changed with the arrival of Hewlett-Packard's DeskJet. The DeskJet was the first printer costing less than $1000 that could match the text clarity, font variety, and graphics detail of a laser printer—and it fit comfortably in almost any workspace. Today, DeskJet owners have it even better. The

DeskJet 500 prints faster and provides better text quality and more font variety than its predecessors, and you can buy it for about $500.

The DeskJet's place in the printer landscape

HP built the DeskJet as a personal business printer for all those documents that have to look really sharp—business letters, short reports, occasional newsletters, anything for which appearance counts almost as much as content. In describing the DeskJet as a "personal" printer, I mean that you don't have to share it with other people—unlike a big office laser printer, the DeskJet can sit on your own desk, attached to your personal computer, available immediately whenever you need it. But this printer is clearly a tool for serious professionals.

By design, the DeskJet has a combination of traits that make it nearly ideal for its intended role. Though it prints at the same resolution as a laser printer, the DeskJet is much smaller and lighter, considerably quieter, and much less costly, all of which make it easier for you or your boss to justify buying a DeskJet for your personal use.

Of course, the DeskJet isn't the printer for every job. For nuts-and-bolts business duties, especially when print volume is high, a fast, sturdy, conventional dot matrix printer is still the most economical and most productive printer you can buy. When you're printing in high volume but you need sharper-looking output than you get from a dot matrix, or if you want to get into desktop publishing in a big way, nothing short of an industrial strength laser printer will do—but the whole office may have to share it.

Inside the DeskJet: Inkjet technology

Key to many of the DeskJet's advantages is its inkjet technology. Like all inkjet printers, the DeskJet employs a tightly-packed array of tiny nozzles to transfer ink to the printed page. Each nozzle squirts its own precisely aimed jet of ink, and the DeskJet creates text and graphics by firing groups of nozzles corresponding to the intended pattern in perfectly timed bursts as the printhead moves sideways across the page.

Of course, there have been plenty of other inkjet printers, the most successful being HP's redoubtable ThinkJet. The DeskJet's real claim to fame is its sharp, high resolution output. With the tiniest ink nozzles going, the DeskJet competes dot-for-dot with the resolution of office laser printers like the LaserJet. Like most laser printers, the DeskJet lays down 300 evenly spaced dots per inch (dpi), both vertically and horizontally, or 90,000 dots per square inch. The dots are so small and they blend together so seamlessly that DeskJet text looks very nearly as clean as what you get from a typewriter or daisy wheel printer. When printing graphics, the DeskJet turns out the same 300-dpi resolution output, and the resulting images are as clear as you can get from any remotely affordable printer. By comparison with lasers, the DeskJet does a better job with solid black areas, since it deposits a uniformly dark swath of ink, while the blacks printed by lasers tend to be splotchy gray.

Actually, although the DeskJet's printhead can lay down no more than 300 dots along an inch of paper, it can be positioned with an accuracy of $\frac{1}{600}$ of an inch in the horizontal direction. Software that takes advantage of this precision can place the dots just where they should go to reduce the jaggedness of curved edges to an absolute minimum.

Because there's no pounding of a metal printhead on a platten, the DeskJet is much quieter than "impact" printers such as standard dot matrix models or the old-style "letter quality" machines (the kind with fixed, completely formed characters on a daisy wheel or ball). During each pass of the DeskJet's inkjet printhead, you hear a gentle rubbing sound, like a very quiet and unobstrusive sanding. In fact, the DeskJet is quieter overall than a laser printer, since there's no continuous fan noise, and nothing like the jet-taking-off whoosh you hear when a laser prints a page.

A quick heft will establish that the DeskJet is also much, much lighter than any laser printer, another reason it's more practical as a desktop companion for your PC. The DeskJet's inkjet print mechanism requires none of the relatively massive parts that make a laser printer bulky, such as the drum and laser engine. The machine weighs a bit over 14 pounds, less than many comparably equipped 24-pin dot matrix printers.

Press hard, you're making five copies

The DeskJet shares one important limitation with all inkjet and laser printers: because the printhead doesn't forcibly strike the paper, the DeskJet can't make multiple-copy duplicates on carbon paper or carbonless forms. For filling out the occasional form, you'll have to scrounge up a typewriter or an impact dot-matrix printer, or make do with your own handwriting. If you have a lot of forms to fill out on a printer, you'd be better off with an impact printer.

Ink and ink cartridges

In spite of its advantages in lower weight and quieter operation, inkjet technology has had a checkered past. You may have heard about an alleged tendency for the ink nozzles to clog, and in fact, this was a frequent problem on early inkjet printers with touchy ink formulas. Since a clogged nozzle can't squirt ink, you'd see a horizontal defect running across every printed line at the level of the affected nozzle.

For the DeskJet design team, one of the major engineering challenges was to ensure that the ink delivery system would not clog as they increased resolution to an unheard-of 300 dpi. The solution they dreamed up was to put the entire printhead with its tiny ink nozzles into a disposable cartridge.

If you have a spare ink cartridge handy, turn it upside down and take a look at the bottom end, so that the green plastic fitting points toward the floor. On that protruding ridge that's now at the very top, you'll see a small, flat, gold-colored rectangle. Remarkably, the surface of that little wafer is the business end of the DeskJet. Drilled by the beam of a super-precise laser, two rows of nearly microscopic holes serve as the ink nozzles. There are 60 nozzles in all, but the DeskJet can only print a swath 50 dots high in one pass of the printhead. Why the extras? For one thing, some of the 50 printable dot positions are represented by a pair of nozzles, one for each direction. The remainder of the extra nozzles simply aren't used at all.

If you look closely, you'll see that the printhead wafer is connected to a multitude of tiny printed circuits that you can trace on that copper-colored ribbon, or flex circuit, over to the front side of the cartridge. There, the little

Anatomy of a Cartridge

The illustration below shows a disassembled print cartridge lying on its back. When installed in the DeskJet, the surface of the little printhead is oriented downward, parallel to the floor. If you lift the cover while your DeskJet is printing, you'll see that ink sprays downward onto the paper.

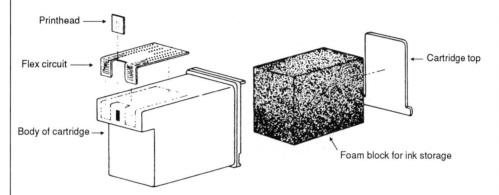

Printhead ⟶

Flex circuit ⟶

Body of cartridge ⟶

Cartridge top ⟵

Foam block for ink storage

To squirt an ink droplet from one of the 50-odd nozzles on the printhead's surface, the DeskJet activates a firing chamber directly beneath the nozzle. The firing chamber consists of a tiny channel for ink within which an even tinier resistor is mounted. Current flowing through the resistor causes it to heat up, vaporizing the ink nearby to produce a vapor bubble. The vapor bubble is in contact with an adjacent droplet of still-liquid ink in the nozzle, and the bubble drives this droplet out of the nozzle and onto the paper. As soon as the droplet departs, a new column of ink is drawn up into the firing channel from a feed channel connecting the printhead to the main chamber of the ink cartridge.

As you can see in the illustration, the ink reservoir is a block of foam sponge that fills the main chamber. This arrangement ensures that the ink remains uniformly distributed and completely liquid.

Whenever the cartridge isn't in use, the DeskJet parks it on top of a *service station* at the far right of the carriage on which the printhead travels. The service station is designed to keep the nozzles from drying out, to protect them from paper dust, and to remove any ink plugs that may have formed. All this is described in more detail in Chapter 2 in the section, "The DeskJet's Service Station."

traces end at round metal contacts which electronically mate the cartridge to the DeskJet proper, allowing the DeskJet to control the firing of each ink nozzle.

Inside the cartridge, ink is stored in a spongy foam material that keeps it evenly distributed no matter how much is left. As the ink nozzles fire, ink is sucked up from the foam into tiny channels leading to the printhead.

As if inventing the mechanical and electronic technologies in the cartridge itself wasn't hard enough, Hewlett-Packard had to come up with an ink to match the cartridge design while delivering excellent print quality. The ink had to print dark, solid blacks, it had to be non-toxic, it had to flow freely without spattering, it had to adhere well without running or spreading on a huge variety of ordinary papers, and it had to keep doing all these things when exposed to extremes of humidity and temperature. Formulating the ink proved to be almost as much of a challenge as was the cartridge design; in fact, the cartridge design had to change to reflect the ink formula, and vice versa.

The ink formulas that HP has used in DeskJet cartridges satisfy all these requirements. However, the original DeskJet ink was water-based, which meant that it smeared if you let it get wet, and that you had to let it dry before touching the page, and that printed pages tended to wrinkle. But with the introduction of the DeskJet 500, HP also came out with a non-water based ink without these drawbacks—and fortunately, you can use the new ink cartridges in any DeskJet model. Like the earlier formula, the newer ink virtually never clogs the printhead. It dries almost instantly on contact with the paper to a rich black, and it looks great on just about any kind of paper you can feed into the machine—while earlier inkjet printers required special papers, you'll get excellent quality from standard bonds and xerographic papers.

Other DeskJet technology

OK, enough about the inkjet angle—the DeskJet offers several other important benefits in addition to the ones that stem from its printing technology. For many people, probably the most attractive of these is the DeskJet's facility with fonts.

We'll cover fonts in detail in Section II. For now, it's worth noting that the DeskJet and DeskJet Plus have only one built-in typeface: typewriter-style Courier, printable in various sizes and styles. Without buying additional fonts, you can print text in several different Courier fonts, the range of choices depending on whether you have an original model DeskJet or a DeskJet Plus. To the Courier, the DeskJet 500 added several fonts in two other typefaces, CG Times and Letter Gothic. With any of these fonts, you can also choose from a generous variety of different characters, ranging from ordinary letters and numerals to foreign language characters to legal and mathematical symbols.

But whatever model of DeskJet you have, you're certainly not limited to the built-in, or *internal* fonts. The DeskJet accepts fonts of your choice both on cartridges or floppy disks, and you can use type-scaling software to print fonts of any size on your printer. With a potentially limitless selection of typefaces, the DeskJet can serve capably for light-duty desktop publishing.

Not a speed demon

As far as speed is concerned, the DeskJet suffers by comparison to laser printers and fast standard dot matrix models, but it's plenty fast enough for its intended role in knocking out letters and short reports. In my time trials, an "average" full page of 10-point letter-quality Courier text took about 50 seconds to print. That gives the DeskJet an actual "throughput" speed of about 70 characters per second (HP rates the letter quality mode at 120 cps, but manufacturers' ratings never take paper handling time into account). The Laser Jet Series II, by contrast, can print plain text at nearly its rated speed of 8 pages per minute, or around 8 seconds per page.

Paper handling

Which brings us to paper handling, another area where the DeskJet shines. The single-sheet paper bin holds about 100 sheets of plain bond or letterhead, and the bin is built into the front of the unit where it's a snap to load. There's also a convenient, built-in, one-at-a-time envelope feeder—you just push the envelope into the guides, press a couple of buttons, and go. The feeding mechanism works smoothly and maintains good alignment, and paper jams are exceedingly rare.

The next time you print a page, take a look at the way those little "flippers" along either side of the output area help push the paper out. This fascinating mechanism is completely unique in the printer kingdom. It's there to ensure that paper covered with drying ink falls smoothly and reliably into the output tray.

The DeskJet does commit one paper-handling gaffe: pages come out face up, so they stack in reverse order. There's also a limitation necessitated by the time it takes the ink to dry: the printer can't be commanded to move the paper in the reverse direction except in tiny increments. Otherwise, the ink would smear. And in case you've wondered, there's no provision whatsoever for pinfeed paper.

Miscellany

A keypad with eight buttons and several indicator lights lets you control several important functions such as paper feeding and font selection directly from the DeskJet's front panel. However, your software will often override the settings on the front panel.

The DeskJet also sports a modest (16K) buffer, a place where incoming data can be parked while it waits to be printed. The buffer could have been larger, perhaps, but it's roomy enough to accept the equivalent of about four or five full pages of single-spaced text in one nearly instantaneous dump. That way, as soon as the last page of your document is sent to the buffer, you can go back to work, while the DeskJet whirs along and finishes printing.

All in the family....

A final DeskJet advantage is that the machine understands most of the same printer commands used by Hewlett-Packard's LaserJet family of laser printers. Because the printer commands available are numerous and quite powerful, they've collectively earned the right to be called a programming language, which HP calls its Printer Command Language (PCL for short). Here's a list of all of HP's PCL laser printers:

- LaserJet (original model)

- LaserJet Plus

- LaserJet 500 Plus

- LaserJet Series II

- LaserJet 2000

- LaserJet IID

- LaserJet IIP

- LaserJet III

- LaserJet IIID

- LaserJet IIISi

- LaserJet IIIP

In addition, a number of other HP printers understand portions of the PCL language. The list includes the ThinkJet, the QuietJet, and the PaintJet, all popular inkjet printers.

For most users, the big benefit of this common command language is that you can generally use the DeskJet with most any program, even if the software isn't specifically designed to work with the DeskJet—just install your software as if you had a LaserJet and you should be in business, although you may sacrifice a few DeskJet features (we'll cover the ins and outs of software compatibility in section III).

For programmers, the command language compatibility of HP's printers means that the same program can be made to work with the entire HP line with little or no modification. Chapter 22 contains an introduction to PCL programming on the DeskJet and DeskJet Plus.

Differences between DeskJet models

While all the DeskJet models print text and graphics at 300 dpi, each model has had several new features distinguishing it from its predecessors. newer DeskJet Plus has several advantages:

- In the original DeskJet, you could only print wide documents "sideways", in landscape mode, with a special font cartridge (in landscape mode, the printed page is oriented so that it is wider than it is tall, as contrasted with the ordinary *portrait* mode—just look at the picture below). The Plus and the 500 come with three built-in *landscape* fonts.

Figure 1-1: *Portrait and landscape pages*

- On the Plus and the 500, fonts can be larger, up to 30 points high. Fonts for the original DeskJet are limited a maximum of 24 points but are usually no taller than 18 points.

- The Plus and the 500 come with built-in Courier italics, while the original requires an optional font cartridge to print italics.

- The 500 adds two new typefaces not found in the earlier models. For business correspondence, there's proportionally spaced CG Times, similar to Times Roman, in 6 and 12 points. For printing financial and database reports, there are three sizes of Letter Gothic.

- The Plus and the 500 let you install up to twice as much memory for soft fonts in the form of optional RAM cartridges (with two RAM cartridges, the Plus and 500 can hold 512K, while the original DeskJet tops out at 256K).

- Text quality of the most commonly used optional fonts, Helv and TmsRmn, was improved in the versions created for the Plus and 500.

- The DeskJet 500 accepts several font cartridges containing attractive, high-quality typefaces such as Univers, Garamond, and Dom Casual; these cartrdiges won't work with earlier DeskJet models.

- The Plus and 500 print text "up to" twice as fast, graphics up to five times faster, according to Hewlett-Packard. In addition, their paper feeding speed is about double that of the original model.

One big change is primarily responsible for the improved speed: as its internal thinking machine, the original DeskJet used a relatively primitive 4 megahertz (MHz) Z80 microprocessor, while the DeskJet Plus and DeskJet 500 use a faster and more capable 8 MHz Z180 chip.

2

DeskJet Hardware

∿

Before you start sending orders to the DeskJet from your computer, you need a working familiarity with the nuts and bolts of the printer itself. Your DeskJet *Owner's Manual* has the instructions you need for unpacking and setting up your printer the first time. There are plenty of diagrams to get you oriented, along with a basic discussion of the panel controls and the DeskJet's minimal maintenance requirements.

This chapter covers some of same ground but adds details the manual leaves out. You'll get background information and practical tips on how to best connect the DeskJet to your computer, on how to use the printer's function switches, and on how the paper feeding system works. You'll also find expanded coverage of the DeskJet's keypad controls along with a brief section on maintenance.

Making connections

To move the information you want to print from your computer to the DeskJet, you need a cable to connect the two, and a place to plug it in on either end. The DeskJet comes with both serial and parallel ports (connectors) built-in as standard equipment. That's fortunate, since almost every computer you'll ever come across will have at least one of these types of ports as well.

With so many computers as potential cable-mates, it can be tough to figure out how to hook things up properly. First, you have to connect the right port on your computer to the right port on the printer, using the right cable. In addition, you may need to change the positions of some of the tiny function switches (known generically as *DIP switches*) at the bottom front of the DeskJet.

As you know, this book concentrates on using the DeskJet with IBM-compatible microcomputers, including PCs, XTs, ATs, PS/2s and all the myriad workalikes and clones. If you have one of these machines, you can skip down to the section "PC to DeskJet" below.

♪ ***Note for Macintosh users:*** *The Mac is conspicuously absent from the* Owner's Manual's *extensive coverage of various makes and models of computers. HP is now marketing a Mac-compatible version of the DeskJet called the DeskWriter. However, it's certainly possible to connect a Mac to an ordinary DeskJet, a procedure described fully in Chapter 21.*

If your computer isn't IBM PC-compatible, you'll still be able to get excellent results with the DeskJet, but it may take more work to make the right connections. The DeskJet *Owner's Manual* for the original model and the Plus had a lengthy section detailing the cabling requirements and function (DIP) switch settings for many computer makes and models, along with other necessary setup procedures. This information was largley dropped from the DeskJet 500 manual, but you will find some help in the *Printer Setup Guide*. If your computer or a similar model isn't listed in the manual, or if you additional questions, you can call the Hewlett-Packard technical support line at 208-323-2551 for assistance.

PC to DeskJet

The one big choice you have to make when connecting your PC- or PS/2-compatible computer to the DeskJet is whether to join the two machines through their serial ports or their parallel ports. Since both techniques work, how do you decide? It's easy: use the parallel method.

In a parallel connection, 8 chunks of printer data travel from the computer to the printer simultaneously, an 8 abreast arrangement, if you will. In contrast, a serial hookup can only send one chunk at a time in electronic single-file. So parallel connections are inherently quicker.

What's more, the "language" of serial communications isn't tightly standardized, so you must be careful to make several special software settings correctly. Otherwise, printer and computer may not be talking the same jive, and your printer may not print. It's not really difficult to make the necessary adjustments, but the potential for error is definitely greatest with a serial hookup.

Is there ever a reason to use a serial connection between a PC- or PS/2-type computer and a DeskJet? The only advantage of serial connections is that you can use a longer cable without risking loss of the information being sent from the computer to your printer. Since you'll almost certainly be placing your DeskJet close to the computer, this is rarely an issue. Unless your parallel port goes dead and you need to keep printing before you can get it fixed, use parallel.

Understanding function switch settings

At the bottom front of the DeskJet, tucked away inside a little recess, lie two sets of tiny switches that have a big impact on how your printer works. If you stand the DeskJet on its hind end and look closely at the switches, you'll see that each set comprises a single component, a little plastic block in which the switches are mounted. Miniature switches packaged together in this way are referred to rather loosely as DIP switches, and you'll find them on many computer products, including most video and memory cards and probably your computer's main circuitboard itself.

HP prefers to call the DeskJet's DIP switches "function switches," which describes their role better. The function switches control several important printer "defaults," the settings that are automatically in effect each time you turn on the DeskJet (you can override many of the defaults with software commands). Among the default settings you can determine with the function switches are the paper or envelope size, the graphics resolution, parameters for serial communication with your computer, the set of characters you can print, and more.

The problems with DIP switches are pretty obvious—they're small and therefore hard to change, and they don't come with a written key to tell you which setting does what. More expensive printers such as the LaserJets have done away with DIP switches, replacing them with a sophisticated front panel control that lets you change default settings and gives you a readout in English to tell you what you're doing. In the DeskJet, you're stuck with the DIP switches. Fortunately, you'll probably need to change them only rarely, if at all.

As it's shipped from the factory, the DeskJet's function switches are set appropriately for most people with IBM-compatible computers. In the Appendix of the DeskJet *Owner's Manual*, you'll find a diagram showing the function switches and how to set them properly to get the default options you want.

Using the Keypad Control Panel

All of the DeskJet's operating controls are located on a simple 8-key keypad on the front right of the printer. We'll cover their use when appropriate in later sections, but we'll touch on them briefly here for quick reference.

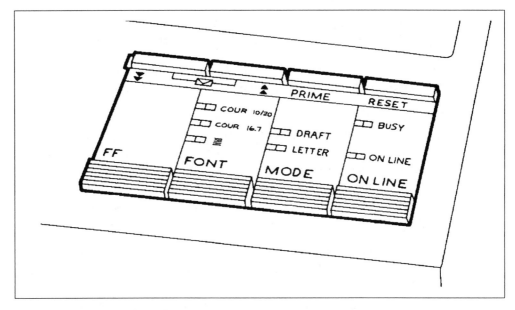

Figure 2.1: *The DeskJet's keypad*

It's important to know that you can access most of the functions available from the keypad via software commands from your computer. In fact, your application programs may override the settings you choose manually with the keypad. However, three keys—UP, DOWN, and PRIME—perform functions that cannot be controlled by software.

Another key point is that your printer offers features that you *can't* control with the keypad. For example, the only way to activate the DeskJet 500's CG Times and Letter Gothic fonts is via software commands.

Keys and Lights

The keypad's eight buttons are divided into two rows, front and back. Between the two rows is a display with several indicator lights, most of which are associated with a particular button.

The four buttons up front are the ones you'll probably use most often, and they're larger. From left to right, the keys in the front row work like this:

The FF (form feed) key ejects the paper currently in the paper path. If there's nothing in the paper path, a page is loaded when you press the FF key.

The FONT button steps you through the fonts currently available, one at a time, allowing you to select the font you want to use for printing. If you've installed a font cartridge in either or both slots, the cartridge fonts become part of the round-robin sequence you step through with the FONT key. On the other hand, you can only select downloadable soft fonts through commands from your computer (see Section II for complete information on fonts).

The active font is indicated by one or more lights above and to the right of the FONT key. If the light closest to the FONT key, the one labelled with a small rectangle of red lines, is glowing, the selected font will print at half size (as you'll learn in Chapter 6, most DeskJet fonts can be used at full size or half size).

On the DeskJet Plus and 500, the light next to the little image of a horizontally-oriented page indicates that the current font is a landscape font, and the page will print sideways. If the landscape light isn't on, an ordinary portrait font is selected. (The terms *portrait* and *landscape* were introduced in Chapter 1 and are discussed in more detail with reference to fonts in Chapter 6.)

The MODE button simply switches the DeskJet back and forth between its best "letter-quality" mode and a faster draft mode, as indicated by the nearby light.

⌘ *Tip:*   *Use the MODE button to switch quickly between draft mode, which saves time and ink, and the default "letter-quality" mode, for finished copies.*

The ON LINE button switches the DeskJet back and forth between two modes: an on-line, "ready to print" mode, and an off-line mode which halts printing temporarily, allowing you to load more paper or select a different font.

The ON LINE indicator light glows when the DeskJet is online and ready, and is off when the printer is offline. The light blinks when the DeskJet runs out of paper during a print job. If this happens, be sure not to turn the printer off, and don't press the RESET button. Instead, just reload the paper tray, and then press the ON LINE button.

If both the ON LINE and BUSY lights are flashing, you have a paper jam. Consult the troubleshooting section in Chapter 23 for how to proceed, but don't press the RESET button if you don't want to lose data waiting to be printed (data may still be lost, however).

The four remaining keys serve less frequently needed functions. They're smaller so you won't press them accidentally, since two of them, RESET and PRIME, will cause problems with a print out. Starting from the left, the back row keys work as follows:

The button at the far left is the UP key and is labelled with a double arrowhead pointing towards the front of the printer. UP advances the paper a tiny distance each time you press it.

The next key to the right is the DOWN key, and is labelled with a double arrowhead pointing toward the rear. It moves the paper back into the paper path a little at a time.

Pressing both the UP and DOWN keys at once loads an envelope into the paper path. You must first place the envelope into position for printing as described in Chapter 18.

Moving to the right, the PRIME key comes next. Its function is to redistribute ink into the printhead's ink channels when clogs occur, ensuring that a smooth, even coating of ink reaches the paper.

⌒ *Caution:* *Pressing PRIME uses a small but measureable amount of ink—don't do it unless there's a real problem with print quality. Also, don't press PRIME while a print job is in progress, since the DeskJet will lose track of where it's printing on the paper.*

The RESET key is located to the far right. Pressing RESET completely restarts the DeskJet, ejects the sheet of paper currently in the paper path, if any, clears the printer's buffer of print data, and reactivates the default font. "Permanent" downloaded fonts remain intact, but "temporary" fonts are also cleared (see the discussion of permanent versus temporary downloaded fonts in Chapter 7).

Finally, there's the BUSY light, which has no associated key. The BUSY light glows steadily when the DeskJet is receiving data from your computer, and turns off as soon as the data flow stops. It blinks when the DeskJet has received data in landscape orientation but hasn't yet printed the page. While the BUSY light is on, the FF, FONT, and MODE buttons don't do anything.

Again, both the ON LINE and BUSY lights flash when there's a paper jam. Consult the troubleshooting section in Chapter 23 for how to proceed, but don't press the RESET button if you want to retain the data waiting to be printed (you may still lose data, however).

Paper feeding

The DeskJet's main paper feeding mechanism is simple and essentially foolproof. You just slide out the paper tray extender, push in a stack of paper with its right side flush against the right side of the tray, and slide the paper tray extender back in. I'll discuss the procedure for loading envelopes in Chapter 18.

✂ *Tip: The DeskJet prints on the side of the paper that's on the bottom in the input tray. If you want to print on both sides of a sheet, place the printed side face up in the paper tray when you're feeding the page in again. Contrariwise, if you want to print the same side twice, put the page in the paper tray face down for the second pass. The edge of the paper that enters the printer first becomes the top of the printed page.*

The Printable Area and the Unprintable Region

For technical reasons, the DeskJet cannot print all the way out to the very edges of a piece of paper. The maximum area on which you actually can print is referred to as the *printable area*. On ordinary 8½ x11-inch letter-size paper, the printable area measures 8 inchs across and 10⅓ inches long. It is bounded by an *unprintable region* consisting of a ⅙-inch margin at the top of the page, a ½-inch margin at the bottom, and ¼-inch margins along the left and right edges of the paper. When you print in landscape orientation, so that text runs across the long edge of the page, the printable area is now

The DeskJet's Service Station

Whenever the DeskJet isn't actively printing, it pulls the cartridge into the service station, a device at the far right of the carriage on which the print cartridge travels.

As the cartridge is parked on the service station, ramps raise a rubber cap so that it contacts the printhead. The cap covers the printhead tightly, sealing out dust, and sealing in moisture so the ink in the nozzles doesn't dry out. To remove paper dust that has accumulated during printing, the service station also has a soft rubber wiper that brushes against the printhead as it moves into or out of the parked position. The wiper scrapes the dust into the thin slots on either side of the printhead. When you throw away the cartridge, the dust gets dumped too.

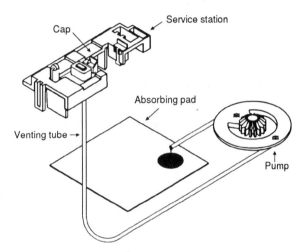

Original service station

In summer 1989, HP introduced a new service station design. Some DeskJet owners had found their ink cartridges running low much too quickly, a problem that was traced to the service station's pump mechanism. In the original design, a flexible tube attached to the underside of the cap maintains high humidity in the cap and is part of a pump system used to clear clogged nozzles. When you press the PRIME button on the keypad, a few droplets of ink are sucked out and drained onto an absorbent pad below. In the new design, the tube and pump have been eliminated. Pressing PRIME agitates the printhead back and forth against the wipers and causes it to spray a small amount of ink into the cap. The results are the same—cleared nozzles—but less ink is wasted. DeskJets with the old service station (those whose serial number prefix is less than 2937) can be upgraded at no charge to the new unit. Order a do-it-yourself kit, part number 02276-677801, by calling HP's Repair Center at 503/757-2002. You can also send your printer to the Center if you prefer.

10⅓ inches wide by 8 inches tall, and the unprintable margins become ¼-inch at the top and bottom, ½-inch on the left, and ⅙-inch on the right. Although you can set larger margins than those that define the printable area, you cannot set make them any smaller.

Care and feeding

Besides being less expensive than a laser printer at the time of purchase, the DeskJet is less costly to maintain. The only item you'll need to replace occasionally is the print cartridge. According to HP itself, the DeskJet requires absolutely no scheduled maintenance.

Ink—Priming the pump

Once in a while, however, you may have to intervene to restore print quality. If print is faded or if dots or lines are missing, and assuming you haven't simply run out of ink, the cure is simple—just press the PRIME button on the keypad. The unit will go through a special sequence to remove clogs from the printhead, restoring the print to its full intensity.

When the ink runs out

Of course, ink in the print cartridge doesn't last forever. HP estimates officially that a cartridge will last 525,000 letter-quality characters of the sizes typically used for body text. That translates very roughly into about 250 single-spaced pages or 500 double-spaced pages. You should get twice that many pages in draft mode. New cartridges carry a $19.95 list price and are available direct from Hewlett-Packard (call 800/538-8787) or from local dealers. Some mail-order houses also carry them, but usually not at tremendous discounts. Cartridges are easy to replace—just snap them in according to the procedure illustrated in the *Owner's Manual.*

Unfortunately, there's no "fuel gauge" to let you know when your current cartridge is running low. The only way you'll know you're running out of ink is when the print starts to fade, and pressing PRIME doesn't restore it.

Keeping your DeskJet clean

HP does advise you to keep the innards of the machine clean. Paper dust tends to build up in the vicinity of the print carriage and could conceivably gum up the works. All you have to do is blow out the dust occasionally. Any ink sticking to the metal platen, the carriage guide, and the paper rollers should be removed with a soft cloth. To clean up ink from the new, non-water based ink cartridges, moisten the cloth with isopropyl alcohol. If you're using one of the original DeskJet cartridges with water-based ink, moisten the cloth with water only.

3

The Brain in the Machine

❧

After you've unpacked your printer and set it up, connected it physically to your computer, and loaded it with paper, the DeskJet is ready to take orders from the computer. Now you, or your software, can tell it what to print and how to print it.

But how do you communicate your instructions to the DeskJet? This chapter will give you a little background about the messages your computer and printer pass back and forth, and how the DeskJet translates these messages into printed pages. While the discussion is a little technical, it will help you to understand some of the quirks in the way your printer works—for instance, why some pages take longer to print than others, and why the DeskJet works better with some programs than with others. With that understanding as a foundation, you'll learn in later chapters how to produce the best possible printed documents in any situation.

Down the wire

Your computer and your printer talk with one another in an electronic language based on a flow of minute, precisely timed voltage fluctuations. The pattern of voltage changes represents a series of numeric codes, which are the letters and words of this electronic language.

In any interchange between your computer and your DeskJet, the PC dominates the conversation: Most of the time, the computer is issuing instructions for the DeskJet to follow. These instructions come in two main types. First, your PC can send codes representing the text and graphics that the DeskJet is actually supposed to print. Second, it can send commands that control other operations of the printer, such as where the text and graphics are to be printed. Occasionally, the printer sends a brief message back the opposite way, to let the computer know, say, that it's out of paper, or that it can't respond to further instructions for some other reason.

Understanding print data

We'll start this discussion of computer-DeskJet communications by looking at the coded information your computer sends when it wants your printer to actually print text or graphics to be printed. These codes are the *print data.*

The DeskJet creates everything it prints out of individual tiny dots of ink. At the level of the printhead, one dot is just like the next, whether it's part of the letter *A* or part of a picture of an eagle in flight. However, there's a considerable difference between the data your computer sends to the DeskJet to print text and the data it sends to print graphics. Thus, there are two types of print data: one type for text, the other for graphics.

Text print data

When you first turn on your DeskJet, it powers up in text mode. In text mode, the computer tells the DeskJet which characters to print using a standardized coding system known as ASCII (for "American Standard Code for Information Exchange"). In the ASCII code, each text character (a letter, numeral, or punctuation mark) is represented by a number between 0 and 255. A capital *A*, for instance, is character 65 in the ASCII code. To get the DeskJet to print that *A*, your computer must send the value 65 in electronic form to the printer.

Now let's look at things from the DeskJet's perspective. Its ultimate mission is to turn on and off just the right ink nozzles at just the right times to create a pattern of dots that you'll recognize as the letter *A*. From this point of view, that ASCII code 65 doesn't help, because it doesn't say anything about which nozzles to turn on, or when the nozzles should start spraying. What the DeskJet needs is electronic intelligence of its own—a behind-the-scenes computer, if you will—that can translate incoming ASCII codes into the sequence of electronic impulses necessary to fire the ink nozzles in the correct pattern. Because the DeskJet has these built-in smarts, when your software requests a letter *A*, it's like signing up for a package tour to Europe—all the little details are handled for you.

Exactly what that letter *A* looks like when it actually gets printed depends on which font is active when the DeskJet receives your command to print it. The active font can be set with the DeskJet's keypad, or through software control, a topic we'll introduce a page or two hence.

The ASCII coding system is almost universal throughout the computer universe, and it's certainly not specific to the DeskJet. Each of the most common letters, numerals, and punctuation marks has a standard numeric value in the ASCII code that almost all printers understand.

But of the 256 available codes, the ASCII system actually defines only 128. That accounts for all the numeric digits, all the upper and lower case versions of the 26 letters, and a good supply of miscellaneous punctuation marks. In addition, certain ASCII standard codes don't represent printable characters at all, but rather signify commands that your computer or printer should follow. But more on that shortly. At any rate, another 128 character codes are undefined in the standard ASCII code. These are frequently used for special characters, such as foreign language characters and mathematical symbols, depending on the font you're using.

Graphics print data

The DeskJet has a very different method for printing graphics than the one it uses for text. In text mode, the ASCII code for a letter or number consists of only a single number, yet the printer translates that one-number code into a complete character made up of hundreds or even thousands of dots on the page, depending on the character and its size. By contrast, when printing graphics, the computer must specifically tell the printer where to put each and every dot on the page. Images created in this way are referred to as *bit-mapped* graphics, or simply bitmaps, meaning that each dot in the image is "mapped" by a single "bit" of data sent by the computer.

In graphics mode, it takes the equivalent of one ASCII character code to produce just eight graphics dots. For this reason, if you wanted to "paint" that letter *A* one dot at a time in graphics mode, you'd need many times the amount of data needed to print the *A* in text mode. The major implication of this vast disparity is that graphics printing is considerably slower than text mode, simply because it requires such a large volume of data. The DeskJet Plus, which is considerably faster than the original model, can print a full page of graphics in about 1½ minutes. Printing a page of text takes only 50 seconds.

The DeskJet does have two built-in functions to speed up graphics printing by compressing data so that fewer bytes need to be sent. In most cases, this helps a little, but not a lot. If you're just interested in filling space as fast as possible, another way to speed things up is to program the DeskJet to use a lower resolution graphics mode (Chapter 22 on programming has the necessary instructions). If you reduce the resolution from 300 dots-per-inch maximum, the DeskJet prints more than one dot for each data bit, so the effective image is larger. Unfortunately, the picture also loses sharpness and clarity.

Object graphics: Not available

As an alternative to bitmaps, computer-generated images can also be stored as *object graphics*, also known as *vector graphics*. Although the DeskJet is not capable of interpreting object graphics, many software programs and some printers are. As a DeskJet owner, understanding object graphics will help you buy and use the right graphics software for your needs.

In the object graphics technique, an image is built up from a composite of separate various shapes, or "objects," such as lines, circles, rectangles, and polygons. The key point is that each of these individual objects is described as a mathematical formula, rather than as a collection of dots. A straight line object, for example, might be defined as starting at a certain point and extending a given distance for a particular length.

In a printer that can handle object-type graphics commands, the objects eventually get translated into a dot pattern, of course. The process is similar to the way a single character code gets converted into a printed character when the DeskJet prints text.

Printers such as the DeskJet that don't understand the language of object graphics can still print images stored by your software in object format. The trick here is that the software itself must translate the objects into bitmapped form, and then send these bitmaps to the DeskJet.

Compared to bitmapped graphics, one of the big advantages of the object variety is that they require far less data. Our hypothetical straight line object might only require a couple of bytes for each part of the line's description (its point of origin, angle of deflection, and length), as compared to hundreds or perhaps thousands of bytes to create an identical bitmapped line. Another point is that a line object always requires the same amount of data, no matter how long it is.

Likewise, all you need to know to draw a circle is the position of its center and its radius—after all, circumference = πr^2, right? Squiggly lines and more complex shapes take fancier formulae, but still occupy less data than the equivalent dot-by-dot bitmap. Overall, an object-type graphics file takes up much less memory in your computer, and much less space when it's stored on disk. For a more extensive look at the pros and cons of the two types of graphics, see Chapter 13.

Printer commands: controlling the DeskJet

In day-to-day use, a printer spends the vast majority of its time actually printing the data you send it—the computer sends a numeric code, the printer interprets it, and out comes the corresponding pattern from the ink nozzles. A few special codes provoke a different response from the printer, however. With these codes, you can command the printer to do something such as change fonts, move the paper, switch from text to graphics mode or vice versa, or even reset itself altogether. In the DeskJet's case, some of the commands that can be sent from the computer duplicate functions on the printer's keypad, but there are many functions that can only be controlled through software commands.

The varieties of printer command languages

Although all printers respond to commands in the same general way, each printer recognizes a different set of specific commands. It's as if each printer speaks and understands its own language. If you send the command that activates a particular DeskJet font to an Epson printer, the Epson will do something else—or just sit there and scratch its printhead. That's why you have to tell your application software which printer you're using before you can print successfully—it's the only way for the program to know that it should be sending its printer commands in the DeskJet language, instead of Epson, NEC, or some other tongue.

In an ideal world, once you told the program you're using a DeskJet, you wouldn't have to worry about printer commands at all. Instead, your application software would take care of the dirty work for you. Say you're using your word processor to write a letter, and you want to emphasize your demand that Al's Great Guys stereo store return your money right <u>now!</u> To print the underline, you should only have to hit the keys that activate your word processor's underlining feature. When it prints your letter, the program would send the underlining command to the DeskJet, without any further intervention on your part.

Printer drivers

For this ideal scenario to work in real life, your program must have a key piece of software called a *printer driver.* A printer driver is a software module tailored to your particular printer that merges into your application program. The driver serves much like an interpreter, translating the program's own codes for, say, underlining, into the corresponding command in the printer's native tongue.

As you can guess, the print quality you can expect when using a particular software program depends in part on how good the program's DeskJet driver is. Many programs come with excellent DeskJet drivers, allowing them to speak the DeskJet language fluently and thereby control all of the printer's more advanced features handily.

On the other hand, some programs have limited drivers, and can speak only a kind of pidgin DeskJet-ese. Others lack a DeskJet driver altogether, and at best will only let you print plain, unformatted characters in a single font.

If you run up against one of these backward programs, you'll have to take matters into your own hands or go without the print features you want to use. Chapter 8 contains an overview of how to get the DeskJet to work best with each application program, and an introduction to using DeskJet commands on your own. In Chapter 4, you'll learn about add-on utilities that can translate between your program and the DeskJet.

DeskJet printer commands

No matter what software or utilities you own, there may be times when you'll need to know how to send commands to the DeskJet yourself, without help from a printer driver. For now, an introduction to DeskJet printer commands will do—when you're ready for the details, see Chapters 8 and 22.

Here's the basic scoop: DeskJet printer commands are numeric codes, just like the ones that represent particular ASCII characters or a bunch of dots in a graphic. However, the DeskJet is primed to recognize a few special code values that signify the beginning of a command, instead of data to be printed.

If you know these special numbers, also known as *control codes,* you have the passwords that give you access to total control of the DeskJet.

In some cases, a single control code constitutes an entire command—the DeskJet receives that one code, takes an immediate action, and goes right back to printing. For example, if you send the code value of 12 (the *form feed* control code) to your printer, the DeskJet responds by ejecting the current page.

But one control code, the *escape character,* works differently. When the DeskJet receives the code for the escape character, the printer pauses and waits for further instructions, in the form of one or more additional codes. These additional codes are not themselves control codes; they would ordinarily represent printable text characters. But when preceded by the escape character, these ordinary codes take on special meaning to the DeskJet.

A command beginning with the escape character is called an *escape sequence.* Escape sequences are much more powerful than one-byte control codes. With them, you can control a multitude of print options. You can select a particular font, change margin settings, load an envelope into the printer, switch to graphics mode, and much more besides.

Escape sequence anatomy

Let's look at an example of a typical escape sequence. The code for the escape character is 27. To turn on underlining, you would send the following sequence to your printer, expressed in decimal numbers: **27 38 1ØØ 48 68**.

To make escape sequences (somewhat) easier to read in print, they're usually written out in the ASCII characters represented by those numbers. Since the escape "character" isn't really a character, it's represented by the abbreviation ^Es_c. Written in this format, the sequence we just examined would look like this: ^Es_c**&dØD**.

Likewise, ^Es_c**(d@** turns underlining off, ^Es_c**(s1S** turns italics on, and ^Es_c**(sØS** turns italics off.

You're probably thinking that escape sequences look like gibberish, and I agree with you. While there is something of a pattern in the various letters and numbers in the escape sequence code, that pattern is hard to trace, and it's not very consistent. But we're stuck with it—escape sequences and control codes are the only commands the DeskJet understands. Again, we'll wade through some of the muck in Chapter 8 and get in chin-deep in Chapter 22.

4

DeskJet Utilities

Batman wouldn't be anywhere today without his utility belt, and DeskJet owners need utility software just as much. Utility programs take the drudgery out of many of the miscellaneous printing challenges that inevitably crop up. In this chapter, we'll look at two main kinds of DeskJet utilities: print spoolers, that speed up your printing sessions, and setup utilities, that let you set up margins, change fonts, and otherwise control your printer almost effortlessly.

Although the utilities profiled in this chapter are distributed through conventional commercial channels, you should be aware that an excellent source of printer utilities is shareware and freeware. There's a vast quantity of try-before-you-buy software available at user group meetings, on electronic bulletin boards, and from a number of mail-order purveyors. It costs little or nothing to test a shareware program, and if you decide to keep it the registration fees are usually modest. Since the first edition of this book was published, quite a few shareware utilities have been written just for the DeskJet. In addition, you can use successfully most of the many utility programs written for the LaserJet family on your DeskJet.

✄ *Tip:* *The best shareware supplier is the Public Software Library. The PSL lists several disks of DeskJet-specific software in its massive library, as well as many generic printer utilities such as print spoolers and setup programs. Call 800/242-4775 or 713/524-6394 for information or a copy of their monthly magazine and catalog.*

Speedup utilities: print spoolers

The DeskJet is reasonably speedy as desktop printers go, but you'll still spend many minutes drumming your fingers as you wait for long documents to print. Do yourself a favor and get a *print spooler* as soon as you can. Print spoolers are software utilities that can drastically cut how much time you wait on your printer. They don't actually reduce the time it takes the printer to pop out the last page of a document, but spoolers do allow you go back to work with your computer long before the print job is finished.

Here's the problem that print spoolers address: your software can send output to the printer much faster than the printer can digest it. The printer needs time to process the data and commands it receives, and even more time to do the actual printing. Software is almost always much faster, and it usually spends most of its time during a print session just waiting to send more data to the printer. In the DeskJet's case, the printer has a small (16K) buffer to which your software can transfer data almost instantaneously. But as soon as that buffer fills up things slow way down. And you'll wait right along with your software—until the printer has accepted all of the software's output, you'll be unable to use your computer.

Print spooler utilities attack the problem by commandeering all the data and commands your software sends to the printer, diverting them to a storage area in memory or on disk instead. Since the transfer doesn't have to wait for the printer, it can occur at top speed. As soon as all the printer output has reached this temporary parking place you get control of your computer again, and you can go on working on your letter, spreadsheet, or what have you. Meanwhile, the spooler takes over the chore of spoonfeeding the data to your printer. The spooler does this behind the scenes as you work, so you can print and work at the same time.

Probably the best known print spooler is PrintCache, featured in the profile just ahead, but any print spooler that works is better than none. If funds are short and you have time to experiment you can give shareware a try. Another option is the print spooler that comes in PC-Kwik's Power Pak, a collection of excellent speedup utilities that can streamline your whole system. In addition to the spooler, the Power Pak tool kit includes a disk caching utility for faster disk performance, the best keyboard speedup program I've tried, and a screen speedup program as well. And the entire package retails for less than PrintCache alone.

You might also consider PrintQ, a print spooler with many more features than PrintCache. Unlike PrintCache, PrintQ lets you view a list of the "jobs" waiting to be printed, change their order, or remove them from the list. And it lets you trap printer output in a file on disk for later printing. Also $149, PrintQ is available from Software Direction at 201/584-8466. Finally, many inexpensive shareware spoolers are available.

✂ *Tip:* *You may already own a print spooler. Windows 3's Print Manager, for example, spools printer output from all your Windows programs, though it doesn't work with ordinary DOS programs you run from within Windows. WordPerfect has a built-in spooler (that only works within WordPerfect), while Lotus 1-2-3 Release 2.3 comes with one you can use within 1-2-3, or from DOS to print plain text (ASCII) files as well as spreadsheets. Finally, DOS' own PRINT.COM is a simple spooler for text files.*

Profile: PrintCache

$149/LaserTools Corp.
1250 45th Street
Emeryville, CA 94608
800/767-8004; 415/420-8777

PrintCache is one of a DeskJet owner's best friends. Above all, the program is fast. The program is designed so that it springs into action as soon as the printer signals it's ready for more data, and only then. By contrast, most other spoolers simply attempt to send the next chunk of data at predetermined intervals, which often means they wait too long.

PrintCache is convenient, too. You can pop up a little window that tells you how much memory you've set aside for temporary spooler storage and how much of your print job has been completed so far. Commands available on the window's menu allow you to empty the spooler buffer, stopping your print job, to eject the current page from the printer, and to suspend printing temporarily. While printing is suspended, PrintCache continues to divert printer data from your software to the buffer. This way, you can stop printing to take a phone call or attend to other business, then pick up where you left off later without losing anything.

As far as I know, PrintCache is the only print spooler that has been adapted specifically for the DeskJet. Since it knows how to translate ordinary graphics printer data into DeskJet compressed graphics data, PrintCache can actually speed up graphics printing by as much as a factor of four. Of course, if your software has already compressed its graphics output this feature has no effect—but very little software does this. (Chapter 22 includes a section explaining the DeskJet's graphics compression modes.)

Setup Utilities

Although it's wise to have a rudimentary acquaintance with the DeskJet printer commands introduced in the previous chapter, there's an alternative to mucking around with escape sequences and control codes when your application program doesn't know how to send the right printer commands for you. Software *setup utilities* let you pick the action you want the DeskJet to perform from simple menus. Instead of typing a row of alphanumeric soup when you want to, say, change to a new font, all you have to do is find the font on the utility's menu and press a key. The utility takes over, generating the correct command for the font change, and automatically sending it to the DeskJet.

In more detail, the functions you can carry out via setup utilities include:

- **Controlling basic printer operations.** Setup utilities often let you load or eject a page, advance the paper, and reset the printer to its default settings, without having to reach over to the keypad.

- **Choosing page settings.** Page settings refer to the characteristics of a printed page: the margins, the length of the paper, the number of lines per page, the orientation (portrait or landscape) and so on. If your application program won't let you set margins, for instance, you can use a setup utility to do the job.

- **Managing fonts.** You probably bought your DeskJet largely because of its ability to print sharp text in many attractive fonts. Woe to you if your application software won't let you select fonts. Since some programs override the choices you make from the keypad, you may be stuck with the DeskJet's built-in fonts, all of which are variants of boring, typewriter-style Courier, even if you've installed a font cartridge.

  A setup utility can make the font change for you, often from within the application program. You won't have to manually key in your font choices or convey your typographic desires via those complicated escape codes. The right utility will download your soft fonts for you and let you switch to any internal, cartridge or downloaded font whenever you like. In fact, some utilities concentrate entirely on font management. Fonts and font management utilities are covered in Section II.

- **Emulating other printers.** Although most new commercial software speaks the DeskJet's language fluently, you may rely on an old version of a program or some shareware that was never equipped with a DeskJet driver. In this case, a utility that translates commands intended for another printer into DeskJet format can make a good solution. With one of these *emulation* utilities, you can set up your application program for a different printer that the program does know how to control, such as a LaserJet or an Epson. When your program starts to print, the emulation utility intercepts commands meant for the LaserJet or Epson, and converts them into corresponding codes that the DeskJet understands. The result is instant DeskJet compatibility. And since emulation utilities do their translations "on the fly," during the actual printing process, they're able to change fonts, margins, and other settings within a document, not just between documents as with some setup utilities.

  DeskJet utilities in emulation category include LaserControl, which emulates Diablo, NEC, Qume, Epson, and IBM Graphics printers, and

Your options include Printer Genius, CSP-PC Printer Control, and LaserControl, as well as the utilities that specialize in font management covered in Chapter 7.

Profile: LaserControl

$150/Insight Development Corp.
2200 Powell St., Suite 500
Emeryville, CA 94608
415/652-4115

LaserControl has a dual mission: to help you set up your printer the way you want it to work, and to emulate other printers when your software doesn't know how to print with a DeskJet.

You can run LaserControl either as a pop-up memory resident utility or as a standalone program. Either way, an easy-to-follow set of menus lets you control DeskJet settings such as font and type style (bold or italics), lines per page, margins, graphics resolution, and so forth. There's also a handy command for ejecting finished pages that are still sitting in the printer, so you don't have to press the FF button.

With LaserControl, the whole setup process can be automatic, so that you don't even have to look at the menus. You can have LaserControl store a file with all your preferred DeskJet settings. At the beginning of a work session, you just tell LaserControl to send the file to your printer by typing **LC** followed by the name of the file on the DOS command line—the DeskJet is instantly ready to go.

LaserControl also lets your DeskJet emulate other popular printers, so that you can use the DeskJet with software that doesn't normally work with it. If a program knows the proper commands for a Diablo 630, an NEC 3550, 5510, or 7710, a Qume Sprint V, an Epson FX-80, or an IBM Graphics printer, it can now work with the DeskJet as well. Obviously, LaserControl can't make your program aware of features such as 300-dpi graphics that are unique to the DeskJet, but at least you'll be able to use the features that are available on the printer you're emulating.

In addition to its setup features and emulating capabilities, LaserControl knows how to get the DeskJet to print justified text (text that aligns perfectly with both margins) using proportionally spaced fonts like TmsRmn and Helv,

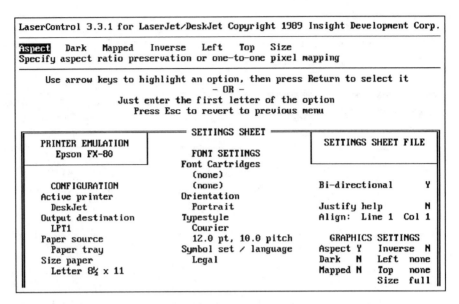

```
LaserControl 3.3.1 for LaserJet/DeskJet Copyright 1989 Insight Development Corp.

Aspect  Dark  Mapped  Inverse  Left  Top  Size
Specify aspect ratio preservation or one-to-one pixel mapping

       Use arrow keys to highlight an option, then press Return to select it
                                  - OR -
              Just enter the first letter of the option
                 Press Esc to revert to previous menu

======================= SETTINGS SHEET =======================
  PRINTER EMULATION                                SETTINGS SHEET FILE
    Epson FX-80             FONT SETTINGS
                          Font Cartridges
                             (none)
    CONFIGURATION            (none)            Bi-directional        Y
  Active printer          Orientation
    DeskJet                  Portrait         Justify help          N
  Output destination     Typestyle           Align:  Line 1   Col 1
    LPT1                     Courier
  Paper source             12.0 pt, 10.0 pitch    GRAPHICS SETTINGS
    Paper tray           Symbol set / language  Aspect Y   Inverse  N
  Size paper                Legal            Dark   N   Left   none
    Letter 8½ x 11                           Mapped N   Top    none
                                                        Size   full
```

Figure 4-2: *Laser Control's main screen. The current menu bar allows you to choose options for graphics printing.*

even when the application doesn't have this capability. One well-known program in this category is WordStar 3.3, though later versions of WordStar can justify unaided. LaserControl also lets you print the screen you're currently displaying in text or CGA graphics mode (see Chapter 19 for more on screen snapshots).

TreeSaver

If you have reasonably good eyesight, you can save time, paper, and that expensive DeskJet ink with TreeSaver DJ. This utility automatically reformats the output from your programs so that two pages fit on a single sheet of paper, printing the text in a minuscule but readable 27-characters-per-inch soft font. This little font also allows TreeSaver to squeeze larger spreadsheet and database reports on a page, and to shrink output to fit on smaller pieces of paper for use with carry-around directories like Day-Timers and Filofax. Treesaver DJ costs $49 and is available from Discoversoft, 415/769-2902.

Shareware DeskJet utilities

A healthy sampling of shareware utilities intended specifically for the DeskJet have appeared since the first edition of *DeskJet Unlimited*. DJ Control comprises a full suite of little programs with which you can control your printer's setup as you work or from a setup file, select soft fonts, and print envelopes and floppy disk labels. Also included are a program that prints a "ruler" with which you can measure in 1/300-inch dots, which is useful if you need to position something accurately on the page using DeskJet programming commands (see Chapter 22).

Other shareware utilities include Landscape Lister, which prints two pages of your file on each sheet of paper in landscape orientation using a small font, without requiring a landscape cartridge; DJSquash, which compresses graphics data on its way to the printer, speeding up printing times; and DJTools, a set of tiny programs that execute specific functions such as switching between draft and full quality print and ejecting a page. All of these shareware offerings are available from the Public Software Library at 800/242-4775.

Profile: LaserTwin

$179/ Metro Software, Inc.
2509 N. Campbell Ave., Suite 214
Tucson, AZ 85719
800/621-1137

LaserTwin could be the only utility software you need to buy for your DeskJet. By getting your modest DeskJet printer to emulate the more powerful LaserJet Series II, LaserTwin gives you superb control over the DeskJet from within the vast majority of contemporary programs. Even if your software is completely ignorant of the DeskJet, you can get great results as long as the program knows how to command the LaserJet. You can, for instance, print any font or any graphics in "sideways" landscape orientation, even though the DeskJet doesn't normally permit this. What's more, you can use any LaserJet downloadable font in a DeskJet document, as long as your application program supports downloadable LaserJet fonts.

The list of programs that benefit from LaserTwin includes all the PC word processors known to humanity, Ventura Publisher, Windows programs like PageMaker and Excel, 1-2-3, and a number of forms preparation products that don't work at all with the DeskJet. If you're skeptical of what LaserTwin can do, get a copy of the promotional brochure—the sample printouts from Ventura and AutoCAD are pretty convincing.

To use LaserTwin, you start by setting up your application software to print to a LaserJet, not the DeskJet. As a TSR, LaserTwin works by intercepting the output destined for that imaginary LaserJet. For each page worth of printer output generated by the program, LaserTwin assembles all the text and graphics data, the printer commands, and the fonts into a high-resolution graphics image of the final page. It then sends out this "bitmap" page image in the form your DeskJet will understand. This process is functionally identical to what happens when you send a page of printer data to a real LaserJet. The only difference is that the LaserJet has a powerful computer of its own, which carries out the page-composition process inside the LaserJet, rather than in your computer. But the LaserJet must still assemble internally a bitmap for each page it prints.

As you can guess, creating the page images and sending them to the DeskJet can take LaserTwin some time, even if you have a fast computer. That's why the utility comes with a print spooler of its own. The printer output from your program and the resulting page images are stored temporarily on your hard disk (which is required). While you go back to work in your program LaserTwin operates behind the scenes to finish composing the pages, and to send them to the DeskJet as fast as the printer can accept them.

LaserTwin comes with a set of downloadable fonts that match the built-in ones on the LaserJet Series II. An optional font pack supplies all the fonts on the LaserJet cartridges available from HP. Besides the improvement in printer control LaserTwin can give you, another advantage for some people is that you can use identical software setups for both the LaserJet and the DeskJet. If your company uses both printers, just install all your software for the LaserJet, pile on the LaserJet fonts, and run LaserTwin when you want to print to a DeskJet.

Drawbacks? Since LaserTwin prints everything in graphics mode, pages of text roll out more slowly than they would if you used the DeskJet's text mode. Also, because it's not a true setup utility, LaserTwin won't help in those situations where the program you're using puts limits on which fonts or formatting commands you can use. If you want the most from a program like this, you may still want want a separate setup utility such as LaserControl or Printer Genius.

Fonts

5

Understanding Typography

Now that you have a printer that can turn out typeset-quality documents right from your desktop, the challenge lies in knowing how to make it live up to its typographic potential. This chapter lays the groundwork for everything you want to do with type and the DeskJet. Like any craft, typography has its collection of special terms, and you'll be introduced to most of the important ones here. You'll learn the difference between a typeface and a font, and the significance of mysterious terms like *serifs, kerning,* and *leading.* You'll also find some practical tips on topics such as how to choose the right font, and how to use type effectively to make your documents look really sharp.

Type fundamentals

When you think about it, it's obvious that every printed character has its own unique design. Compare these three sets of symbols carefully:

$$AQ \quad AQ \quad AQ$$

I guess you can see that all three specimens consist of the letters *A* and *Q*. But what makes each character design distinct from its counterparts? For one thing, their proportions—width compared to height—are a little different. See how the thickness of the *strokes*—the lines that make up the characters— is different from character to character. Notice too that this thickness, the *stroke weight,* changes within some of the characters. To get even more detailed, notice that the lines in each *A* trace different paths, and that the tail of each *Q* joins the main part of the character at different angles and at different places.

One other aspect of character design is worth pointing out. The *A* on the left has little lines or bars extending out from the main parts of the character. The *A* on the right, by contrast, is just straight lines, and doesn't have these bars. The term for these little lines is *serifs*. A character without them is a *sans serif* character (sans means "without" in French).

The imaginary horizontal line upon which the characters rest is called the *baseline.* The bottoms of rounded characters such as *o* sometimes extend below the baseline slightly. Of course, a few lowercase characters, such as *g*s and *p*s, have long downward strokes called *descenders.* Similarly, the upward strokes of letters such as *h* and *l* are known as *ascenders.* Ascenders usually end at the same height as the tops of uppercase letters, but in some cases are taller.

Typefaces

The term *typeface* designates a complete set of characters, all sharing a similar design. A single typeface encompasses as many letters, numbers, punctuation marks, and miscellaneous symbols as the typeface designer wishes to create. When you consider all the variations of letters used in all the European languages, all the symbols used in mathematics and scientific notation, and the tremendous range of special punctuation marks, you can see why some exhaustively complete typefaces include several hundred characters.

Typeface designers strive to impart a consistent appearance to all the characters in the "face," so that they look like they belong together. In a given typeface, the various characters will have similar proportions, their strokes will be roughly comparable in width, and the strokes will vary in width in a similar fashion.

Typefaces are often broadly classified as serif or sans serif since the characters in a typeface all usually either have serifs or don't have serifs. Among serif typefaces, the appearance of the serifs is an important distinguishing design element. In some fancy typefaces, serifs aren't enough, and the designer adds ornate flourishes and curlicues.

Another way to classify typeface designs is based on relative width of the characters in the face. *Monospaced* typeface designs, such as Courier and Letter Gothic, consist of characters which are all the same width. Monospaced typefaces were originally created for typewriters, where each metal bar had to be the same size. With a combination of large serifs and extra white space, a skinny little *i* fills up just as much room on a line as a wide *w*.

♪ **Note:** *Hewlett-Packard refers to monospaced typefaces as fixed pitch faces. The two terms are synonymous.*

In *proportionally spaced* typefaces, the width of each character varies according to the taste of the designer. Proportionally spaced faces generally look classier and more professional than the monospaced variety. They're easier to read, and they let you fit more characters on a page since there's no wasted space around the *i*s, *l*s, and *t*s. Numerals in a proportionally spaced typeface are usually monospaced, in order to make columns of numbers line up.

Here are examples of monospaced and proportionally spaced typefaces:

```
This text is printed in
the monospaced Courier
typeface. Notice how
each character lines up
with the one above it.
That's because they're
all of equal width.
Courier is a popular
typewriter typeface.
It's built into the
DeskJet.
```

This text is printed in proportionally spaced Helvetica. In this typeface, nothing lines up from line to line, since each letter has a different width. Helvetica is said to be the world's most frequently used typeface. HP's Helv is one of many imitations of Helvetica available for the DeskJet.

Still another typeface classification system revolves around a face's intended function. *Text* or *body* faces are for long blocks of text, and are designed for easy reading. *Display* faces are meant to arrest the reader's attention, and are used in larger sizes to make headlines, titles, and other snippets of text stand out. *Decorative* or *novelty* faces are so flashy and strongly stylized that they may distract attention from your message, but they're fun to use and can set a special mood. Then there are *symbol* faces for non-text purposes. Here are some examples:

Benguiat is a Display Typeface.

You can print in Savage, a novelty font, if you have Publisher's Powerpak.

Here are characters from a musical symbol typeface:

Finally, *typeface families* are collections of two or more typefaces of very similar design, but different in some aspects. Along with the regular version of a typeface, a typeface family may contain italics, boldface, compressed (squished horizontally) or expanded (stretched) versions. Other characteristics, such as the character proportions, the presence and type of serifs, and so on, remain roughly the same.

Confusingly, the members of a typeface family are often referred to as *type styles*, suggesting that they represent variations on a single basic typeface. In the DeskJet's case, that's partly true, because the printer can render any font in boldface (more on this in Chapter 6). But to print in italics, the DeskJet needs a separate italics font. Don't worry, we'll be defining the term "font" in just a moment.

Understanding typeface names

Typeface designs can't be copyrighted, but their names can. That's why so many typefaces that look the same are marketed under different names. Font vendors who don't want to pay to license the "real," original version of a face can easily create their own faithful imitation. All they have to do is more or less trace the outlines of the original typeface's characters and give the result a new name. Though the vendor can't sell the copycat typeface as the original, he or she is free to describe the imitator as "similar to" Times Roman, Helvetica, or whatever the original face is legally called. Even HP has taken this approach with its TmsRmn and its Helv. SWFTE's versions of the same typefaces are Roman and Helvette.

Fonts

In everyday speech and in most magazine articles on DTP, the terms "font" and "typeface" are used interchangeably, which is fine for most purposes. But there is a difference that can be important when you're shopping for type for the DeskJet.

Defined accurately, a typeface is the *design* for a set of characters, while a font is that design turned into a specific subset of characters, or *character set*, at a specific size (the way typographers measure font size will be described shortly). In the poem below, you can see examples of several different fonts. They look a lot alike because they're all based on the same typeface, but each font is a different size:

Here is one font.

Here is another.

Based on Times Roman,

All four are like brothers.

We'll get to the character set part of the font definition in a moment. For now, let's concentrate on the practical reason for differentiating between the terms typeface and font. When you buy a font for the DeskJet, you're getting the ability to print at only one size. In other words, you must buy a different font for each size at which you want to print. True, you may find several fonts, all of the same typeface, in a commercial font package. That means you'll be able to print at several different sizes—but not necessarily at any size you please.

But all this nit-picking goes out the window when you're talking about scalable typefaces, with which you can create your own fonts at any size you like. Although standard DeskJet typefaces are not scalable, you can buy special type-scaling utility programs that work perfectly well with the DeskJet. More on these in Chapter 7.

Character sets

A character set is a particular collection of character symbols selected from all those available in a typeface. A character set for a computerized font rarely contains all the characters in its typeface. There's a simple reason for this: the ASCII code system used by your PC and the DeskJet can only accommodate 256 characters at a time, while many complete typefaces include more than 256 characters. At any rate, this means that two fonts that start with the same typeface and type style and are the same size are still technically different fonts if they contain different character sets.

The DeskJet sports 19 built-in character sets, and some optional fonts offer additional character sets besides. For more details, see "DeskJet character sets" later in Chapter 6.

Font size

Type size is expressed with two separate terms, point size and pitch. *Point size* refers to how high the characters are, measured from the top of the highest ascender to the bottom of the descenders. A *point* is a typographer's unit of measurement very nearly equal to ⅟72nd of an inch. That means there are about 72 points to an inch. Just for completeness, 12 points make a *pica*, and you can therefore tap out 6 lines of pica type within a vertical inch on that old typewriter.

Pitch is a the number of characters that will fit side-by-side in an inch, measured horizontally across a line of text. Another way to look at pitch is as a measurement of the width of individual characters—the larger the pitch, the more characters fit in on a line of text, so the skinnier they have to be. A pitch value only makes sense when you're referring to monospaced type—in proportionally spaced typefaces, the number of characters per inch depends on which characters you're talking about.

There are still more typographic terms you'll run across frequently, many of which pertain to the way text is spaced and positioned in your document. We'll get to the most important of these concepts in a bit, but we'll linger on the topic of fonts for a little longer first.

Choosing and using fonts

You bought the DeskJet to make your documents look better, and a lot of the improvement will come from your printer's ability to print text in a variety of high-quality fonts. But to get the results you're expecting, you need to know how to select the right fonts for a given document, and how to use them effectively.

How to pick the right font

Just like wine connoisseurs, dyed-in-the-wool typographers can go on forever discussing the subtle strengths and weaknesses of each specimen of their stock-in-trade. In the typographer's case, the subject is fonts, which are unabashedly described with jargon such as "even color," or "warm and friendly, not overbearing."

For most people, though, choosing a font doesn't have to be a full-time preoccupation. Heed a few basic guidelines, and you can't go wrong.

Fonts for body text

For text passages of any length, your main priority in choosing a font is to find one that's easy to read. Here are some of the font characteristics that influence readability:

1.Simplicity. The font's typeface design should not call attention to itself.

2. Size. A font that's too small is obviously hard to read, but overly large fonts can also require too much effort from your reader. In most situations, you should use a font in the range of 9 to 14 points. If you have to go smaller to cram a lot of copy into a small area, use a typeface whose lowercase letters are tall, as measured by the height of a lower case x (this distance is thus referred to as the *x-height*). By contrast, a smaller x-height is better when you're filling a vertically long column, as in a newsletter or newspaper.

3. Weight. Use a font based on a typeface of medium stroke weight. If it's too light, it won't stand out from the background. If it's too heavy, the extra thickness tends to obscure the empty areas within the characters (the *counterforms*), which help the reader recognize the character.

4. Uniformity of strokes. The stroke thickness of the font's typeface should be fairly uniform. If not, the thin strokes will verge on invisibility, the heavy strokes will obscure character definition, and the contrast between them will cause a scintillating effect that further reduces readability.

5. Slant. Use upright fonts instead of italics (slanted) ones for long stretches of text. Italics slow the reader down, but they're good for emphasizing a word or phrase.

6. Serif versus sans serif. Both types of typefaces can be equally legible, depending on other characteristics, but custom may make your reader prefer one or the other. In the U.S., serif typefaces have long predominated.

Typefaces well-suited to body text are legion. Some of the perennial favorites include Times Roman (TmsRmn or Dutch), Helvetica (Helv or Swiss), and Palatino. This book is set in ITC Garamond.

Fonts for display text

For headings, emphasized quotations, or other brief passages, you're freer to use more stylized display typefaces for their inherent visual appeal. Readers attracted by the look of the type will be willing to make a little more effort to get the message, as long as the text is short. On the other hand, it's perfectly acceptable to stick with a simple typeface for display text, and just use a larger-sized font. In many books, for example, headings are set in good old Helvetica.

Beyond these very general guidelines, the choice of typeface is a matter of personal taste. If you feel uncomfortable with that responsibility, take the easy way out: buy HP's TmsRmn and Helv in a smattering of sizes, or their equivalents from another vendor, and leave it at that (we'll cover the forms in which you can buy fonts in Chapter 6).

Designing with type

It's not enough just to pick your font. You also have to decide how you're going to use it in your document. Among the design issues you need to consider are how to mix fonts, how to create emphasis, and how to space and position your text for best readability and optimal overall appearance. While matters of art and taste can hardly be codified, there are some simple rules that will help you avoid the most glaring errors.

Mixing fonts

Limit the number of typeface families in a document. Just because the DeskJet gives you the ability to mix fonts freely in a single document doesn't mean you should do so. What's great about having a variety of fonts to pick from is that you can choose the one or two that best suit the tone and meaning of your document—not that you can fill your document with a distracting melange of different faces. Like ornate individual typefaces, frequent typeface changes attract attention to the type itself, distracting the reader from the meaning of your text.

For most documents, one or two typeface families should suffice. For example, a common practice is to use a serif face for the body of your text, and a sans serif face for the headings. When in doubt, go with the smaller number of typefaces.

Use typefaces that contrast significantly when you want to indicate the differences in function between various sections of text. The right reason to use multiple typefaces is to highlight the difference between, say, headlines and the body of the text, or between a general discussion and a supporting collection of dense facts and figures. But when you do decide that a typeface change is in order, make sure the typefaces you juxtapose are significantly different. Again, a good starting point is to use a serif face for one function, a sans serif face for the other.

Use even point size multiples. Again, the "point" in varying type size is to emphasize the differences between different portions of your text. You want the reader to notice the size contrasts, at least on the subconscious level. Don't make it hard to distinguish them—no two fonts in the same document should be closer than two points apart. For example, you might select a 12 point font for your main ideas, and a 10 point font for explanatory material the reader might want to skip.

☁ *Caution: When you want to emphasize a point, stay away from underlining, and above all don't use all capital letters. Both reduce readability significantly.*

Use italics instead of underlining to emphasize important phrases. Typists adopted underlining to indicate emphasis primarily because typewriters can't produce italics or boldface, but underlining tends to make text look cluttered and crowded. The DeskJet can print both italics and boldface, so you don't need to underline unless you really want to for some special reason.

Even more important, AVOID USING ALL CAPITAL LETTERS TO CREATE EMPHASIS. MORE THAN ANY OTHER FACTOR, ALL-UPPERCASE TEXT REDUCES THE READABILITY OF YOUR COPY. (Seen enough?) The uniform height of the letters makes it very hard for the eye to distinguish individual characters. What's more, all-uppercase passages take up considerably more space than ordinary text.

Spacing and positioning text

The vertical distance between lines (the *leading* or *linespacing*) is one of the most important factors in creating a readable block of text. Most word processors and desktop publishing programs put in too little leading for you, with the result that the text is overly dense and hard to read.

Leading is measured in points, measured from the baseline of one line to the next. You'll often see it written with the typeface's point size—a 12 point face with 14 points of leading is expressed as 12/14, for example.

Although the optimal amount of leading varies from document to document and from typeface to typeface, a good place to start is with leading of at least 120% of the typeface's point size. For 9- to 11-point type, use 1 to 3 additional points of leading; add 2 to 4 points of leading to 12 point type; and so on. Add more leading for long lines of text, for bold or sans serif faces, and for faces that have strongly contrasting stroke weights.

When a block of text is *justified*, the horizontal boundaries of all the lines in the block are aligned with one another. The most common "unjustified" alternative is *ragged right*, in which the lines are flush on the left, but vary in length on the right.

Ragged right text is easier to read, because the spaces between letters and words are even, and because the varying line lengths serve as reference points when the eye looks for the beginning of the next line. Still, try not to make the text *too* ragged on the right, or your reader will get distracted by the striking shape of the column.

Justified text gives your document a formal "published" appearance. Almost all word processors can automatically justify your text for you, but they don't all do an equally good job of it. Justification is achieved by several methods: you can hyphenate words, you can increase the space between the words (the *wordspacing*) and between the individual letters (the *letterspacing*). You must use these techniques carefully, though, since too many hyphens create clutter, and too much space breaks up the flow of the text, making it harder to read. If you use justification, you'll have to look at your document closely after it's printed to make sure these problems aren't severe.

Whether or not you justify, wordspacing and letterspacing are important for optimum readability. When words are too far apart, the eye has to hurdle the gaps and reading slows down. The wordspacing should be smaller than the leading, or the eye will move down the lines instead of across. To fit a given amount of text into a defined space, adjust the wordspacing, not the letterspacing, whenever possible.

Letterspacing should above all be even, to allow the eye to "glide" over the words without jerky movements. You may want to adjust the letterspacing to create an effect that's not too light or too dark. In general, you can space letters more closely in brief passages—headlines and the like—than in the main body of your text. The process of evenly adjusting the letterspacing for a group of characters at the same time is known as *tracking*.

Kerning is used to tighten or loosen the space between two adjacent characters. It's a common practice because the ordinary spacing alloted to some characters becomes too large when the characters are paired with certain others. For example, consider the capital *T* and the adjacent *h* in the word "The." The typeface is designed so that when you print the *T*, enough room is left so a tall character like the *h* won't touch it. The space alloted to the *T* doesn't change if you erase the *h* and substitute a short *o*, but the space is now too big, since the *o* can nestle in under the bar at the top of the *T*.

Kerning corrects this problem. It's especially useful for type you print in large point sizes of type, where the extra spaces become more noticeable. Some word processors let you kern manually, and the major desktop publishing programs will do it for you automatically as well.

The length of each line is another factor that influences readability. For long passages, choose a combination of line length and font size so that each line contains about 55 to 70 characters, or about 9 to 12 words.

6

DeskJet Fonts

∾

In concept, a DeskJet font is a particular set of characters in a particular typeface that you can print at a specific size. In practical terms, however, a font is something built into the printer, or something you buy on a disk or as a cartridge. This chapter introduces you to the way your printer handles fonts in general and to each of the forms of DeskJet fonts in particular. Later in the chapter, you'll also find a section on cartridge fonts. Chapter 7 is devoted to soft fonts, the kind you buy on disks, and related font alternatives.

Types of DeskJet fonts

In the past, when someone talked about a DeskJet font, they meant the standard text-mode font as defined by Hewlett Packard, the kind that are built into your printer. Recently, however, breakthroughs in software technology have brought an entirely different kind of font to the fore, the kind generated from scalable typefaces. We'll spend a lot of time on scalable typefaces in Chapter 7, and it's important you understand them before you invest in a font library. In this chapter, however, we'll focus on the standard DeskJet fonts.

Standard text-mode DeskJet fonts are stored in three different places in your printer, but they all work in exactly the same way otherwise. The three types of standard fonts are:

Internal fonts: Every DeskJet has a limited complement of fonts permanently hardwired into the printer. The DeskJet Plus has several internal variations of Courier fonts not available on the original DeskJet, and the DeskJet 500 includes a few CG Times and Letter Gothic fonts as well.

Cartridge fonts: The DeskJet has two slots just behind the keypad controls on the right, intended for optional font cartridges sold by HP. Each cartridge permanently stores font data for one or more fonts. Once you've placed a font cartridge into a slot, you can select the cartridge fonts from the keypad or via software commands, just as if they were built into the printer. You'll find more information on using cartridge fonts later in this chapter.

Soft fonts: Another way to add fonts to your DeskJet is to buy them in the form of files recorded on floppy disks. To use these *soft fonts*, you must download the font files from your computer to the printer, where they're stored in the memory of special RAM cartridges you must first install. Once you've downloaded a soft font, you can select it via software commands, but not via the keypad. Although a bit less convenient than cartridge fonts, soft fonts are usually a better buy. You'll find a complete discussion of the pros and cons of soft fonts along with instructions for using them in Chapter 7.

How the DeskJet handles fonts

In the printer, a standard DeskJet font is stored as a big collection of data representing the dots that must be printed to construct each character. The DeskJet keeps all this font data in its equivalent of a table, in which the set of dots for each character is referenced by that character's unique code number.

Although the DeskJet can store many fonts simultaneously, only one of them can be active for printing at a time. When you ask the DeskJet to print a particular character, it looks up that character's dot data in the active font table. The data tells it which dots to print, and out comes the character you wanted.

To print text in another font, you must first *select* the new font (we'll see how that's done in a moment). In response, the printer shifts its attention to the data table for the new font. When the next printable ASCII code comes along, the DeskJet takes its instructions for printing the character from the new font table, and the letter or number you see on the page reflects the change.

DeskJet font capabilities and limitations

Although the DeskJet was the first printer for under $1000 to offer 300-dpi text printing in a wide array of fonts, it does have limitations when it comes to font selection. This section summarizes what you can and can't do with DeskJet fonts.

Character spacing

Fonts for the original and Plus lack the character-to-character spacing (kerning) information present in 500 fonts—so you can't use 500 fonts with earlier models.

Font size

The DeskJet is capable of printing a relatively limited range of font sizes. You'll hear various opinions about the maximum possible point size of DeskJet fonts, but all of them are based on the same basic facts: Your printer can cover an area of only 50 dots high in a single pass of the printhead. Since a dot is $\frac{1}{300}$-inch, this means you can print no more than $\frac{1}{6}$ of an inch, or 12 points, on one pass. To allow for larger fonts, the original DeskJet can print characters using two passes of the printhead, for a total height of 100 dots (24 points). The DeskJet Plus can do even better, as it can make as many as four printhead passes to print a character. Unfortunately, however, DeskJet fonts can't usually be 200 dots (48 points) tall—another limitation gets in the way. On both models of the printer, a single character can be no *wider* than 127 dots. Except for novelty fonts whose characters are very tall and skinny, this width limitation restricts the size of DeskJet Plus fonts to about 30 points.

✂ *Tip:* *If the top and bottom portions of tall characters are out of alignment, you can cure the problem by setting the DeskJet to print unidirectionally. Normally, to save time, the DeskJet prints continuously as the printhead moves in both directions across the page. However, some DeskJets are unable to maintain precise alignment between the left-to-right and right-to-left passes of the printhead, a defect that shows up when printing characters larger than 50 dots high. In the unidirectional print mode, the printhead goes all the way back to the extreme left side of the carriage at the beginning of each pass, ensuring proper alignment. To switch to unidirectional mode, use a setup utility or send the escape sequence ESC&k0W to your printer.*

One way to make larger fonts suitable for headlines is to remove all the lowercase letters. As you'll recall from Chapter 5, a font's overall point size is measured from the top of the tallest ascender to the bottom of the lowest descender. Since uppercase letters have no descenders, an all-uppercase font can be enlarged to fill the space that would normally be taken up by the descenders of the lowercase letters. This method works best for the original DeskJet, permitting fonts up to 30 points tall (see Chapter 7 for sources of these and other soft fonts). While the same technique could theoretically be used to make 60-point DeskJet Plus fonts, the width restriction means that many of the characters would be too narrow.

✂ *Tip:* *You can print text characters as graphics to get around the size limitations on DeskJet fonts. For details, see the section "Graphics fonts" in Chapter 7.*

Font options: half-size, boldface, and draft mode

In Chapter 5, you learned that a regular Courier font and boldface Courier are two different fonts, technically speaking, and likewise, that while 12-point TmsRmn and 24-point TmsRmn look very similar, they too exist independently. Now it's time to learn the DeskJet's exceptions to the rules.

Built into the DeskJet are software routines that can transform any font in a variety of ways. For example, most DeskJet fonts can be scaled by the printer to half its labelled size. If you have a 12-point Helv on board, you can print it at both 12 and 6 points by sending the correct command to the DeskJet. The same holds true for boldface fonts. In this case, the printer simply makes each character one or two dots wider when you request the boldface version of the font.

The drawback of these automatic modifications is that they're mechanically applied to every character without a human designer's for each individual character. As a result, the resulting type doesn't look as crisp as you get from a font originally designed for the smaller size or for bold printing. If you want the best possible text quality from your printer, you'll need to buy, load, and select genuine bold fonts, rather than relying on the DeskJet's automatic bolding feature.

✂ *Tip: If you've installed a font that permits automatic boldface and a separate genuine boldface font of the same typeface and size, the command for boldface printing will turn on the automatic bolding feature instead of selecting the real bold font. Print quality will suffer as a result, and characters may not be spaced properly. There's no way to solve this problem short of redefining the information in the fonts themselves so that the automatic bolding feature is turned off. This is a technically demanding job, but your font vendor may be able to assist you.*

You can view the DeskJet's draft mode as another one of these automatic font transformations. In draft mode, some of the dots in each character are omitted. The resulting type is gray rather than solid black but still very sharp, and ink consumption is reduced substantially.

Although the DeskJet can theoretically print any font at half size, in boldface, or in draft mode, you can only use these automatic modifications on fonts that permit them. Each font contains separate settings that turn the half-size, boldface, and draft mode options on or off. If the font allows automatic bold printing, it will also include a setting telling the DeskJet whether to add one or two dots to create the bold effect.

Italics

The DeskJet does not have an automatic italicizing feature. To print text in italics with the DeskJet, you need a separate italics font, period.

Landscape fonts

Although the DeskJet can print text in its "sideways" landscape orientation, your selection of fonts is limited in this mode. The DeskJet Plus and 500 models feature built-in landscape Courier fonts. Font cartridge K supplies these same landscape Courier fonts for the original DeskJet, while cartridge L has several landscape versions of Courier and Letter Gothic. Both Courier and Letter Gothic are monospaced typefaces—it's not possible to print proportionally spaced text in landscape mode. The printer does accept downloaded landscape soft fonts as long as they're monospaced.

✄ Tip: *To print in landscape mode with an original model DeskJet, you must install landscape cartridge HP22707K or HP22707L. Do not use the K cartridge in the DeskJet Plus, since the printer already has these fonts built in.*

To understand these limitations, it helps to know how the printer manages sideways printing. There aren't really any separate landscape fonts. Instead, the DeskJet just rotates the characters of a regular monospaced font counterclockwise by 90°. However, rotating the individual characters is the easy part. The real trick is to print them in the correct places on the page.

Remember that the DeskJet printhead always moves from side to side across the page it's printing, never up and down, and that you always feed paper lengthwise into the printer. In landscape mode, the part of the paper printed first—what would be the top in portrait mode—becomes the right side of the page. Obviously, it follows that the last part of the page to exit the printer is its left side. In other words, the first character you would read, the one at the top left margin, gets printed on the very last pass of the printhead. Clearly, the DeskJet cannot print the characters in the order in which they are received from your software. Instead, the printer must store a page worth of text in its buffer before it can begin to print a landscape page. Then, for the first pass of the printhead, it sifts through the buffer to find and print one character from each line in the text, the one that belongs at the right margin of the page (of course, a given line may not have a character at the right margin). For the next pass, it picks out the character from each line that belongs in the next column to the left, and so on.

To figure out which character belongs where on the page, the DeskJet relies on the simple assumption that each character occupies an equal amount of space horizontally, along a line of text. There's not enough RAM in the DeskJet's buffer to store and manipulate spacing specifications for each character on an entire page, nor is the printer programmed to make the necessary calculations. This explains why landscape fonts must be the monospaced kind.

⌒ **Caution:** *In landscape mode, printing starts only after the DeskJet has received a full page of data or a form feed command (explained in Chapters 8 and 22), or after you've pressed the FF button on the keypad. This is because the DeskJet must know where the data for the page ends in order to figure out where to place the landscape characters. If you send less than a full page of data to the printer without a form feed command, the BUSY light will blink to indicate that the data has been received, but printing won't begin until you press the FF key.*

♪ **Note:** *By the way, although the DeskJet technically can't print graphics in its own landscape mode, many software programs are able to achieve the same results. The trick is to rotate the graphic into the sideways orientation within your computer, then send the resulting image to the DeskJet in portrait mode. The printout looks the same as if the DeskJet had its own landscape mode.*

DeskJet character sets

You'll recall from Chapter 5 that part of a font's definition is its character set, the specific set of symbols the font contains. A sampling of the DeskJet's 19 built-in character sets are shown in Appendix B. Some optional fonts offer additional character sets besides. A quick scan of the Appendix will show you that most character sets start with all the ordinary letters, numbers, and punctuation marks, and then add special characters suited to a specific purpose: foreign languages, mathematics and engineering, or character-based graphics. On the other hand, some character sets (and the typefaces from which they're drawn) consist entirely of special symbols such as math symbols, character graphics, little pictures, bar codes, or musical symbols.

A character set that tries to offer something for everybody is the one used for screen displays in the IBM PC and thousands of workalike computers. This set is reproduced in the DeskJet's internal fonts, and is known as the PC-8 set in DeskJet parlance. Most users find the selection of characters adequate, though there are the critics who say that in trying to please everyone, the PC-8 character set satisfies no one. For everyday business use, the PC-8 character set does have a few glaring omissions—the trademark, registered trademark, and copyright symbols (these can be found in the DeskJet's Legal character set, by the way).

✄ **Tip:** *Use the DeskJet's Legal character set to print the trademark (™), registered trademark (®), and copyright (©) symbols.*

Selecting the font of your wont

The simplest way to select the font you want to print with is via the FONT button on the DeskJet's keypad. Just press the button repeatedly until the desired font you've activated the desired font. When you've selected the right font, its indicator light glows.

Often, however, you'll want to change fonts by way of software, rather than with the keypad. For one thing, any soft fonts you've downloaded to your DeskJet are inaccessible with the FONT button, and you can only select them via printer commands from the computer. Nor is the FONT button effective when you want to switch fonts within a document—there's no way you could hit it at the right time. In this case, you have to manually place the commands for changing fonts at the right locations in your document, or let your software program send the commands for you. In some cases, you may find it simply more convenient to select fonts with software, so you don't have to reach over and press the FONT button.

An introduction to font selection commands

When you select a font from the keypad, you're setting all its attributes—typeface, point size, pitch, and so forth—at once. To select a font via printer commands, however, you or your software must set each of these attributes independently using separate escape sequences. For example, to specify the typeface of the font you want to activate, you must send the DeskJet an escape sequence calling for that typeface by its code number (every typeface has one). You'd send another escape sequence to specify the font's size, and still another to indicate italics or boldface.

♪ **Note:** *Actually, as you'll learn in Chapter 7, there is a way to select a font with a single command in some circumstances, but it's not as reliable as specifying each font attribute separately.*

Even though each font attribute can theoretically be controlled independently through printer commands, don't get the idea that you can break the rule about a font having a fixed point size and pitch. While there are separate commands for each font attribute, you can only select the attributes that are available in the specific fonts you've installed. If you order up a nonexistent point size, for instance, the DeskJet will simply substitute the font closest in size to your request.

Obviously, having an application program or a setup utility issue the commands to select your desired font for you is far more convenient that doing it yourself. But in the event that you need to select fonts on your own via printer commands, you'll find complete instructions in Chapter 22.

Using font cartridges

Font cartridges are without question the most convenient format for adding optional fonts to your DeskJet. They're a no fuss, no muss solution—just plug in a cartridge and you're instantly ready to print using any of the cartridge fonts. The drawbacks are that you're stuck with the particular fonts that come on the cartridge, and that cartridge fonts cost more per font than do soft fonts.

Be sure that the font cartridge you plan to buy will work with your DeskJet model. Cartridges designed for the original DeskJet are compatible with any later model, but the reverse isn't true: many of the more recently released cartridges won't work in the original DeskJet. And there are some font cartridges that only work with the 500.

You can buy font cartridges from HP and from at least one third-party font supplier, Elesys (most third-party font vendors sell soft fonts instead). Elesys' cartridges are a great value, offering lots of high-quality fonts at very attractive prices. The Elefont Desk Cartridge contains 68 different fonts in sizes from 5 to 16 points drawn from the CG Times, CG Triumvirate, Prestige Elite, and Letter Gothic typefaces. The Elefont Headline Cartridge has 28 Times and Triumvirate fonts from 11 to 30 points high. And there's a Landscape Cartridge with 68 fonts from four monospaced typefaces in sizes from 3.5 to 28 points. They sell for $99 apiece, and you can buy them in pairs and save about $20. Call Elesys at 800/637-0500 or 408/747-0233; the address is 529 Weddell Drive, Sunnyvale, CA 94089.

Font cartridge anatomy

Inside a font cartridge, the font data is stored in permanent form on ROM (read-only memory) chips. At the bottom of the cartridge is an electronic connector that goes into a mating slot in the printer, and lets the DeskJet communicate with the ROM fonts.

The label from a typical cartridge is pictured below in Figure 6-1. Just under the HP logo, the label lists the cartridge number. This number is simply HP's own catalog number for the cartridge, but I guess it's a better name than something like "SX-900 Plus." Under the part number in tiny print is a short message indicating the character sets available for the fonts in the cartridge.

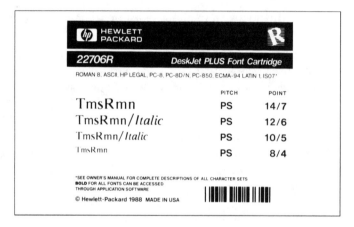

Figure 6-1: *A DeskJet font cartridge label*

Most of the cartridge label is devoted to a list of the fonts contained in the cartridge. The name of each font is printed as a sample of what the font looks like at actual size. Then comes a column for pitch (note that most monospaced fonts can be printed at either of two pitches). The pitch column reads PS for proportionally spaced fonts, since these fonts don't have a set pitch value. Finally, there's a column for the font's point size. Again, many fonts can be printed at full- or half-size, and you'll see both sizes on the label if that's the case.

Installing font cartridges

⌒ ***Caution:*** *Never install or remove a font cartridge when the DeskJet is turned on.*

Remember one critical point about installing and removing font cartridges: don't do it when the power is on. Otherwise, there's not much that can go wrong with a font cartridge. Once the slot cover is off, you just pop the cartridge in the slot, connector side down, like toast in a toaster—you can't even plug it in backwards. For me, the hardest part of the installation is taking off the little plastic piece that covers the slot. You can't do it with your fingers— use a small flatblade screwdriver, a rounded dinner knife, or the tip of a pen instead. You can install a single font cartridge in either slot, and you can put cartridges in both slots at the same time.

⌒ ***Caution:*** *There is one combination of cartridges that won't work: don't install a landscape cartridge and the Epson emulation cartridge at the same time.*

Accessing cartridge fonts

Since there's a direct electronic connection between a font cartridge and the DeskJet, cartridge fonts act just as if they were part of the original equipment of your printer. You can select a font on any installed cartridge by pressing the FONT button on the keypad repeatedly until the indicator light next to the font's abbreviation on the top of the cartridge glows.

If you're trying to select the half-size version of the desired font, keep pressing the FONT button until both the font's indicator light and the indicator closest to the FONT button (the one marked with a series of several red lines) are glowing. If you're selecting a landscape font, press the FONT key until both the font's indicator and the indicator for landscape mode glow. You can also access cartridge fonts using printer commands as detailed in Chapter 22.

7

Using Soft Fonts and Scalable Type

∾

Once you get hooked on the idea of using fonts creatively, you won't be satisfied by the limited selection of fonts available built into the DeskJet and on cartridges. For the variety you want, you must turn to soft fonts and other software-based font solutions. The best choice for most people is an on-the-fly typeface scaling system. But we'll look at all the options in this chapter.

Just in case you missed the definition earlier in the book, soft fonts are standard DeskJet fonts supplied on floppy disks. To install them in your DeskJet, you transfer or *download* these files to the printer, much as you do when you print ordinary text or graphics files. Once they reach the DeskJet, soft fonts are stored in the memory provided by special RAM cartridges you must add to the printer first.

Although conventional soft fonts often come in sets, you're still buying them in predetermined, fixed sizes. In other words, if the set you buy doesn't have a 13-point font, you can't print in 13-point type. You can avoid this limitation by buying *font generator* software instead. Font generators let you create your own soft fonts in as many sizes as you like, and often allow you to add snazzy special effects to the fonts. You then download the new fonts to your DeskJet just as you would regular soft fonts.

But the most flexible and convenient software-based font alternative is to use on-the-fly *typeface scaling* software. These packages produce text at just about any size you specify while you print, doing away entirely with the need for individual soft fonts. Some typeface scaling systems let you add special effects as well. And since you don't need separate fonts for each size you want to print, you save lots of disk space.

Typeface scaling systems (let's just refer to them as "scalable fonts") do have some potential disadvantages, which we'll cover in the appropriate section later in this chapter. Still, scalable fonts are generally your best bet in DeskJet type. To use them, you must meet one key criteria: your word processor, desktop publisher, or other application software must be compatible with the scalable fonts you're using. But if you rely on WordPerfect, Microsoft Word, Ventura, Microsoft Works, or any Windows program for your printouts, you won't be missing much if you skip all the material on regular soft fonts and font generators and go directly to the section on scalable fonts.

Soft fonts

Soft fonts can claim three major advantages over fonts that come on cartridges: variety, flexibility, and lower cost. Although they aren't quite as cheap or convenient as scalable fonts, they'll work with almost any software, and can offer slightly higher quality in some cases (we'll return to the quality issue in the section on scalable fonts).

If you look only at the HP catalog, you wouldn't know that a large variety of typefaces are available in soft fonts for the DeskJet, far more than you can get on cartridges. At this writing, HP sells only three soft font packages, representing various sizes of just three very conventional typeface families. Turn to the third-party font suppliers, though, and you'll find a much larger range of soft font offerings encompassing many different typeface designs, from ordinary text faces to ornate decorative faces. What's more, it's possible to convert any of the huge number of LaserJet soft fonts to DeskJet format. Though font quality suffers slightly in the conversion process, this opens up a vast cornucopia of typeface possibilities (more on LaserJet to DeskJet font conversions later in this chapter).

Even if you don't covet infinite typeface variety, you'll enjoy greater flexibility with soft fonts. You can mix fonts from one package with those from any other, even from another font supplier. By contrast, the particular set of fonts on a cartridge is permanently fixed. Let's say you have a DeskJet Plus and you want to print a newsletter using 30 point TmsRmn for the headlines, 10 point Helv for the captions, and 12 point TmsRmn for your body text, a common set of font choices. Unfortunately, there's no combination of two font cartridges that offers all three fonts. Buy HP's TmsRmn/Helv soft font package, however, and you can download just the fonts you need from all those in the assortment.

From most suppliers, soft fonts also cost much less per font than do cartridge fonts. Many font vendors sell soft font sets with several different typefaces represented in each set. Font packages that generate soft fonts from master outlines (see the section on font generators later in this chapter) give you the ability to create as many different size fonts as you like, within the range allowed by the DeskJet—and all for one price.

The bad news

For all their good points, soft fonts also have some drawbacks compared to cartridge fonts. For one thing, they take up lots of room on disk, room that you might want to use for programs and files instead. Another difficulty is that you have to customize printer drivers for your soft fonts, a process that tends to be complicated and time-consuming. Finally, soft fonts must be downloaded to your printer, which also takes time. You'll learn how to minimize these problems later in the chapter.

Getting started with soft fonts

In order to use soft fonts, you'll have to take care of several preliminaries. First, you'll need to purchase additional memory for your DeskJet in the form of RAM cartridges. Next, you'll probably want to install the soft fonts you use most often on your hard disk, if you have one. Finally, you'll need to plan and implement a strategy for downloading the fonts to your printer.

Adding RAM cartridges: a must for soft fonts

⌒ *Caution:* *You must add at least one RAM cartridge to use soft fonts in your DeskJet. DO NOT install or remove RAM cartridges while the DeskJet is on.*

Before you can even begin to work with soft fonts, you must bolster your DeskJet's memory capacity. As it comes from the factory, the DeskJet can't accommodate even a single soft font. To use soft fonts, you must install at least one optional RAM cartridge in the machine. RAM cartridges are available in 128K and 256K models, but the latter work don't work in the original DeskJet. You can mix or match the two kinds of RAM cartridges in the PLUS. RAM cartridges are available from HP and, for less money, from Elesys (800/637-0500; 408/747-0233).

The RAM cartridges install in the same slots used for font cartridges, located just behind the main keypad controls on the printer's right side. To install a RAM cartridge, remove the plastic panel covering one of the slots with a small flatblade screwdriver. Then insert the RAM cartridge so that the connector on the bottom of the cartridge plugs into its counterpart at the bottom of the cartridge slot.

Sources of soft fonts

⌒ *Caution:* *Be sure the soft fonts you buy work with your DeskJet model. Soft fonts for the original DeskJet will work in any model, but those marked for the Plus work only with the Plus or 500, while DeskJet 500 soft fonts work only with that machine.*

Soft fonts specifically intended for the DeskJet are a bit scarce. HP offers only a handful of soft font packages. One advantage of HP's soft fonts is that they're recognized by the printer drivers of some application software—few, if any, printer drivers offer built-in support for third-party soft fonts. HP does supply a font downloading utility with its soft font packages.

Probably the most popular DeskJet soft fonts are the ones marketed by Elfring Soft Fonts. A sample of Elfring's 30-point uppercase-only Roman is included in the soft font sampler in Figure 7-1. You can buy a set of fonts covering multiple sizes from one typeface, or pick from collections organized by function: headlines, spreadsheets, and so on. Elfring also sells an excellent font management utility called TSR Download, profiled later in this chapter, and a utility for selecting font options such as boldface and half-sized printing.

There are other ways to obtain DeskJet soft fonts. You can generate your own at any size you like using one of the font generating systems we'll look at later. Another source of DeskJet fonts is the vast catalog of LaserJet fonts: an inexpensive utility covered in this chapter can convert almost any LaserJet font to DeskJet format. Hundreds of LaserJet fonts are available from legions of suppliers. In fact, you can obtain many LaserJet fonts for free from user groups and electronic bulletin boards such as CompuServe.

Understanding font filenames

It's very easy to accumulate so many soft fonts that you lose track of which is which. After all, you need a separate font file for each unique combination of typeface, point size, and style (regular or italic). DOS allows only 11 characters total in a filename, not enough space for a full description of all the font's characteristics.

Making the best of a bad situation, HP has ordained a coding scheme for naming DeskJet (and LaserJet) soft fonts. True, font names that follow this convention still look like gibberish. However, once you know the code you can learn a lot about a font from its name, and it will be much easier to find the font you want in a crowded directory on you hard disk.

⌒ **Caution:** *Unfortunately, many soft font suppliers don't follow HP's font naming convention. If you use such fonts you'll just have to learn whatever naming system the vendor dreamed up, or rename the files to conform to the HP code.*

Here's the pattern for soft font filenames in HP's coded system:

AABBBCDD.EEF

and two examples:

TR12ØMPN.DJP

CO145XØ8.DJP

The first two characters in the name, *AA* in the pattern, are an abbreviation for the font's typeface. In the examples, **TR** stands for Times Roman, and **BW** for Broadway.

The next three characters, represented by *BBB* in the pattern, give the font's size, in half-point increments. You have to imagine the decimal point between the second and third characters in this group. In the first example, the characters **12Ø** indicate that the font is 12.0 points high. In the second example, **145** means the font is 14.5 points high.

The sixth character, *C* in the pattern, stands for the font's style, weight, or both. **M** in the first example indicates an ordinary medium weight, upright font, while **X** in the second example signifies a bold-italic font. Here are the style and weight designations you'll see most often:

M	Medium
R	Regular
B	Bold
I	Italic
L	Light
X	Bold italic

(M and R are roughly synonymous)

The seventh and eighth characters in the name, represented by *DD* in the pattern, tell you what sort of character spacing the font employs. The letters **PN** in the first example indicate that this is a proportionally spaced font. If you find numbers instead of letters in this position in the name, as in the second example, they mean that you're dealing with a fixed space font. In the example, **Ø8** indicates this is a 8 pitch font.

ELFRING'S 30-POINT ROMAN FONT

Elfring's 24-point Helv

Here is a Garamond-like LaserJet font converted to DeskJet format.

Here is 18-point Abbey from SWFTE.
It's another LaserJet conversion.

**SWFTE's version of 18-pt. Cooper Black.
Yet another LaserJet conversion.**

This is MoreFont's
26-pt. Opera, outlined.

26-pt. Showtime
with a fountain fill.
Also from MoreFonts.

Figure 7-1: *A DeskJet soft font sampler, printed on a DeskJet. The page has been reduced by 18 percent.*

Now we come to the font name's extension, starting after the period in the name. The first two letters of the extension, *EE* in the pattern, tell you what character set the font contains. Common character set abbreviations include:

DJ   Fonts that include all the standard DeskJet character sets
IB   IBM PC screen set, same as PC-8
LG   Legal
M#   Math, # is the number of the specific math set from 0 to 9
R8   Roman-8
SF   Various older LaserJet soft font sets
US   US ASCII

The final character refers to the font's orientation, portrait or landscape. That's *P* for portrait, *L* for landscape. Since DeskJet soft fonts always have the portrait orientation, the last letter in any font's filename extension should always be **P**. Landscape soft fonts are available for LaserJets, however.

Mastering soft font challenges

Soft font users face three major challenges: soft fonts require lots of disk storage space, they need custom software drivers, and you have to download them to the DeskJet. Let's look at each of these requirements and consider strategies for coping with them.

Soft fonts and disk space

As you'll remember from Chapter 6, DeskJet fonts are bitmapped fonts, meaning that they specify the location of each and every dot in each and every character. With all the data required to represent all those dots, a font takes up a lot of room in the DeskJet's memory. The actual amount of memory consumed by a font depends on its size (since larger characters have more dots than smaller ones), the typeface design, and the number of characters in the character set. The range is usually between about 6K for 6 point fonts through about 15K for 12 point fonts to 45K or so for the 30 point fonts you can print on the DeskJet Plus.

Each soft font takes up a little more space on disk than it does in the DeskJet's RAM. When you consider that you need a separate soft font file for every point size, it's easy to see how you can wind up devoting several megabytes on your hard disk to a modest soft font collection.

Minimizing soft font storage space

A file compression utility can help reduce the amount of disk space you devote to your soft font library. You'll probably find that you use some of your soft fonts only occasionally. With a compression utility such as ARC, PKZIP, or LHA, you can "squeeze" these down to half their original size or less. Whenever you want to print with one of the compressed fonts, you just uncompress it and download it to your printer. These utilities are available as shareware from the Public Software Library (800/242-4775) or on Compu-Serve.

✂ *Tip:* *One way to cut disk space requirements dramatically is to use scalable fonts. MoreFonts and Glyphix create and download the specific font you request from small master typeface outlines as you print. The outlines are stored on disk, but not the fonts generated from them, which saves you lots of disk space.*

Managing your soft font files

Because soft font files are large, it's most convenient to store them on a hard disk, where they'll be accessible without having to shuffle and swap floppy disks. Downloading from a hard disk goes much faster, too. Assuming you do have a hard disk, the best way to keep track of your DeskJet soft fonts is to create a special directory for them. Making a new directory called **FONTS** is simple:

1. Switch to the root directory of your hard disk. If your hard disk is drive C, type

   c:(↵), then cd \(↵).

2. Now type the command **md \fonts(↵)**. The disk will chatter as DOS creates the directory you've specified.

Once the directory is ready, copy all the font files you use regularly there, where it'll be easy to find them when you need them. You may want to store soft fonts you use only occasionally on floppy disks, so they don't consume space on your hard disk that you could use instead for additional programs or documents.

Soft fonts and printer drivers

You may as well face the fact that it can be difficult or impossible to mix your soft fonts freely in a given document. The problem is that the DeskJet drivers in most programs are only set up to handle a limited number of soft fonts.

As you'll recall from Chapter 3, a printer driver is a supplementary software module that you must install into your main application program to get the program to work with your printer. The driver functions much like an interpreter, translating the commands a program uses for functions such as font or margin changes into the corresponding codes in the printer's native tongue.

As far as fonts are concerned, the driver detects the places in your document where you've switched from one font to another, and issues the corresponding font selection commands to the DeskJet when it's time to print that part of the file. A really good driver will even download the new font if it hasn't already been sent to the printer. In addition, the driver supplies the program with spacing information for each character in the font. The program uses this spacing information, called a *width table*, to format the text properly, so that the characters are positioned properly within the margins you've set up.

In the days before laser printers, computer printers had very few fonts, and a program could get by with one simple driver for each printer (still, that made for a tremendous number of drivers). With jillions of optional fonts in the picture, though, things get even more complicated. Since each typeface has a different numeric code and each font has a different width table, two DeskJets with two different sets of optional fonts are almost like two separate printers. Depending on your software, you may need a completely different driver for each set of optional fonts you install.

When you're talking about hundreds of fonts from many different suppliers, it's clearly impossible for anyone to write a DeskJet driver that will work with every available soft font. The DeskJet drivers that come with most application programs can only access the cartridge and soft fonts sold by HP, and often only a limited selection of these. That means that to get your program to print using your particular collection of soft fonts, you're going to have to come up with a custom driver somehow.

Many word processing programs, including WordPerfect and Microsoft Word, allow you to create your own drivers tailored to your soft fonts. Unfortunately, the process is difficult, time consuming, and fraught with the possibility for error. If you own one of these top-selling programs, your font vendor may let you off the hook by providing you with a special utility that creates custom soft font drivers for you. If you use a less popular program, though, you'll probably have to develop your own driver, assuming the program permits you to do so. Consult the program's publisher or ask your font supplier for help.

Downloading soft fonts

The remaining challenge with soft fonts is that you have to download them, a process that's a little tricky and can certainly be time consuming. These days, many application programs download your soft fonts for you, once you install the correct driver. If your program is capable of doing the downloading, all you have to do is tell it where you've stored the fonts you've used in your document (in other words, in which disk drive and directory they're located). When you give the print command, the program downloads the fonts called for without any further effort on your part. Microsoft Word and WordPerfect can both download soft fonts automatically.

Unfortunately, there are plenty of other programs that can't download soft fonts. What's more, it often makes sense to do your own downloading, even if your software can take care of the job. One reason is that the downloading process takes time. If you use a particular set of downloaded fonts for most of your documents, you can download all the fonts in the set when you first turn on the DeskJet each day. That way, your software just has to switch from one font to the next, rather than going through the whole downloading process again each time you select a new font. (Remember this, though: even if you never change the soft fonts you use during a given day, turning off the DeskJet clears the printer's memory, wiping out any soft fonts you've downloaded.)

If you don't rely on your application program to do your font downloading for you, you have two alternatives: you can do it yourself with DOS commands, or you can enlist the help of a font management utility. I heartily recommend the downloading utilities—they make the job almost painless. Still, I'll cover both methods in a moment, after some background on how the DeskJet keeps track of the downloaded fonts.

Soft font ID numbers

The DeskJet requires that every downloaded font be assigned a unique identification number during the downloading process. This ID number isn't permanently matched to that particular font. Instead, it's assigned arbitrarily at the time the font is downloaded either by you, if you're downloading from DOS, or by whatever software does the downloading for you. The ID number can be anything from 0 to 32767. Once the font has its ID number, an application program or utility can select it by that number with an escape sequence (or you can do the selecting yourself, as described in Chapter 22).

Though you can use the same ID number for different soft fonts if you like, only one font with a given number can be resident in the DeskJet at any one time. If you assign an ID number that's already in use to a new font, the previously downloaded font will no longer be accessible.

Permanent versus temporary soft fonts

Another choice that must be made at downloading time is whether the font will be assigned to permanent or temporary status. "Permanent" fonts remain intact when the printer receives a "soft reset" command, which many programs send every time they start or finish a printing job. You can still erase a permanent font from the DeskJet's memory, but to do so you must send a specific command to erase one or all of the current soft fonts.

To make the font you're downloading permanent, an appropriate escape sequence must be sent to the DeskJet immediately after the font itself has been downloaded. If you don't issue this escape sequence, the font you've downloaded will automatically be considered "temporary," and the DeskJet will erase the font from memory when it receives the soft reset command.

Either way, of course, all your soft fonts will vanish from the DeskJet's memory when you turn the printer off.

Managing DeskJet font memory

Even if you install the maximum amount of soft font RAM possible, 512K for a DeskJet Plus, you may have much less useable font memory than you think. This problem is especially noticeable with larger soft fonts—often you'll be unable to install a few large fonts whose total memory requirements are far less than what's apparently available.

The explanation lies in the design of the DeskJet's font memory circuits, which can only be accessed in 64K blocks. Although a large font can spill over from one block to the next, the character data you're actually using cannot cross a 64K boundary. That means that some large fonts simply won't fit in the DeskJet.

In addition, the DeskJet puts the font being downloaded into the largest free memory space still available, even when that's an inefficient decision. For example, if you have a 256K RAM cartridge you have four separate 64K blocks of memory available for font storage. If you download four 30K fonts, the DeskJet stores each one in its own 64K block, leaving 34K available in each block. So, although there's theoretically 136K left free in the cartridge, you can't download any additional font that's larger than 34K.

✗ *Tip:* *To fit the maximum possible number of fonts into the useable memory space, download your soft fonts in decreasing order according to their memory requirements. The best way to maximize the number of fonts you can download into your RAM cartridges is to download the largest soft fonts first, then the next largest, and so on. Let's see how this would have worked with the fonts in the example above. If you had started by downloading your largest font, say a 60K font, and had then downloaded a 40K font, you would still have had enough room for four 30K fonts—two would have fit in each of the two remaining 64K blocks of RAM.*

Downloading soft fonts from DOS

In essence, downloading a font file to the DeskJet using DOS commands is as simple as copying a file from one disk drive to another. Unfortunately, the process of downloading fonts from DOS is complicated by several factors. For one thing, you have to assign a font ID number to each font you download, and then keep track of these numbers yourself. For another, you must send an escape sequence to the printer before you download the font itself. Once the font is transferred, you must send another escape sequence to assign either permanent or temporary status to the font.

The major problem here is that on the DOS command line, you can't type the escape character, the one that begins every escape sequence (the escape character is ASCII code 27 in decimal notation and is represented by the symbol ← on your screen). The easiest way to get around this problem involves creating a batch file containing the escape character. Chapter 9 has all the details on controlling the DeskJet from DOS using this method, but I've summarized the instructions you'll need for soft font downloading here.

Before you begin, make sure you know the full filename of the font you want to download, as listed in the disk directory, and that you know the path (the disk and directory) where the font file is stored. For the rest of these instructions, I'll assume that your font is named TR120RPN.DJP and that it's parked on hard disk C: in the FONTS directory. The complete path and filename would then be *C:\FONTS\TR120RPN.DJP.*

The first step is to create the special file ESCAPE containing the escape character. Chapter 9 has the instructions in the section "The ESCAPE solution." Then, with the DeskJet powered up, connected, and online, you're ready to do the download. First, you must send the initial escape sequence that tells the DeskJet to expect a soft font download. Here's how:

1. Switch to the disk and directory where your fonts are stored by typing **c:**⏎, then **cd \fonts**⏎.

2. At the DOS prompt, type

copy escape+con lpt1 ⏎

When you press ⏎, the cursor will drop down to the next line on your screen.

3. Now type

*c7D

This escape sequence tells the DeskJet to assign a temporary ID number to the font you're about to download, in this case 7. You can use any number you like between 0 and 32767 as long as it's not in use already by another font (don't type a comma for numbers larger than 999). Make note of the number you assign, because you'll need it to select the font for printing.

4. Press (F6) followed by (↵) to send the escape sequence to the DeskJet.

Now download the font itself. On the DOS command line, type

copy c:\fonts\tr12Ørpn.djp lpt1 (↵)

This is the same COPY command you use to copy a file from one disk to another—the difference is that you've specified the printer port as the destination for the copy. As soon as you press (↵) to start the download the disk will chatter as DOS sends the font file to the DeskJet. When the download is complete, you'll see the message:

1 File(s) copied

If you want the font you've just downloaded to remain "permanently" in the DeskJet's memory until you specifically erase it, or turn the printer off, you must finish the download by sending an escape sequence. If you just want to use the font once and don't mind if it gets erased, the DeskJet will automatically assign the font to temporary status. See the section "Permanent vs temporary soft fonts" earlier in this chapter for more on how permanent and temporary fonts work.

You'll need the ESCAPE file again to make the font permanent. Here are the steps:

1. On the command line, type

copy escape+con lpt1 (↵)

Just as before, the cursor drops down to the next line.

2. Type

*c5F

3. Press (F6) then (↵) to send the command to the DeskJet. You've just protected the downloaded font against accidental erasure.

Downloading multiple fonts

You can download as many fonts as the DeskJet's RAM cartridge memory will hold—just repeat the above steps for each font in turn.

If you have specific sets of soft fonts that you use frequently, you can automate the downloading process for each set with a batch file. Again, Chapter 9 gives details on how to create batch files for controlling the DeskJet. As with all batch files, your font downloading batch file should be named with the .BAT extension. For example, you might call it FONTSET1.BAT.

For each font you want the file to download, enter the following three lines in your file:

echo ←*c#D >lpt1

copy /b *fontname* **lpt1**

echo ←*c5F >lpt1

In place of the word *fontname* above, type in the font's complete path and filename. Substitute a number between 0 and 32767 (don't use commas) for the # symbol in the first line as the font's temporary ID, using a different number for each font you download.

☊ *Caution:* It's critical to use the ECHO command instead of COPY on the first and third lines. COPY would read those *'s in the escape sequences as DOS wildcards, and would try to copy files on your disk whose names end in c# D and c5F. Also, be sure to enter the > before lpt1 on the first and third lines, but not on the second line.

For example, suppose you want to create a batch file to automatically download two fonts stored in your DJFONTS directory. If the fonts are named

named CEN18RB0.DJP and PAS16RB0.DJP, your batch file should contain these lines:

```
echo ←*c10D >lpt1
copy /b \djfonts\cen18rb0.djp lpt1
echo ←*c5F >lpt1
echo ←*c11D >lpt1
copy /b \djfonts\pas16rb0.djp lpt1
echo ←*c5F >lpt1
```

Notice that I've arbitrarily assigned the temporary font ID numbers 10 and 11 with the first echo command for each font. You could use any other numbers instead, as long they don't conflict with those already in use by fonts you've previously downloaded.

To download the font set using your new batch file, all you have to do is type the name of the batch file at the DOS prompt, and press ⏎. In our example, you'd type **FONTSET1**⏎.

Downloading with font utilities

Now that you have some background on how the DeskJet handles your soft fonts in its memory, it's time to get practical. How do you actually download the fonts? The easiest and most reliable way is with the help of a good font management utility. Downloading with a font utility is as simple as finding the desired font on a menu and pressing a key. In addition, font utilities often have lots of extra features for helping you keep track of your fonts, and for making the downloading process seem faster.

In choosing a font management utility, you can opt for one which concentrates entirely on the font-related functions, or you can rely instead on one of the general purpose setup utilities that also has font management capabilities (these were described in Chapter 4). Either way, an ideal font utility should above all be easy to use—otherwise, you might as well do the downloading yourself with the DOS commands described in the next section. Specifically, look for these characteristics:

You should be able to control all the utility functions using simple, easy-to-follow menus.

The utility should automatically list the names of all the DeskJet soft fonts on your disk(s) for you, so that you can choose the fonts to download simply by picking their names from the list. If you have to type in the font names yourself, you'll waste time keeping written records of the names and doing the typing, and it's easy to make mistakes.

The utility should enable you to download sets of routinely used fonts all at once directly from the DOS prompt, without having to specify each font one by one from the menu. Typically, a program with this feature creates a separate file containing the names of the fonts you want in your set. When you give the command to download your font set, the utility then reads the file to see which fonts it should download.

At your option, you should be able to operate the downloading either as a standalone program (so you can reserve as much computer memory as possible for your application program) or as a pop-up memory resident (TSR) utility (so you can download fonts without leaving your application).

The two best font utilities for the DeskJet are BackLoader and TSR Download, each of which rates a profile here. In addition to these two programs, many downloading utilities for the LaserJet will work adequately, including some available as shareware.

Using your soft fonts

Downloading your soft fonts to the DeskJet is only half the battle. The other major hurdle you'll face is selecting the soft font you want to use, so that you can print your text in that font. Whenever possible, use your application program to select the font you'll be printing with. If your program lacks a driver for your soft fonts, your next best bet is to use a font management utility. If all else fails, you'll have to select them yourself from within your application or via DOS commands. Use the general approach for sending commands to the DeskJet outlined in Chapter 8, and see Chapter 22 for the details on using the font selection commands.

Profile: BackLoader 2

$89 /LaserTools Corp.
1250 45th St., Suite 100
Emeryville, CA 94608
800/767-8004; 415/420-8777

The supreme DeskJet font management utility is BackLoader, now in release 2. BackLoader makes using soft fonts so much quicker and easier that you should consider buying it even if all your application programs can download soft fonts for you.

Like most DeskJet utilities, BackLoader is a memory resident program, and you can pop it up whenever you need it. But where other font utilities do their downloading when you ask them to—which seems to make sense— BackLoader takes a different tack. It starts by downloading all your most frequently used fonts to the DeskJet, so they'll be there when called for. Then, as you print each document, BackLoader monitors the printer output from your program. When it detects a font selection command, BackLoader checks its list of all the fonts currently installed in the DeskJet. If the font is already available in the printer, BackLoader just passes the font command on. On the other hand, if the font isn't yet installed, BackLoader downloads it on the spot. If there's no more room in the DeskJet's memory for another font, BackLoader removes the fonts you've used least recently until the new font will fit.

All this assumes that your application program knows enough about the DeskJet to send the right font selection commands in the first place—in other words, that the program has a driver that allows it to work with your soft fonts. But even if your program doesn't know Courier from Cooper Black, you can still change fonts to your heart's content with BackLoader.

This very powerful feature relies on simple "tags" you define as abbreviations for your fonts. For instance, you might define the tag ~6 as an abbreviation for a 10 point Times Roman italic font, and ~7 for 10 point regular Times Roman. To use the italic font in a document, you would type **~6** just before the word you want printed in italics, and **~7** after it. When BackLoader detects the tag in your printer output, it downloads the corresponding font, if necessary, and then selects it. The tag technique allows you to vary fonts in almost any kind of printed document, whether it's a spreadsheet, an accounting report, or a database. Of course, since the application program doesn't know what you're up to, it can't control the spacing of individual letters, and you may not get properly aligned columns and margins if you vary fonts within a block of text or a table.

BackLoader also lets you use the same method to insert any printer command in any document. Once you've defined the control code or escape sequence, you just enter an easy-to-remember (and easy-to-type) abbreviation in the file, and BackLoader will see to it that the DeskJet gets your orders.

Such outstanding service is impressive enough, but it's only half of the story. When BackLoader downloads a font, it doesn't take complete control of your PC. Instead, it works in the background, sending a small chunk of the font data out every few fractions of a second. Where this comes in handy is when BackLoader is downloading that set of frequently used fonts at the beginning of a session, or if you choose to manually download a font. Instead of staring at your screen for a minute or two as you wait for the download to finish, you'll be returned to your work moments after it gets started. As you work, BackLoader will continue to send the fonts to the DeskJet, but you'll hardly notice the interruptions.

BackLoader 2 even makes the process of cataloging your soft fonts automatic. Since it can search your entire hard disk for font files, you don't have to keep your fonts in one directory, if that's your preference. You do have to tell it which cartridge fonts you've installed, if any. Finally, BackLoader 2.2 works in concert with FaceLift for WordPerfect, a scalable font driver for Word-Perfect, to manage ordinary soft fonts and the scalable kind simultaneously.

Profile: TSR Download

$45/Elfring Soft Fonts
P.O. Box 61
Wasco, IL 60183
708/377-3520

Another excellent font management utility for the DeskJet, and a real bargain, is Elfring Soft Fonts' TSR Download. Mr. Elfring sells the best collection of DeskJet soft fonts available, as well as a family of similar products for LaserJet printers.

Only $45 gets you a copy of TSR Download, and for just $30 more you can add a full set of DeskJet fonts, Elfring's imitations of Times Roman and

Helvetica in sizes from 8 to 30 points. The 30-point fonts contain only numerals, punctuation marks, and uppercase letters, so they work on the original DeskJet as well as the DeskJet Plus. Also available are printer drivers and font installation kits for WordPerfect, Microsoft Word, WordStar, PC-Write, Q&A, and other applications, allowing you to use your soft fonts with these programs without sweating the technical details.

But back to TSR Download. As its name indicates, this is a pop-up memory resident utility, but it can also be run as an ordinary non-resident program if you prefer. The program reads your soft font files, displaying them in a list of plain-English descriptions, not inscrutable filenames. To download one or more fonts, you start by marking them on the list. While you're making your selections, TSR Download displays a running total of their memory requirements in the DeskJet along with the memory consumed by any fonts that have already been downloaded. When you're ready to download, a quick choice from a menu sends the marked fonts off to the printer. Once you've downloaded your fonts, you can select any of them as your default font. The program also lets you remove fonts from the DeskJet's memory when they're no longer needed.

As an alternative to pop-up downloading, you can use TSR Download's font list to create files containing the names of your favorite sets of soft fonts. To download one of these sets, you supply its filename when you run TSR Download. The program will transfer the fonts to the printer and then quit, without becoming memory resident.

An accompanying program, FONTCAT, prints a complete listing of all your soft fonts, showing each font's name, typeface, point size, and so on. Another plus with TSR Download is that its manual includes a succinct primer on soft fonts.

Though it's primarily intended for managing fonts, TSR Download lets you control other important aspects of DeskJet setup as well. You can eject a page, reset the printer, switch from portrait to landscape mode and back, and choose the number of lines per inch.

Converting LaserJet fonts to DeskJet format

LaserJet owners can choose from literally hundreds of different soft fonts, but DeskJet users are stuck with relatively few. You can stake a claim in the LaserJet typographic gold mine with LJ2DESK, a utility that converts LaserJet fonts to a format the DeskJet can understand. This solution isn't perfect, but it's more than good enough for most people.

The reason you can't use LaserJet fonts on a DeskJet isn't because HP set out to deprive you. Instead, the design team recognized that LaserJet-format fonts wouldn't have produced optimum text quality on the DeskJet because of inherent technical differences between the two printers. For one thing, the LaserJet reads font bitmaps horizontally, while the DeskJet reads them vertically. More important, a dot printed by the LaserJet is slightly oblong, while one printed by the DeskJet is closer to being perfectly round, meaning that the same dot pattern would result in slightly different character appearance on the two printers. HP therefore decided to create a new font format that would give the highest possible text quality on the DeskJet.

The big question is whether you would have noticed the difference between that "highest possible" quality and the second-best quality you can get from LaserJet fonts. For most people, the answer is probably "no." Although close scrutiny will reveal that the converted fonts have more of the jaggies than true DeskJet fonts do, the characters are still quite sharp. Besides, having hundreds of fonts to choose from, many of them free for the asking, should make up for the loss of quality.

A couple of obvious limitations confront any font conversion utility for the DeskJet. One is size—you can't convert fonts that are larger than the DeskJet can print. Another is the fact that the DeskJet doesn't accept downloaded landscape fonts, so LaserJet landscape fonts won't work either.

✄ *Tip:* *To use LaserJet fonts without these limitations, turn to the LaserTwin emulation utility profiled back in Chapter 4. Rather than converting the fonts to DeskJet format, LaserTwin uses them to build its own graphic image of the page, including text, just as a real LaserJet would. It then sends this page in graphics mode out to the DeskJet. This way, you can print LaserJet fonts of any size or orientation.*

Profile: LJ2DESK

$52/S.H. Moody & Associates
P.O. Box 299
San Luis Obispo, CA 93406

LJ2DESK is a complete solution to the challenges of LaserJet-to-DeskJet font conversion. In addition to the conversion program proper, the package comes with several great utilities that make it much easier to choose the fonts you want to convert and to use them once they're in DeskJet format. If you use soft fonts from any source, whether or not you're interested in converting LaserJet fonts, you should add LJ2DESK to your utility collection.

LJ2DESK carries out the conversion process before you print, creating permanent DeskJet font files you can store on your disk. To save memory and downloading time, you can pick out particular characters from those in the original LaserJet font, omitting the ones you don't plan to use. During the conversion you can make adjustments in the positioning of each character relative to the baseline, and in the font's x-height, the height of a lowercase *x.* LJ2DESK can convert up to 100 fonts in a single pass. All the fonts prepared by LJ2DESK are formatted so that you can print them on the DeskJet at half size, in boldface, or both. You can set up the program to generate fonts in the proper format for any of the three DeskJet models.

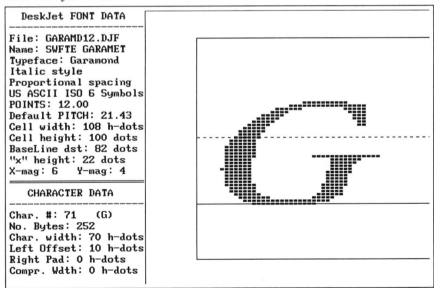

```
DeskJet FONT DATA
--------------------
File: GARAMD12.DJF
Name: SWFTE GARAMET
Typeface: Garamond
Italic style
Proportional spacing
US ASCII ISO 6 Symbols
POINTS: 12.00
Default PITCH: 21.43
Cell width: 108 h-dots
Cell height: 100 dots
BaseLine dst: 82 dots
"x" height: 22 dots
X-mag: 6    Y-mag: 4

   CHARACTER DATA
--------------------
Char. #: 71    (G)
No. Bytes: 252
Char. width: 70 h-dots
Left Offset: 10 h-dots
Right Pad: 0 h-dots
Compr. Wdth: 0 h-dots
```

Figure 7-2: *The FONTVIEW utility lets you examine any DeskJet or LaserJet font.*

Several other utilities come with LJ2DESK. Before you convert the font, you can use FONTVIEW to display the original font's characters one by one on a graphics monitor. That way, you can decide which characters you want to convert, or whether you want to convert the font at all. When FONTVIEW is finished, it displays the complete escape sequence you'd need to send to select that font. You can also view DeskJet fonts with FONTVIEW, as shown in the illustration in Figure 7-2.

Then there's the FONTWID utility. FONTWID is a necessity for using the converted fonts with your word processor or desktop publishing program, but it should be in your library even if you don't ever plan to use a LaserJet font. FONTWID reads any LaserJet or DeskJet font file and constructs a width table containing all the information you must supply to your word processor when you create a custom driver for the new font. Without the width table, the word processor won't be able to space the characters properly, and will botch formatting chores such as letterspacing, centering, and justification. If you ever have trouble finding width table information for any DeskJet font, turn to FONTWID. Rounding out the LJ2DESK package are a font downloading utility, a simple batch file that prints out a font's complete character set, and a program that converts LaserJet fonts to half-width, allowing you to make taller fonts suitable for headlines. Utilities that automatically create the proper drivers for your soft fonts for WordPerfect and Microsoft Word are also available.

Scalable fonts

Ordinary soft fonts may be more flexible than the cartridge variety, but they still limit you to printing at fixed point sizes, and you're stuck with the hassle of downloading your fonts to the printer. The best way to overcome these shortcomings is with a typeface scaling system, which consists of software and master typeface outlines.

Conventional DeskJet soft fonts are distributed as separate, ready-to-download files for each point size. In a TmsRmn soft font collection, for example, there'll be one file for the 12 point font, another for the 14 point font, and so on. You must download the specific font file for each point size you want to print, and you can't print in 13-point TmsRmn at all, because there's no file for a 13-point font in the set.

Unlike these conventional fixed-size fonts, a *scalable typeface* can be printed at almost any size you like. In a scalable typeface, each character is represented not by a collection of dots but by a mathematical description of the character's outline. When you decide to print a character at a particular size this master outline is scaled to the requested size. Only then is the outline filled in with the necessary dots so that it's ready to be printed.

Pros and cons of scalable fonts

This approach has some real advantages. One important benefit is the flexibility that comes from being able to print any size font without having to track down and buy the right font file. Another is that you don't have to download the fonts to your DeskJet—the font scaling software takes care of sending the necessary instructions to your printer. Finally, a scalable typeface outline takes up far less room on disk than do a complete set of fixed-size soft fonts.

On the other hand, font scaling systems face a challenge in maintaining the quality of the generated fonts across the entire range of point sizes that are possible. To scale a large character, for example, you can't just double the number of dots in a small character, because smooth curves would take on a jagged, stairstep appearance. Instead, you have to add more dots to fill in the rough edges. Likewise, you can't start with a large character and shrink it down—if you'll try, the result will have too many dots, and will be smudged-looking and maybe even unreadable.

To avoid these problems, a typeface scaling system has to use complex software routines to convert the master outline to a font that's optimized for a particular size. People may tell you that the characters in a good conventional soft font look better than scaled characters, since a human being rather than a program has decided where to put the dots. But most of the typeface scaling systems do the job quite well, and you'll be hard pressed to tell the difference between a "handmade" soft font and a scaled font.

On-the-fly typeface scaling systems do all the work of scaling the typeface outline to the requested size and filling it in with dots while you print. Some create and download conventional soft fonts, but most place the DeskJet into graphics mode, and then send the actual dot patterns that make up the characters to your printer. Both give excellent results. Either way, you only have to store the typeface scaling software and the master outlines on your hard disk, not finished font files totalling many megabytes.

I should note the disadvantages of scalable fonts. For one thing, there's the potential for lower quality mentioned a moment ago. For another, the process of scaling the fonts on the fly takes longer than downloading prefab fonts. Finally, you can use scalable fonts only with the most popular application programs, or with programs that have font scaling technology built in.

Scalable typeface formats

The availability of font scaling software has made working with type dramatically easier, but it brings with it a frustrating limitation: each font scaling system only works with one typeface format. There's no direct way, for instance, to use a PostScript typeface with either version of FaceLift. To help you keep things straight, here's a listing of the typeface formats most commonly used by PC software:

- PostScript Type 1: Until 1990, this was Adobe's proprietary format for PostScript typefaces, and it produces the best possible quality from PostScript printers. It's now in the public domain and is widely used by other vendors. ATM requires Type 1 fonts.

- PostScript Type 3: This is the "second class" PostScript typeface format, producing somewhat lower quality output than Type 1s. Despite its inferior quality, most PostScript typeface vendors had to rely on the Type 3 format until recently.

- Fontware: The format used by Bitstream's older font generator, Fontware.

- Speedo: The format used for on-the-fly scaling by Bitstream's FaceLift products.

- TrueType: TrueType is a complete page description language compatible with PostScript. TrueType typefaces incorporate additional information than do their PostScript counterparts about the way the resulting fonts are to be used. On-the-fly scaling for TrueType faces will be built into the next version of Windows, 3.1.

- Compugraphic: The format used by HP's Type Director II.

Atech AllType

The developers of Publisher's Powerpak have a solution to the incompabilities between typeface formats, a kind of Rosetta stone of digital typography. Though I haven't yet tried it, AllType is supposed to convert typeface outlines back and forth between all of the major formats: PostScript Type 1 and Type 3, Fontware, Speedo, TrueType, Compugraphic, and more, as well as Atech's own format, of course. If AllType works as claimed, you'll be able to buy the best font scaling system for your needs, without worrying about which typefaces are available in the format it requires. AllType costs $79 and is available from Atech Software, 5964 La Place Court, Suite 125 Carlsbad, CA 92008, 800/748-5657 or 619/438-6883.

Choosing a font scaling software package

Since eight or more font scaling systems work with the DeskJet, it can be tough to choose the right one. In addition to comparing price, use the following points to make the decision:

1. Start by narrowing the list to the font scalers that work with your own programs. If you want to use scalable fonts within Microsoft Works, for example, you're limited to Publisher's Powerpak. If you use Windows, on the other hand, you still have many choices.

2. Decide on the kind of typeface outlines you want to start with. In general, each font scaling system relies on a single kind of typeface outline (SuperPrint is the exception). Since you'll be stuck with the typefaces available in that format, be sure you'll be happy with their variety and quality. For example, if you covet Adobe Type 1 PostScript fonts you'll want either the Adobe Type Manager (ATM) or SuperPrint to print them on your DeskJet. You may want to print foreign alphabets or special characters which are available only in a particular typeface format, and that will determine your choice of a font scaler.

3. Compare the quality of the font scalers themselves. The key considerations here are how fast the scaling process is, how much memory the scaling software consumes, and the appearance of the printed output.

Font scalers for Windows

If you rely on Windows 3 as your software "environment," you have at least six different type scaling systems to choose from. All work reliably, but they differ widely in features, price, and output quality. You'll find details on Adobe Type Manager, FaceLift for Windows, SuperPrint, and HP's DeskJet 500 Scalable Printer Driver in Chapter 10 on Windows. Two other scalable font systems that work with Windows, MoreFonts and Publisher's Powerpak, are covered in this chapter, since they work with DOS programs as well.

Font scalers for DOS

While most of the action in scalable fonts is in the Windows arena, a few packages bring the benefits of on-the-fly font sizing to popular DOS programs. Publisher's Powerpak, MoreFonts, and Glyphix all offer DOS-based font scaling solutions that work with one or more non-Windows programs.

Publisher's Powerpak

At this writing, the most versatile typeface scaling solution shy of full-blown PostScript is Publisher's Powerpak from Atech Software. Powerpak performs on-the-fly scaling for more programs than any other package. Versions are available for Ventura, First Publisher, Windows (the Windows version of Powerpak can scale printer and screen fonts to any size from within any Windows program), Microsoft Word, Microsoft Works, and, of course, WordPerfect. And more optional typefaces are available for Powerpak than for any other low-cost font generating product. While the bulk of Atech's own typeface designs are only mediocre in quality, many of them are unique faces you can't find elsewhere, and they're inexpensive. For more esthetically pleasing characters, you can choose from a healthy sampling of faces drawn from the respected Monotype library.

Powerpak works as advertised. Installation is effortless (I never once looked at the manual), and you print from within your application just as you normally would. Any Powerpak typeface (imitations of Times, Helvetica, and Courier come with the package) can be printed in a variety of special styles, such as thin, condensed, and outlined. Working while you print, Powerpak scales the master typefaces to whatever sizes you've requested in your document, sending the resulting characters to the DeskJet in graphic form (see "Graphics fonts" below). In the most recent releases, quality has been improved with the addition of "hinting," guidelines that help the program decide how to adjust the shape of small characters for optimal appearance.

Unfortunately, you have to pay full price for each version of Powerpak you buy, although the different versions can share typefaces. Of course, the fact that Powerpak must scale the characters before it prints them slows down the printing process a bit. Another drawback to keep in mind is that you can't mix regular DeskJet fonts with Powerpak fonts in the same document.

MoreFonts

MoreFonts, a font generator from MicroLogic Software, is one of the best values in DeskJet fonts. For one low price, MoreFonts comes standard with 14 typefaces that you can turn into fonts in any point size the DeskJet can print: up to 23 points for the original DeskJet, and 45 points for the DeskJet Plus via limited character sets. But MoreFonts doesn't stop there: font downloading, screen fonts for applications that display in graphics mode, and special font effects are all part of the package. And to that list, the most recent versions of MoreFonts add on-the-fly font scaling for Windows, WordPerfect, and Microsoft Word.

While their quality doesn't match what you get from Bitstream or Adobe, the typefaces supplied with MoreFonts cover a lot of typographic territory, and they're far less expensive. The core of the set is two complete typeface families, creditable imitations of the ever-popular Times Roman and Helvetica. The members of each family include Italic, Bold, Bold Italic, and regular faces. Five display faces, including MoreFonts' versions of Broadway, Cooper Black, Coronet, University, and Bodoni, are provided for eye-catching headlines and titles. There's also a version of Letter Gothic, a monospaced sans-serif typeface whose narrow characters often make it a better choice for reports than Courier.

What's more, your fonts aren't limited to plain all-black characters. During font generation, any of the available typefaces can be gussied up with a variety of special effects. For example, you can select from eight patterns for the interiors of the characters—the parts that are normally solid black—including stripes, a wood grain effect, "starry night," and so forth. In addition, you can add shadow effects ("drop shadows") or outlines of varying thickness. If you have a graphics monitor, you can see sample characters to get a good idea of how your custom font will look in print. Figure 7-3 shows an example of a MoreFonts screen showing a gaudily dressed-up rendition of the MoreFonts Showtime typeface (the Broadway imitation).

The most convenient way to use MoreFonts is as an on-the-fly font scaler, but it works that way only in Windows and the two leading word processors. With each of the other programs it supports, MoreFonts generates the fonts you select ahead of time as standard DeskJet soft fonts, and then automat-

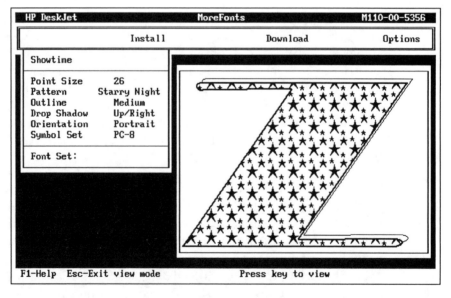

Figure 7-3: *MoreFonts lets you view the special effects you're adding before you actually generate the font.*

ically installs them into a customized driver for that program. MoreFonts will make the necessary printer drivers for XyWrite, First Publisher, and MultiMate, so you can go right to work with these programs without worrying about the messy details of width tables and so on. Actually, you can use it this way with Windows, WordPerfect, and Word as well.

When used with Windows, MoreFonts' on-the-fly scaling routine is actually faster than any of its competitors, and it's also one of the most frugal with memory. On the other hand, setting it up is somewhat cumbersome, since it requires you to use both Windows and DOS utilities.

But the main MoreFonts program, which runs in DOS, is as easy to use as it is powerful. You control the whole program from an intelligently designed drop-down menu system using either the keyboard or the mouse. With thorough context-sensitive help always available, you can dispense with the manual once you've installed the program.

Glyphix

Glyphix is a popular and inexpensive font generating system that works very well with the DeskJet, with many of the advantages of MoreFonts. You can create fonts in any size that suits you from a variety of master typefaces, either ahead of time as soft font files, or on the fly at print time. Glyphix gives you special effects too. You can choose reversed type, various shades, stripes, and shadows for any font you generate.

Glyphix goes MoreFonts one better in letting you break the DeskJet's 30 point font size limit. When you want to print text in a font larger than 30 points, Glyphix translates the characters into graphics and sends the resulting data to your printer. The result is just as good as if you'd used a built-in DeskJet font.

If you're a Microsoft Word or WordPerfect user, you'll appreciate the trouble SWFTE has gone to in tailoring special drivers for your word processor. The Word and WordPerfect drivers let you make full use of all your Glyphix fonts, including special effects, from these programs. In addition, they give Glyphix the same sort of DeskJet memory management capabilities as BackLoader. With Word or WordPerfect, Glyphix knows which fonts have already been downloaded, and automatically downloads only the ones you need when your document calls for them. Likewise, it deletes rarely used fonts to make room for new ones when necessary. Unfortunately, all these features work only with Glyphix fonts, so you're on your own if you want to mix them with fonts from other vendors.

FaceLift for WordPerfect 1.5

Bitstream built its business on Fontware, a font generating system that creates conventional soft fonts prior to printing. But the times have changed, and most people clearly prefer the convenience of on-the-fly font scaling at print time. Bitstream is obliging them with a new typeface format called Speedo that permits high-speed scaling without demanding much memory. Speedo typefaces are being built into application programs such as Lotus 1-2-3 Release 2.3, but Bitstream itself has come out with two of its own on-the-fly scaling products, FaceLift for Windows (covered in Chapter 10) and FaceLift for WordPerfect.

The WordPerfect version works with both 5.0 and 5.1. You need FaceLift release 1.5 or above—the first incarnation didn't work with the DeskJet. Setting up the utility takes some work within WordPerfect. In fact, the process is much like installing WordPerfect for the DeskJet discussed in Chapter 11. After the preliminaries, however, your FaceLift fonts are available with WordPerfect's Base Font command, just like any other WordPerfect font would be. And FaceLift for WordPerfect lets you use something like 750 different characters in your documents, including foreign language characters, math symbols, graphics characters, and so on. After you've created the document, WordPerfect's standard Print command calls FaceLift to life. During a momentary pause, FaceLift scales the selected fonts to the correct size and sends the resulting graphics data to the DeskJet.

Font generators

I use the term "font generators" to refer to software packages that, at your command, create standard DeskJet soft fonts from master tyepface outlines. A font generator works much like an on-the-fly font scaling system, in that it can build fonts of any size you request. The key differences are that you must explicitly create each font you plan to use ahead of time, before you actually print, and you must ensure that the fonts get downloaded to the DeskJet at or prior to print time.

Clearly, font generators are less convenient than on-the-fly font scalers. And you're still saddled with maintaining a big collection of soft fonts on your hard disk. But there's one key reason you may want to use a font generator: font scalers aren't available for all application software. If you use a word processor, spreadsheet, or other program that isn't compatilbe with a scalable fonts system, a font generator is the only way to avoid buying a separate soft font for every size you might ever want to use.

We've already covered two excellent font generating packages, Glyphix and MoreFonts, in the section above on font scaling. Two others, intended exclusively for before-hand font generation, are Type Director II and Fontware.

Type Director 2.0

If you need a way to generate soft fonts at any size and an on-the-fly font scaler isn't viable for your situation, the best DeskJet font management utility is Type Director. Developed by AGFA Compugraphic Corporation, a major typographic company, and distributed by Hewlett-Packard, Type Director generates printer and screen fonts based on Compugraphic outline typefaces. The program will also install them for you automatically into many popular applications.

Compugraphic's type library encompasses about 1700 outline typefaces, although HP currently sells only a small selection of them. Working from any of these outlines, Type Director can create LaserJet soft fonts of any size between 4 and 200 points in 1/4-point increments, and containing any of 17 character sets. All work fine when downloaded to the DeskJet. Type Director will also create matching screen fonts for Ventura Publisher and all Windows and NewWave applications.

One of the nice things about Type Director is that it lets you define custom reduced character sets by picking out the particular characters you need from any of the main character sets available with the package. Reduced character sets conserve disk space and printer memory, an advantage you'll notice most with larger fonts. Another plus is that it takes less time to generate a font that contains a reduced character set than to make one that has the full set.

Besides making the fonts, Type Director can install them into Windows, NewWave, WordPerfect 5.1, and Microsoft Word 4.0 and 5.0. Alternatively, Type Director can create the TFM files used in HP's new AutoFont system. AutoFont-compatible programs are able to install soft fonts automatically into their printer drivers by reading these TFM files.

Type Director includes several utility functions as well. It can download a predetermined list of fonts to your DeskJet. You can also have the program list all DeskJet and screen fonts, even those not created by Type Director, in any application's directory. From the list, you can delete unneeded fonts simply by highlighting them and hitting a key.

Adobe Font Foundry

They took a long time in getting around to the vast LaserJet market, but Adobe Systems, creators of PostScript, finally came up with a way to sell their wonderful PostScript typefaces to LaserJet owners. Adobe ignored the DeskJet, but you can still get PostScript text on your printer with a little extra work.

What you need is the Type Foundry utility, which now comes standard with every Adobe typeface package for the PC. First, you generate LaserJet fonts from the PostScript typefaces you're interested in. Then, with the LJ2DESK utility described earlier in this chapter, you convert those LaserJet fonts into DeskJet format and download them to your printer.

Fontware

Bitstream's Fontware is the best known and most widely used font generating product for LaserJets, and the line of Fontware typefaces is extensive and probably of higher quality than any other kind of computer type you can buy. Unfortunately, the WordPerfect version of Fontware is the only one that generates DeskJet fonts. In addition, the quality of Fontware's DeskJet fonts isn't as high as that of its excellent LaserJet offerings. Still, since the WordPerfect Fontware starter kit is inexpensive—only about $30—it can't hurt to give it a try.

Font effects

If you're looking for something really distinctive in the way of a typeface, why not create your own? Actually, I'm not suggesting that you design a new typeface from scratch, but what you might want to try is doctoring up an ordinary typeface with a few special touches. A judiciously applied special effect or two can turn a humdrum typeface into a one-of-a-kind standout.

With the right software, you can replace the normally solid black of the characters with shades, lines, or even random patterns, you can draw bold outlines around the letterforms, and you can add shadow effects or patterns around the letters. Some typographic purists frown on this sort of thing, but if you like the results, you're free to use your creations wherever you see fit.

Owners of LaserJets and PostScript printers have far more options in choosing software for font special effects. So far, only the MoreFonts and Glyphix font generators described earlier in this chapter let you perform such trickery, and only on their own fonts. For the LaserJet, the best font effects program available is called, well, Font Effects. Font Effects isn't available for the DeskJet, but you can convert LaserJet fonts modified with the program to DeskJet format using the LJ2DESK utility.When you use MoreFonts, Glyphix, or Font Effects to create special effects, the resulting characters comprise real fonts that you print in the DeskJet's standard text mode.

Another route to special font effects is through graphics mode. Graphics programs such as Corel Draw and Artline not only let you add patterns, outlines, and shadows to the characters you type, but they also let you change the outlines of the characters themselves. In this case, though, you have to enter all the text you want to print with the effects into your graphics program—you can't print a word processor file in the modified font. And if you use Windows and ATM (see Chapter 10), consider Twist and Shout!, a utility specially designed to provide a variety of special font effects through graphics mode.

Graphics fonts

As you know, the DeskJet puts rather serious limits on how large a normal font can be—roughly 18 points with the original model, and 30 points in the DeskJet Plus. Unfortunately, even 30 points is too small for attention-grabbing headlines. But there is another way to add large letters to your document: as graphics.

Most people think of graphics as recognizable pictures of something, but there's nothing to stop you from creating a graphic in the shape of a letter. And just like any other DeskJet graphic, a graphical letter can be any size you like, up to a full page. Check out some of the examples in Figure 7-4. By the way, most of the font scaling packages discussed earlier in this chapter and in Chapter 10 work by switching the DeskJet into graphics mode and printing the text as graphics.

As the illustration suggests, size isn't the only limitation you can overcome using graphics-based text. Since the character images are graphics rather than conventional text, you can play with their shapes and patterns to your heart's content. You can stretch, shrink, or otherwise distort them, rotate them or arrange them along a curve, fill them with stripes or polkadots, or stack multiple copies of them on top of one another.

Of course, most people aren't very interested in designing letters themselves. But you don't have to. Graphics programs typically come with a range of typefaces and let you enter the characters by typing them directly from the keyboard. Once you have the letters on your screen, you can modify them with the same commands that you use to edit other graphics. If you think you might want to buy a graphics program for creating classy headlines, one of your best bets is Corel Draw. Corel Draw comes with a host of great typefaces that print well on the DeskJet, and it's an excellent general purpose drawing program as well.

Once you're happy with the way your graphical letters look, you save them on disk (be sure to use a file format that can be read by the application program you'll be using to assemble and print your final document). The easiest way to incorporate graphics with ordinary text is to use a desktop publishing program, since it's specifically designed for that job. But it's also possible to merge text and graphics with many conventional word processors, including Microsoft Word, WordPerfect, and WordStar.

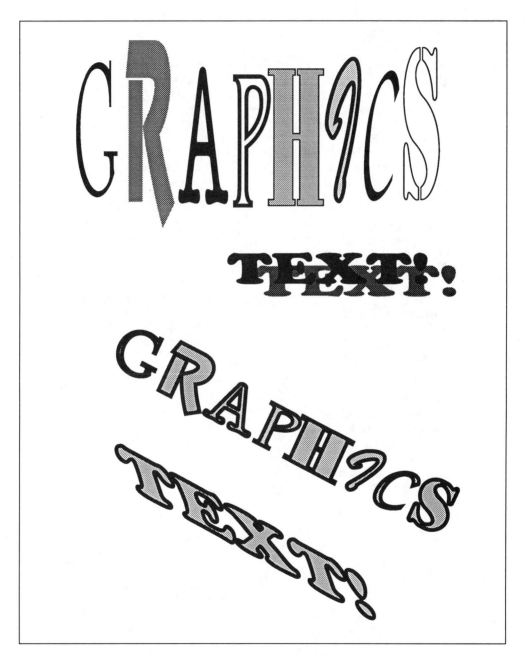

Figure 7-4: *Text created as graphics in Corel Draw*

Access: Font utilities

Type Director Version 2.0/$40
AGFA Compugraphic Division
Agfa Corporation
90 Industrial Way
Wilmington, MA 01887
508/658-5600
Distributed by Hewlett-Packard
Boise Division Marketing
Boise, Idaho 83707
800/538-8787

Font Effects/$95
SoftCraft, Inc.
16 N. Carroll St. #500
Madison, WI 53703
608/257-3300

MoreFonts/$99.95
MicroLogic Software, Inc.
6400 Hollis St., Suite 9
Emeryville, CA 94608
800/888-9078

AllType/$79
Publisher's Powerpak/$79
Typefaces $29.95-$79.95
Atech Software
5964 La Place Court, Suite 125
Carlsbad, CA 92008, 800/748-
5657 or 619/438-6883.

Glyphix/$99.95
SWFTE International
P.O. Box 219
Rockland, DE 19732
800/237-9383; 302/658-1123

Twist and Shout!/$99
Adobe Font Foundry/
Free with Adobe PostScript
typefaces
Adobe Systems, Inc.
1585 Charleston Road
Mountain View, CA 94039
800/833-6687; 415/961-4400

Fontware Starter Kits/free–$39
FaceLift for WordPerfect
Typefaces/$129
Bitstream, Inc.
Athenaeum House
215 First Street
Cambridge, MA 02142
800/522-3668; 617/497-6222

Application Software

8

Working With Applications

~

With this chapter, we begin a long section devoted to helping you get the most from your DeskJet with your application programs, so that your printed documents will look as classy as possible no matter what programs you use.

In this preliminary chapter, you'll learn fundamentals that will help you achieve harmony between the DeskJet and almost any program. Major topics we'll cover include how and why to choose the best DeskJet driver available for your software, and, when drivers fail you, the various methods for sending printer command from within an application program.

The remaining chapters of the section cover ways to get the most from your DeskJet using DOS and the most popular application programs ranging from word processing to spreadsheets and databases to graphics and desktop publishing.

Choosing a DeskJet driver

Without exception, the safest, smoothest route to excellent results with the DeskJet is to use a program that comes with a good DeskJet driver of its own.

You'll recall that printer drivers are special software modules specific to your particular printer that "dock" into your main application program. A driver serves as the interpreter between your program and the printer, translating what the program wants to print into commands the printer can understand. A well-written DeskJet driver will let you access both text and graphics modes, mix internal, cartridge and soft fonts in the same document, control spacing of your text and resolution of your graphics, and tap the improvements available in the DeskJet Plus.

Since the first edition of this book was published, the DeskJet has established itself as one of the most popular printers around. All the major applications now supply decent DeskJet drivers. My job is therefore much easier.

But there are still times you may find yourself using a program without an adequate driver for your printer. Perhaps you're using an older program and either there's no upgrade available or you don't want to pay for the new version. Or perhaps there are certain printer features that your program's DeskJet driver doesn't handle perfectly. A small toolbag of utilities (covered in Chapters 4 and 7) and software tricks (introduced in this chapter) will get you through these tight spots.

How to get the DeskJet to work with any program

The chapters to come coverspecific applications and how to use them with the DeskJet for best results. For now, let's look at the approach that the head-scratching DeskJet owner should take when confronting the generic application program. Here are the steps to follow:

1. Consult your software owner's manual to see if the program comes with a printer driver designed for the DeskJet. If you own a DeskJet Plus or 500, try to find instructions that pertain specifically to that model—otherwise, you may give up some of the features of your improved printer.

In addition to reading the main manual, be sure you also look for any supplementary instructions, and for a README file on the program disk, that may contain further printer advice. Software vendors are always playing catchup to make sure that their programs can work with with popular new printers. Even if there's no mention whatsoever of the DeskJet in your software documentation, a DeskJet driver may have been created since the manual was printed.

If the program does come with specific support for the DeskJet, read the description of what DeskJet features you can and can't use. Often, you'll face limitations such as being only able to print with certain fonts. If the driver supports every feature of your DeskJet model, you're home free. If you find some limitations, skip to step 4.

2. If you don't find specific DeskJet instructions listed anywhere, call the software publisher, and ask if they've come up with a DeskJet driver yet. If so, the publisher will send it to you for free or for a nominal fee. (On second thought, even if the program does have a DeskJet driver, call the vendor anyway—they may have a newer, better version of the driver to send you.) If the publisher confirms that there's no DeskJet driver, it's on to step 3.

3. If your software just doesn't supply a DeskJet-specific printer driver, your next best bet is to install a LaserJet driver instead. The LaserJet long ago became as much a standard as any other printer model, and every program worth its salt comes with a LaserJet driver. Since the DeskJet understands most of the same commands that control the LaserJet, you can usually substitute a LaserJet driver for the missing DeskJet one with good to excellent results.

Using a LaserJet driver, you'll certainly be able to print text, but the characters may not be spaced properly. Graphics files may print just fine, or not at all, depending on the program. Test the system, take note of any problems you find, and skip to step 4.

♯ Tip: *To get reliably superior printouts using a LaserJet driver, use the LaserTwin utility profiled in Chapter 4. LaserTwin is a LaserJet emulation utility that lets your DeskJet print any page a LaserJet can handle.*

4. If the DeskJet or LaserJet driver you've adopted won't let you achieve the printed results you want, or if you're using some stoneage program that doesn't even support the LaserJet, you have two choices. First, consider using a utility such as BackLoader (Chapter 7), which lets you place DeskJet commands in any document, or LaserControl (Chapter 4), an emulation utility that makes the DeskJet emulate a number of common printers, one of which the software probably does recognize. If you don't want to use a utility, go on to step 5.

5. If all else fails, you'll have to send the necessary commands yourself. If your program permits, you can add the printer commands within your document, a process discussed in the remainder of this chapter. If not, you must send the commands via DOS, as described in Chapter 9.

Doing it your way

The rest of this chapter is devoted to an introduction to DeskJet commands (control codes and escape sequences) and how to use them in conjunction with application programs to get the printouts you want. First, you'll learn about the various ways you can send printer commands from different applications. Then we'll look at some of the most important escape sequences.

♪ Note: *Chapter 22 on DeskJet programming describes all of the commands individually and in detail. Even if you don't plan to write your own drivers or standalone programs for the DeskJet, you may want to read Chapter 22 once you're familiar with the basic commands.*

Escape sequences

Back in Chapter 3 you met your first escape sequence, the one used to turn on underlining. It's time for a closer look at the underlining command and what each of the characters in that escape sequence do. Here it is again, printed first in the format usually used for escape sequences: ^{E}s$_c$&dØD and then in decimal notation: **27 38 100 48 68**. Reading from left to right, there's a one-to-one correspondence between the two printed versions of our sequence. ^{E}s$_c$ represents the escape character, code 27. The ampersand is code 38, the lowercase *d* code 100, and so on.

Unfortunately, as you can see immediately, the code numbers HP chose for the escape sequences don't translate into printed characters all that well—the notation looks dense and inscrutable. And besides being hard to read overall, HP's code uses some letters and numbers that look too much alike. For example, many escape sequences use the lower case letter l (that's "el," as in "lois lane" or "lex luthor"). Of course, a lower case "l" looks much like the numeral "1" (one), a number that also appears frequently in escape sequences.

It's a perfect setup for making horrendous mistakes in entering these codes. The stopgap solution HP came up with was to print the "els" in cursive. But in HP publications, you're on your own when it comes to distinguishing upper case "O"s (ohs) from "0"s (zeros). In this book, however, I'll use Ø (a zero with a slash through it) to represent zero, and an ordinary O for capital *O*.

Even without the mistaken identity problems, DeskJet escape sequences are simply unattractive jumbles, with nothing mnemonic about them. Upper and lower case letters, numbers, and miscellaneous punctuation marks seem to appear randomly. Actually, there is a trace of a pattern in the coding system, which you can read about in Chapter 22. The practical point is this: be sure you concentrate on your typing while you enter escape sequences, and proofread very carefully.

Printer commands for the sorcerer's apprentice

The available DeskJet commands are so numerous and powerful that they can be considered a special-purpose programming language. But for most everyday text printing chores, a handful of printer commands will suffice.

Being able to change fonts, margins, and type style *within* a document is the most important reason for learning how to use printer commands. If you want to italicize one word in a line, and then underline another in that same line, like this:

Joyce's *Ulysses* is a <u>thick</u> book.

you must find a way to send four commands to the printer within the stream of characters on that line. One escape sequence must come just before the italicized *Ulysses* to turn on the italic font, and another immediately after to restore the ordinary font. You then have to bracket the underlined <u>thick</u> with a second on/off pair of escape sequences.

So, what you need is a way to place or *embed* printer commands directly into a document at the point in the file where they are to take effect. However, if the reason for embedding commands in a file makes sense, the method is not so obvious. The problem is that you can't just type in the necessary codes from your keyboard. Even though you have keys labelled (ESC) and (CTRL), pressing these keys won't do the trick—application programs use them for their own commands, as you well know.

Unfortunately, there's no standard system for sending commands to the DeskJet (or any printer, for that matter) that will work in all application programs. Yes, the computer eventually has to deliver the right codes to the printer cable, but how you tell it to do that varies significantly from program to program. And a good many programs make no provision for printer commands at all. As always, the best way to find out how your software works is to consult the owner's manual. If the program permits you to send printer commands to your DeskJet, there should be a reference in the index to "printer commands" or "escape sequences." Meanwhile, though, the following discussion should prepare you for what you'll find in the manual.

♪ ***Note:*** *If your program does not permit you to embed printer commands in your files, you can still control many printer features from DOS. See Chapter 9 for details.*

Some programs have a special mode just for the purpose of embedding printer codes. You give a particular command that signals the program to interpret the next keystrokes you type as printer codes, instead of acting on the keys as it normally would. When you're finished entering the printer codes, you press another special keystroke to return to normal program operation. In WordPerfect 5.0, for example, you type the keystroke sequence (SHIFT)(F8) **4 6 2 1** to activate the Printer Commands feature, then type in the printer codes themselves. When you're through typing printer commands, you press (F7) to return to your document.

Programs that use this system may let you enter the printer commands themselves in several different ways. In some cases, you simply type the associated keys. For example, in the text editor Brief, you press the (ESC) key to embed the numeric value of the escape code in your file (in Brief, as in most other programs that use this system, you see the escape character ← on your screen). On the other hand, other programs including WordPerfect require you to type in some or all of the code numbers digit by digit, as discussed in the next few paragraphs.

In programs that don't have a special mode for entering printer commands, you may be able to embed the necessary codes typing them directly into your file preceded by a particular character such as the backslash (\). When the program detects this special character, it knows to send the characters that follow directly to the printer. You still can't type "unprintable" characters such as escape or the control codes, so you have to enter them as numerals.

Lotus 1-2-3 Release 2.2 and earlier, and many other spreadsheets and databases work this way. In 1-2-3, the escape sequence for turning underlining on would be embedded in a spreadsheet file as \Ø27&d1D.

The numerals **Ø27** represent the numeric value of the ASCII code for the escape code. When 1-2-3 reads this value as it prints the file, it send will a code 27 as single byte of data to your DeskJet, not separate bytes for the codes for "Ø", "2," and "7." Since the rest of the entries in the sequence are ordinary keyboard characters, you can enter by typing them directly.

Some programs require you to enter the entire sequence of printer code values in numeric form, even the codes for characters you'd be able to type directly on the keyboard. In a program of this type, you'd have to type in the escape sequence for underlining shown above as \Ø27\Ø38\1ØØ\Ø49\Ø68.

Using common printer commands

Now that you know how to embed printer commands in your documents, the question remaining is which commands to use. Here's a quick introduction to the escape sequences and control codes you'll need most often. Again, these and all the other escape sequences and control codes are covered in detail in Chapter 22.

Underlining

The DeskJet offers several different underlining options, all of which are detailed in Chapter 22. To cut down on the confusion, only the escape sequences for the standard type of underlining are listed here. To underline a word or phrase, you embed a pair of escape sequences in your text, one immediately before the passage to be underlined to turn underlining on, and one immediately after the passage to stop the underlining.

ᴱs_c&dØD   Turn underlining on

ᴱs_c&d@   Turn underlining off

Here's an example of underlined text, followed by the file that produced it showing the embedded escape sequences.

The rain in Spain falls <u>mainly</u> on the plain.

The rain in Spain falls ᴱs_c&dØDmainlyᴱs_c&d@ on the plain.

Printing bold text

As you'll recall from Chapter 6 almost any DeskJet font can be printed in boldface. Here are the escape sequences that turn boldface type on and off:

^{E}s$_C$(s3B   Begin boldface printing

^{E}s$_C$(sØB   End boldface, return to ordinary text

To print the line

A motion to adjourn is **always** in order.

your file should read

A motion to adjourn is ^{E}s$_C$(s3Balways^{E}s$_C$(sØB in order.

Printing italic text

The DeskJet understands two escape sequences related to italics: one to switch from ordinary straight up-and-down characters to slanty, italicized text, the other to switch back to regular characters.

⌒ ***Caution:*** *You can only switch to italics with the simple command you're about to learn if you have an italics font installed in your printer that's otherwise identical to the font you're currently using (same typeface, point size, character set, and so forth). Note especially that the original DeskJet's internal font set does not include an italic version of Courier, a deficit that was corrected in the DeskJet Plus.*

To print a word, a phrase, or an entire page in italics, surround the passage with these codes:

^{E}s$_C$(s1S   Enable italics

^{E}s$_C$(sØS   Italics off

For example, to print the second verse of Genesis as rendered in the King James Bible,

And the earth was without form, and void;
and darkness *was* upon the face of the deep.

your file should look like this:

And the earth was without form, and void;
and darkness ^{E}s$_C$(s1Swas^{E}s$_C$(sØS upon the face of the deep.

Printing super- and subscripted text

To print one or more characters above or below the normal text baseline, embed the following escape sequences around the characters to be super- or subscripted:

^{E}s$_c$(s1U Turn on superscripting

^{E}s$_c$(s-1U Turn on subscripting

^{E}s$_c$(sØU Turn off super- or subscripting

So, to print

$$E = MC^2$$

your file should look like this:

E = MC^{E}s$_c$(s1U2^{E}s$_c$(sØU

Setting margins

With the proper escape sequences, you can reset the margins as often as you like within a single document.

^{E}s$_c$&a#L Left margin

^{E}s$_c$&a#M Right margin

Margins are measured in columns, so replace the # in the above sequences with the numeric value of your desired margin, in columns. The size of a column depends on the current print pitch. You can use Table 8-1 to figure out the column number for the margin you want.

Pitch	Column for Desired Margin		
	.5″	1″	2Æ
5	2	5	10
10	5	10	20
16.67	8	16	33
20	10	20	40

Table 8-1: *Column settings for various margins, to be used in escape sequences*

For fractional margins greater than an inch, add the column numbers for the component measurements. For a 1½ inch margin at 10 pitch, for example, you'd send the escape sequence $^{E}s_{c}$&a15L (15 = 5+10).

Changing page orientation

In portrait mode, the long edge of the paper runs vertically, and you have lots of lines but not so many columns. In landscape mode, the long edge is oriented horizontally, so you can fit long lines, though not as many on a single page.

The DeskJet is capable of printing in either orientation, although in the landscape orientation only a very few fonts are available, and you can't print graphics at all. The DeskJet Plus has a couple of built-in landscape fonts, but you need a landscape font cartridge for the original DeskJet. If you do have landscape fonts installed in your printer, selecting landscape mode automatically selects the one that's most like the font you were using in portrait mode, so you don't have to specifically select a font unless you want to.

To switch from portrait to landscape or vice versa within a document, here are the escape sequences you'll need (the l's are lowercase "el"s):

$^{E}s_{c}$&l1O   Select landscape orientation

$^{E}s_{c}$&l∅O   Select portrait orientation

Creating a page break

If you want a new section or chapter in your document to start at the top of the page, you'll need to send a command that makes the DeskJet eject the current page and start in again with the next one. The command in question is the form feed, or Ctrl-L, a one-byte control code with the ASCII value of **12**.

Selecting print quality

As you'll recall, the DeskJet can print text using a razor sharp, letter quality mode, or in a faster but somewhat less impressive-looking draft mode. In most cases, it's easier just to lean over and hit the MODE button on the keypad. But if you do want to change modes via software, the necessary escape sequences are:

^{E}s$_C$(s2Q   Letter quality mode

^{E}s$_C$(s1Q   Draft mode

Choosing fonts

Chapter 6 introduced you to the techniques for selecting fonts via printer commands, but the details are complicated. Although I'll leave the full disussion of font selection commands for Chapter 22, the italics and boldface commands given above qualify as commands in that category.

9

Controlling the DeskJet from DOS

❧

Although there are quicker, easier, more elegant ways to get the DeskJet to do your bidding, sometimes your best bet is to control the printer directly from DOS. Two situations in which it's handy to communicate with the DeskJet from DOS immediately come to mind. Here's the first: you'd like to print a short DOS text file directly from the DOS prompt, without going through the bother of loading the file into your word processor first. Unless you want to reformat the file, you don't gain anything by printing a DOS text file from your word processor, and you lose time as you wait for the word processor to get itself started and then to import the file.

The second scenario involves sending printer commands to the DeskJet. Let's say that to print a particular document to your liking, you need to switch to another font or set new margins before you start printing. The problem is that you're using WERDS.EXE, a backwards application program that doesn't have a DeskJet driver, and doesn't allow you to embed your own escape sequences directly in the file.

A better-than-nothing solution is to send the DeskJet setup commands from DOS, and then run your application and print the document. You'll have to be content with the same font, margins, and other settings for the entire document, but at least you aren't stuck with the printer settings in effect before you started.

Printing DOS text files

Plain DOS text files are everywhere. Good examples are the READ.ME files that software companies often place on program disks, and the files you download from an electronic bulletin board (such as CompuServe) or e-mail (electronic mail, such as MCI Mail) system.

A plain text file is the kind that looks like it's supposed to— not full of strange characters scattered wildly around the screen—when you view it on the screen with DOS's TYPE command (see your DOS manual if you're unfamiliar with TYPE). The reason is that DOS text files consist entirely of ordinary characters stored in ASCII code format, and have none of the special formatting codes peculiar to a particular program.

The simplest way to print a plain text file from DOS is by COPYing it to the printer. If your file is called OPUS.TXT, you type

copy opus.txt lpt1:⏎

♪ *Note: All the examples of sending escape sequences and control codes from DOS assume your printer is connected to LPT1. If you've connected via another port, substitute that port's DOS name for lpt1 in the DOS commands shown in the examples.*

If you want to get a little bit fancier you can use DOS' PRINT program. PRINT is a memory resident program that starts the printing process and then returns you to the DOS prompt immediately, so you can go on with your work as printing proceeds.

❀ *Tip:* *COPY and PRINT work fine with the DeskJet, but you have to remember to send any setup commands yourself ahead of time. If you have a favorite font or use a standard set of margins, you can automate the entire printing process, including sending the DeskJet commands and printing the file itself, with a single batch file.*

Sending printer commands from DOS

Sending DeskJet commands directly from DOS is simple, as long as you know a couple of tricks. The main challenge is this: you can't type the critical control codes on the command line. Fortunately, there's an straightforward way to sidestep this obstacle. Before we get to the solution, though, let's spend a little more time explaining the problem (if you want the brass tacks, skip to the section "The ESCAPE solution" below). Here's the situation: When you type the keys that correspond to DeskJet commands, DOS itself responds immediately, taking some action and gobbling up the commands for good. To see what I mean, you might want to sit down in front of your computer and start the beast, so that the DOS prompt is on the screen.

As you'll recall from Chapter 8, typing the (ESC) key at the DOS prompt doesn't produce the escape character on your screen. If you're at the computer, try it. A slash appears and the cursor moves a line lower, but you won't see the ← that represents the escape character.

The same sort of thing happens when you try to enter most of the control codes. When you press the necessary keys ((CTRL) plus a letter key) DOS takes some kind of action, or does nothing, instead of placing the control code character on your screen.

For example, try pressing (CTRL) J, which is supposed to produce an ASCII code value of 10, the line feed code (you'll find a table of DeskJet control codeS in Chapter 22 on DeskJet programming.) When the DeskJet receives a code 10, it stops printing and advances the paper by one line.

But when you press (CTRL) J, you won't see a code of any kind on the command line. Instead, DOS follows the line feed command itself, and simply moves the prompt and cursor one line down on the screen.

Actually, you can enter one or two of the ten DeskJet control codes on the command line. But that's hardly enough to bother with.

The ESCAPE solution

If we can't enter our precious special codes directly in DOS, how, then, can we get the codes to the DeskJet? With special files containing the codes prepared ahead of time, that's how. At a minimum, you should create a file called ESCAPE containing the escape character and it alone. Using a technique you'll learn shortly, you'll be able to combine this file and characters you can type at the keyboard to send any escape sequence to the DeskJet from DOS.

♪ **Note:** *If you want to use DOS to send other DeskJet control codes such as the form feed command to start a new page, you'll need a separate file for each code. You'll find details in the "Batching It" section below.*

To create ESCAPE, you'll need a word processor or text editor that can store files in plain ASCII format, without any special formatting codes. All the major word processors—and most of the minor ones—have a command for saving files in ASCII format. Another absolute requirement is that your word processor or text editor must not automatically add a carriage return and/or line feed character at the end of every line. The ESCAPE file must consist of the escape character only, not the escape character plus a carriage return or line feed (see the tip below if your word processor fails this test).

In addition, your word processor or editor must allow you to enter non-keyboard characters such as the escape character. In most word processors, you do this by holding down the (ALT) key and typing the ASCII code for the character you want to enter on the numeric keypad. To enter the escape character, for example, you hold down (ALT), type 2 then 7, and release the (ALT) key. The escape character, ←, appears in the file.

◠ **Caution:** *When entering characters using the Alt key, you must use the number keys on the numeric pad, not the ones on the row above the letters. It doesn't matter whether or not the Num Lock function is on.*

To create the ESCAPE file, start a new file and enter the escape character at the very first position in the file (don't move the cursor). Without doing anything else, save the file with the name ESCAPE. That's all there is to it. Similar files for other control codes are a little longer than one character.

✄ *Tip: If your word processor doesn't meet all the requirements listed above, you can create the ESCAPE file using a combination of a DOS function and a utility program. At the DOS prompt, type COPY CON ESCAPE and press ⏎. Now type* **e** *(actually, any single character would do) and immediately press* (F6)*. Then press ⏎ to create the 1-byte ESCAPE file containing only that e. Now load a disk utility program such as the Norton Utilities and use the hexadecimal edit function to change the value recorded in the file from 65 for the e to 1B for the escape character, and then save the file.*

Using ESCAPE

Once you've created the ESCAPE file, you can use it to send any escape sequence to the DeskJet from DOS. Here's how:

1. At the DOS prompt, type

    copy escape+con lpt1

2. Type in the remainder of the escape sequence. Remember, although an escape sequence starts with the non-typeable escape character, the rest of the sequence consists of ordinary keyboard characters that you can type in directly.

3. Press (F6) followed by ⏎ to finish your entry and send the escape sequence to the DeskJet.

✄ *Tip: You can automate the process of sending escape sequences from DOS using batch files. See "Batching it" below.*

For example, to send the escape sequence that turns on boldface type, you would type:

copy con escape+con prn
(s3B
(F6)
⏎

See Chapter 8 for a discussion of the most commonly used escape sequences, and Chapter 22 for a complete reference to all DeskJet commands.

Batching It

Whether you want to send DeskJet commands, download fonts, or print DOS text files without a word processor, *batch files* can help you do the job much faster. A batch file Is a predefined series of standard DOS commands that DOS executes for you, so you don't have to type them in yourself each time. If you like, you can think of a batch file as a simple program that gets DOS to do your bidding.

To run a batch file, all you do is type its name on the DOS command line, and then press ⏎, just as if you were running an ordinary program. When you execute the batch file, DOS reads the file and carries out its commands one line at a time, exactly as though you were pounding them out on the keyboard.

Let's take a simple example. Since you can send files to your printer using the DOS command COPY, a batch file that automatically prints two files might contain these commands:

```
copy c:file1 lpt1:
copy c:file2 lpt1:
```

If you named this batch file PRNTFILE, you would type PRNTFILE⏎ at the DOS prompt to run it. You could rerun the file as often as you want the same files.

Obviously, batch files make using a set of a frequently used DOS commands much quicker and less prone to error. For our purposes, batch files are great for the DeskJet commands you use most often. For example, you might create one batch file for setting margins, and a collection of separate batch files for selecting your favorite fonts.

Creating DeskJet batch files

There are two basic ways to create batch files: directly from DOS using the COPY CON command, or via a word processor or text editor. The COPY CON method has the advantage of being instantly available, since you don't have to wait for your word processor to load. In fact, you don't even need to have a word processing program at hand. However, although the COPY CON method works for printing files, you can't use it to enter control codes or escape sequences. For that, you'll have to use a word processor. Besides, a word processor makes it much easier to edit your file, especially if the file is longer than one line.

Either way you go, the one essential—other than avoiding typing errors in the command—is that you name the file properly. The first eight characters of the filename can be anything you want, but you must use .BAT as the filename extension.

⌒ **Caution:** *All batch files must have .BAT as the filename extension. Valid batch file names include 1.BAT, E.BAT, COPYFILE.BAT, and so on.*

Creating a batch file with COPY CON

Here's how to use COPY CON to create the PRNTFILE.BAT batch file for printing two files, shown in the above example:

1. Switch to the disk drive and directory where you wish to store the batch file.

2. At the DOS prompt, type

copy con prntfile.bat⏎

The cursor will jump down a line to the far left margin of your screen.

3. Type

copy c:file1 lpt1⏎
copy c:file2 lpt1⏎

4. Press (F6)

You'll see the characters ^Z on the screen.

5. Press (↵). Your batch file will be saved on the disk, and you'll get the message **1 File(s) copied** from DOS to confirm it.

Creating batch files with your word processor

To create batch files with a word processor or text editor, THE program you use must be capable of saving files in plain ASCII format, without any special formatting codes. It must also let you type in symbols like the escape character that aren't represented on the keyboard. Most of the well-known word processors, including WordPerfect, Microsoft Word, and PC-Write meet these criteria. For batch files, it's all right if your word processor automatically adds a carriage return at the end of each line.

With most programs, you use the (ALT)-numeric pad method described above in the section "The ESCAPE solution" to enter the codes you can't type. Some word processors have a special command for entering non-keyboard characters—you give the command first, and then use whatever method is provided for entering the codes.

Using the ECHO command

In batch files, you should use the DOS command ECHO to send your escape sequences and control codes to the DeskJet, not the COPY command. Some DeskJet escape sequences include the * character, which COPY interprets as a filename *wildcard.* Instead of sending the * to your printer, COPY will look for files on your disk whose name begins with the escape character and ends with the characters following the * in the escape sequence. ECHO correctly sends the * to the DeskJet. Note that you must type the DOS redirection symbol > before the printer designation (lpt1 in the examples). Do not use the redirection symbol with the COPY command.

Making a batch file

The overall process of creating a batch file with your word processor IS no different than creating any plain ASCII text file: start your word processor, open a new file, type in the characters, and save the file.

For practice, try creating the batch file BOLD.BAT for switching to boldface type:

　1. Start your word processor and open a new file. If your program wants you to name the file before you start typing, call it BOLD.BAT.

　2. Without moving the cursor (it should be at the the first position in your new file, the top left corner of the screen work area), type *echo* and press the spacebar.

　3. Next, use whatever method your program allows to enter the escape code, ASCII value 27. In most cases, you'll just hold down the (ALT) key while you press **2**, then **7** on the numeric keypad. When you let up the (ALT) key, a ← symbol representing the escape character should appear in your file.

　If your program provides a different method for entering non-keyboard characters, use that method instead.

　3. Now type the following string of characters: (s3B >lpt1. The ">lpt1" sends the command to the printer when the batch file is executed.

　4. Without moving the cursor or typing any more characters (do not even press (↵)), save the file in plain ASCII format. If you haven't yet named it, call it BOLD.BAT.

You can use this technique to create batch files for all the commands you use regularly, including those that use control codes other than the escape character. For example, to create a file that sends the form feed control code to eject the current page from the DeskJet, you would:

　1. Start a new word processor file called FF.BAT

　2. Type **echo** and press the spacebar

3. Press (ALT) and type **12** on the numeric pad, then release the (ALT) key. The ♀ symbol, representing the form feed character, should appear on your screen.

4. Press the spacebar, then type **>lpt1**. The completed line should look like this:

echo ♀ >lpt1

5. Save the file.

Combining commands in batch files

You can combine as many separate commands as you like in a single batch file. For example, you could create a SETUP.BAT batch file that sends a form feed command, sets a 1" left margin, and switches to boldface type. The contents of this file would be:

echo ♀ >lpt1
echo ←&a12L >lpt1
echo ←(s3B >lpt1

A generic batch file for escape sequences

You won't want to bother with creating a separate batch file for every possible escape sequence you can send to the DeskJet. Instead, the method described in "The ESCAPE solution" above will do for escape sequences you use only occasionally. However, you can speed up this technique by creating a batch file to do all the repetitive typing for you.

Using either the COPY CON method or your word processor, create a new batch file called DJ.BAT. The file should contain this one line:

copy escape+con prn

To use this file, type **dj** at the DOS command line and press (↵). You'll be dropped down to a new line where you can type in the rest of the escape sequence. Press (F6), then (↵) to send the escape sequence to the DeskJet.

Batch files for printing text files

Batch files are handy for printing DOS text files. If you have a favorite font or use a standard set of margins, you can automate the entire printing process, including sending the DeskJet commands and printing the file itself, with a single batch file.

Using the word processor method, create a batch file named PRINTDJ.BAT that looks like this:

```
if %1==stop
echo ♀ >lpt1
echo ←(s3B >lpt1
copy %1 lpt1
:stop
```

Once you've saved the file, you can print a letter called BOXTOPS.TXT with your preferred font, margins, and so on, by typing printdj boxtops.txt⏎ on the command line.

This batch file relies on a couple of tricks that we haven't covered yet. In the first line, the notation *%1* refers to the filename you type on the command line after "printdj". When DOS reads the batch file, it substitutes what you typed for every *%1* it finds in the batch file.

In the example batch file, the *if* statement on the first line determines whether you entered a filename to be printed. If you didn't type anything, this line causes DOS to skip everything else and pick up the batch file at the last line, labelled *:stop*. Since there are no further lines after the *:stop*, the batch file simply finishes without doing anything.

If you did type something following "printdj," it's on to the heart of the batch file. The next two lines in the sample PRINTDJ.BAT are for the DeskJet commands you want to send before printing the text file. The ones shown send a form feed command and select boldface type, but you can substitute any DeskJet escape sequence or control code you prefer, and you can add as many commands as you like. Each command must be on a separate line.

The line that begins with *copy* gets down to business and prints the file. As you can see, this line also includes a *%1*, which means that DOS will print whatever file you chose when you started PRINTDJ.BAT.

Batch files within batch files

Before you create your own version of PRINTDJ.BAT, there's one more potentially time-saving wrinkle you should know about first: a batch file can execute another batch file. If you've already created batch files for individual DeskJet commands, you don't need to retype the commands themselves in PRINTDJ.BAT. Instead, the file should look something like this:

```
if %1 == stop
FF
BOLD
copy %1 lpt1
:stop
```

That concludes our look at DOS batch files and ends this chapter as well. Although it's generally easier to control the DeskJet with your application program's built-in commands or with a printer setup utility, you can access almost every feature of your printer with the techniques you've learned here.

10

Microsoft Windows

∾

Windows 3.0 is one of the most successful pieces of software ever introduced. One of Windows' big drawing cards is the notion of *device independence*. When a software developer creates a Windows program, he or she doesn't have to worry about how to make the program work with all the different monitors, mice, and printers that are on the market. Instead, the developer just concentrates on getting the program to work with Windows. When the user of the program wants to print, for example, Windows takes care of interacting with the user's particular printer.

This arrangement works great, as long as someone has developed a Windows driver for the printer in question. The driver gets installed into Windows, not into a particular Windows program, and all Windows programs will work with the printer once the driver installation is complete. But by the same token, if the driver has any limitations, all your Windows programs will have to put up with them—the quality of the driver determines how effectively you can take advantage of that printer's features.

Windows and the DeskJet

Fortunately, the driver for the DeskJet that comes with Windows 3 suffers from very few limitations. You can set it up for any of the three DeskJet models, and it automatically knows which internal fonts your model comes with, and which font cartridges it can use.

Better yet, it knows about soft fonts, and can install most soft fonts automatically for you. The driver lets you access all the other major DeskJet features as well.

In addition, HP has created a separate Windows driver that provides scalable fonts for the DeskJet from any Windows program (scalable fonts are defined in Chapter 7). Although this driver is called DeskJet *500* Scalable Printer Driver, it works with any DeskJet model—albeit slowly with the original DeskJet. This driver is free from HP.

Tip: *You can get the latest version of either DeskJet driver for Windows directly from HP at no charge. Call 303/353-7650.*

Finally, if you're willing to pay for the privilege, you can choose from five other scalable font drivers for Windows that work with the DeskJet. All of them allow you to print graphics as well, either by working in concert with Windows' standard DeskJet driver, or by taking over graphics printing themselves. Additionally, you can get simulated PostScript output for text and graphics with one of the PostScript interpreter packages profiled in Chapter 20.

Installing the Windows DeskJet driver

To get Windows and your DeskJet working together, your two main tasks are to install the the DeskJet driver and then to configure the driver for your DeskJet. You complete this mission using Control Panel, a vital little program that comes with Windows. Control Panel lets you alter a number of Windows features, including screen colors, keyboard setup, mouse response time—and what we're interested in here, printer setup.

There are two ways to run Control Panel for printer setup. You use one when you're installing the Windows for the first time, the other when you're adding a new printer driver to an existing Windows installation.

First-time Windows installation

If you're installing Windows 3 for the first time, you simply follow the standard installation procedure outlined in your Windows manual using the Setup program on your "Setup" disk. The printer installation step comes after you've already chosen the correct computer type, display adapter, keyboard, and mouse, and after most of the Windows files have already been copied to your hard disk.

At this point, Setup automatically starts the Windows Control Panel program and opens the Printers dialog box, shown in Figure 10-1. You're now ready to install and configure the DeskJet driver, as detailed in "Installing the DeskJet driver" below.

Adding a DeskJet driver to an existing Windows setup

If the need arises, it's easy to add the DeskJet driver after you've already installed Windows itself. There are two main reasons you might want to do this. Either you bought your DeskJet after you installed Windows, or you want to replace an older driver with an updated version that adds new features and corrects earlier flaws.

To add a new printer driver after you've installed Windows, you must run Control Panel yourself. Use one of these three methods:

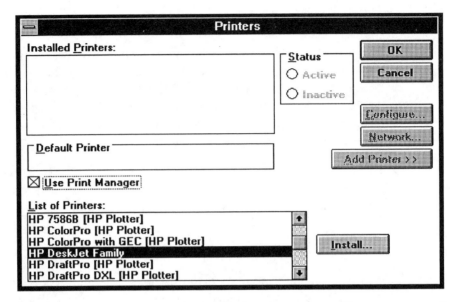

Figure 10-1: Pick out the DeskJet on the list of printers you'll see as you install Windows.

- In Program Manager, double-click on the Control Panel icon.

- In File Manager, double-click on the Control Panel file (CONTROL.EXE).

- In either Program Manager or File Manager, choose the Run command, type **control** then press **W**.

As soon as Control Panel is running, double click on the Printers icon to bring up the Printers dialog box, shown in Figure 10-1. Now go on to "Installing the DeskJet driver" below.

Installing the DeskJet driver

At this point you should have the Printers dialog box on screen. Notice that the scroll box at the bottom left offers a list of all the printers you can install (if it doesn't, click on the Add Printer button). The time has come to install the DeskJet driver, which includes features specifically for the DeskJet.

⅜ *Tip:* *If you plan to print from Windows using a driver not listed in the scroll box, such as Publisher's Powerpak or SuperPrint, it's a good idea to install the extra drivers as soon as you've finished installing the regular DeskJet driver. Follow the instructions in the driver's manual. Likewise, if you plan to use Windows with other printers besides the DeskJet, or with a PostScript emulation package, you should install all the necessary drivers when you first install Windows. You'll follow essentially the same steps laid out here, modifying them as appropriate for your other printers.*

Here's how to install the DeskJet driver:

1. Scroll through the list to the entry *HP DeskJet Family* and click on it to select it as shown in Figure 10-1.

2. Click on the *Install* button.

3. What happens next depends on whether a DeskJet driver already resides in your Windows directory. This would be the case if you previously installed a different DeskJet printer or compatible, or if you installed an earlier version of the DeskJet driver and now want to replace it with the latest update. If no DeskJet driver already exists on your hard disk, you'll skip to step 4. If a DeskJet driver is present, Windows will ask you whether you want to reinstall the currently installed driver or replace it with a new one instead. Click on *Current* for the existing driver, *New* to replace the existing driver with a new version. If you choose *Current*, Windows completes the installation at this step, and you can skip to *Using Print Manager* below.

4. You'll now be asked to insert the floppy disk containing the driver you want to install. Put it in the drive and choose OK. Windows adds the DeskJet driver to the list of installed printers at the top left of the dialog box. If this is the first driver you've installed, Windows automatically lists it as Active. If another driver is already active, the DeskJet driver will be listed in the box as Inactive.

5. If you install two or more printer drivers you'll want to choose one of them as the default printer, that is, the printer Windows will use for printing until you change to another default printer.

What's the difference between the default printer and the active printer?

Since Windows 3 lets you assign more than one printer to each printer port, it needs a way to know which printer you'll be printing with when you use that port. This is the *active* printer. There's a separate active printer for each printer port.

The *default* printer, on the other hand, is the one printer of all those you've installed that Windows will actually use for printing (until you choose a new default printer). In other words, if you want to print a document on a different printer, you must make that printer the default printer first. You can have only one default printer no matter how many printer ports you're using.

The default printer must be active. If you've installed, say, three printers on the same port and have chosen one of them as the default, you can't make another of the three the default printer without making it active first. And here's a key point: when you do switch a printer's status from inactive to active, Windows automatically makes the newly activated printer the default, if the previous default was assigned to the same printer port.

On the other hand, when you activate a printer assigned to a port other than the one used by the current default printer, the default does not change. Windows will still print to the current default printer until you change the default. You can choose a new default printer or change the activity status of a printer at any time except when you're actively printing—it's OK to make the switch between print jobs during the same Windows session.

To choose active status for a printer, select the printer in the Installed Printers list, then click on the button labelled *Active* beside the list at the top of the Printers dialog.

There are two ways to choose a new default printer:

- If the current default printer is assigned to the same printer port as the printer you now want as your default, you highlight the new default's name in the Installed Printer list and click on the *Active* button. Windows activates the second printer and simultaneously designates it as the new default while inactivating the old default.

- If the new default is assigned to a different port than the current default, you must first make the new default the active printer for that port. Then double click on the new default's name in the Installed Printers box. Alternatively, you can highlight the name and press (ALT)-down arrow. You'll see the driver name appear in the area labelled "Default Printer."

⌒ **Caution:** *The "Active" printer may not print. Since you can have more than one active printer (one for each printer port), simply making a printer active does not ensure that Windows will send your next print job to that printer. Only the current default printer ever prints.*

Using Print Manager

Before you leave the Printers dialog, you have one more decision to make: whether to use the Windows Print Manager. Print Manager is a print spooler, which means it lets you get back to work before a print job finishes (see Chapter 3 for more on print spoolers).

Like most spoolers, Print Manager will accept a series of print jobs from separate programs, printing each in its turn. But it also lets you view a list of the documents waiting to be printed, change their order in the "queue," cancel them individually, or stop the printing process temporarily.

Print Manager really does cut down on the time you spend waiting for your printer. In general, you should check the box labelled "Use Print Manager" at the lower left of the Printers dialog. The only exceptions:

- if you want to print as fast as possible, and don't care if you can't use your Windows programs in the meantime

- if you've installed SuperPrint or another alternative print spooler

- if you're printing over a network

- if you have too little room left on your hard disk for Print Manager to function effectively

To activate Print Manager, click in the box labelled *Use Print Manager* so that an X appears in the box, as shown in Figure 10-1.

♪ *Note:* *Print Manager doesn't work with Non-Windows programs . When you print from a non-Windows program that you're running within Windows, Print Manager stays out of the picture.*

Configuring the printer driver

With the driver installed, your next job is to configure it properly for your particular system. Here's how:

1. Click on the *Configure* button. You'll see the Printers - Configure dialog box, shown in Figure 10-2. Here, you tell Windows which communications port the printer is connected to. By default, the first parallel printer port, LPT1, has been selected for you. If the printer is connected to another port, select that port in the scroll box.

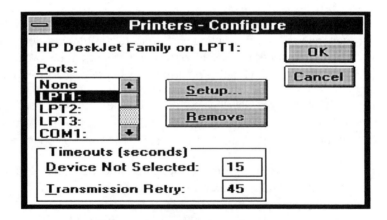

Figure 10-2: *The Printers-Configure dialog*

❊ *Tip:* *Windows 3 permits you to assign more than one printer to the same communications port. However, only one printer can be active at a time. To activate a different printer, go back to the Printers dialog box (click on OK in the Printers - Configure dialog), select the currently active printer, and click the Inactive button. Then select the printer you want to activate and click Active.*

◠ *Caution:* *You must reinstall your fonts if you change printer ports. See "Copying fonts to another port" below.*

> 2. Next, look at the options in the "Timeouts" section of the dialog. These determine how many seconds Windows will wait during a print job before it starts popping up messages that something is wrong with your printer. *Device Not Selected* decides how long Windows waits before telling you that the printer is off-line, while *Transmission Retry* controls how long Windows waits before deciding that the printer isn't receiving the output data. Change either value by clicking on it, deleting the current number, and typing in a new one.

♪ *Caution: Setting serial port parameters* *If you've opted for a serial connection, you'll need to check several serial communication parameters. You might as well do it now, before you forget. Go back to the main Control Panel screen by clicking on OK twice (in both the Printers - Configure and Printers dialogs. Then double-click on the Ports icon. In the Ports dialog, choose the icon for the COM port (serial port) to which your printer is connected, then click on Settings. In the box that appears, check the values to be sure that they match the printer's settings for speed, parity, and so forth. The default values, shown in Figure 7-4, should be correct if you've installed the DeskJet according to the instructions in the User's Guide. Choose OK twice to return to the main Control Panel window, choose Printers, and click Configure to re-open the Printers - Configure dialog.*

> 3. From the Printers - Configure dialog, click on the Setup button to open a dialog full of setup options for the driver, shown in Figure 10-3. We'll call this the Setup dialog, though it's labelled HP DeskJet Family.

> 4. Click on the first option, *Printer,* to open a drop-down list box containing all the DeskJet compatible models the driver works with. Scroll down to the DeskJet DeskJet selection and click on it to select it. The remaining options change so that they correspond to the DeskJet's features.

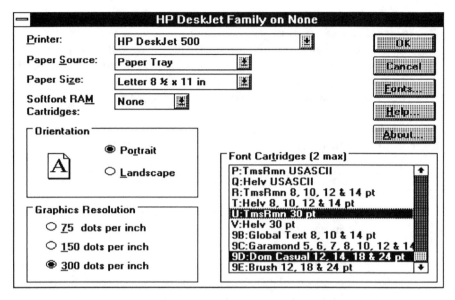

Figure 10-3: *The Setup dialog for the DeskJet driver.*

5. Set up the remaining options to match your DeskJet and your preferences:

- *Paper Source*—choose the tray you want Windows to feed paper from.

- *Paper size*—select the paper size you've loaded.

- *Softfont RAM*—select the value that matches the total amount of RAM cartridge memory you've installed.

- *Orientation*—select portrait or landscape mode.

- *Graphics resolution*—choose between 75, 150, or 300 dots per inch.

- *Cartridges*—the Windows driver knows that the DeskJet only has two cartridge slots, so you can select any combination of two of the cartridges displayed in the scroll list at the lower right.

6. If you want to use soft fonts within Windows, go on to "Choosing soft fonts" below. If not, you're finished. OK all the printer dialog boxes in turn. If you're installing Windows for the first time, Setup will take you to the next installation step. If Windows is already installed, you'll end up back at the main Control Panel window. Use the *Close* command to exit Control Panel and return to Program Manager.

Choosing soft fonts

You can select and configure soft fonts for the DeskJet when you first install Windows and as often as you like thereafter. To work with soft fonts, start from the Setup dialog box discussed in the previous section and click on the *Fonts* button. You'll see a new *Printer Font Installer* dialog shown in Figure 10-4.

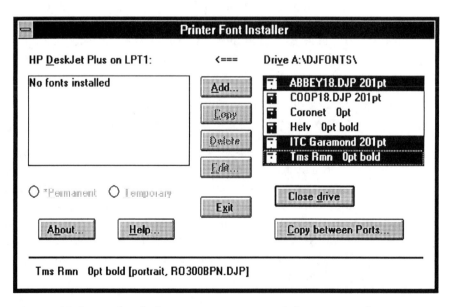

Figure 10-4: *Use this dialog to manage your soft fonts in Windows.*

To install new soft fonts:

1. Click on *Add Fonts* (the same button that reads "Close drive" in Figure 10-4.

2. Windows will ask you to insert a floppy disk with the new fonts disk. If your fonts are on a floppy, put it in the drive and click OK. If you've previously copied the fonts you want to install to your hard disk, you can type in the directory where the fonts are stored instead, and then click *OK*. Windows finds all the font files on the floppy or in the font directory and displays them in the list box at the right, as shown in Figure 10-4.

3. If the font you wanted to install isn't in the list, click on *Close drive*, then *Add Fonts* again to specify a different disk or directory.

4. When Windows has located the correct fonts, select the ones you want to install by clicking on them. Notice that the actual disk filename of the selected font now appears in the lower left hand corner of the box. You can select any combination of fonts in the list. As soon as you've selected at least one font, the *Add* button turns black.

5. Click on *Add* to install the selected fonts. They'll appear in the left hand window.

6. Windows assumes you want the installed fonts to be downloaded as temporary fonts, meaning that they get deleted every time the printer receives a soft reset command (which many programs send each time they print). If you prefer, click the *Permanent* button to download the fonts "permanently," meaning they'll stay in memory after a soft reset. Windows reminds you of the implications of your choice the first time you select a permanent font. See Chapter 7 for more on temporary versus soft fonts.

Editing font names

If you like, you can edit any installed font's name as it appears on Windows' font menus. Select one or more fonts listed in the lefthand box, then choose *Edit*. In the dialog that appears type in the new name you want. You can select permanent or temporary download status for each font here as well. If you selected more than one font to edit, click the *Next* button after you finish with each font to go on to the next one.

Since you can edit more than one font at a time, it's easy to rename all the fonts in a typeface. Select all the fonts you want to rename, click edit, and then click the box at the bottom of the Edit dialog labelled "Changes apply to all selected fonts." After you edit the name for the first font and click OK, all the selected fonts will receive the new name.

⟨⟩ *Caution:* *Unless you're truly a font expert, don't fool around with the choices "Font ID" or "Family"—you can screw up the way Windows accesses the font, or cause conflicts with other fonts.*

Copying fonts to another port

When you install soft fonts in the Windows DeskJet driver, you're installing them for a specific printer port, the one assigned in the Printers - Configure dialog. If you decide to connect your DeskJet to a different port, you have to change the port assignment in the Printers - Configure dialog, of course, but you'll also have to reinstall your soft font collection for the new port. The *Copy Between Ports* command gives you an easy way to do this, by transferring fonts already installed on one port to another port. You can move the transferred fonts, meaning that they are removed from the original port, or copy them, meaning that they're duplicated on the new port but remain on the old port as well. You can find details on how to use this option by choosing *Help* on the Printer Font Installer dialog.

Finishing installation

Once your soft fonts are installed and set up the way you want them, you're finished with installation of your DeskJet driver. Click *Exit* to leave the Printer Font Installer dialog, then OK each of the remaining printer-related dialogs in turn. Once you've OK'd the final dialog, Printers, you'll either be taken to the next installation step (if you're installing Windows for the first time) or to the main Control Panel window (if Windows is already installed). In the latter case, exit Control Panel to return to Program Manager.

Modifying printer settings

Windows makes it easy to modify the settings on your DeskJet printer driver at any time. If you plug in a different font cartridge, install more memory, add new soft fonts, or want to switch from portrait to landscape mode, all you do is reconfigure your DeskJet driver with the same printer-related dialog boxes we've already talked about. Just run Control Panel, choose the Printers icon, select the DeskJet driver, and choose *Configure* to access the first dialog in the series.

Using alternative Windows printer drivers

While Windows' own driver for the DeskJet does a creditable job, several alternatives are faster, more flexible, or both. The big advantage of all of these optional drivers is their ability to scale fonts to any size you need at the time you print. All of them can make generate corresponding screen fonts, so that you can see your document on the display as it will appear in print. One package, SuperPrint, also improves both the speed and quality of graphics printing. In this section, we'll look at Adobe Type Manager, FaceLift for Windows, and SuperPrint, as well as HP's own scalable font generator for Windows and the DeskJet. Two other Windows-compatible font scalers, Publisher's Powerpak and MoreFonts, are covered back in Chapter 7.

The DeskJet 500 Scalable Printer Driver

The DeskJet 500 comes with a special driver for Windows called the DeskJet 500 Scalable Printer driver. If you use this driver in place of the standard DeskJet, you can scale any AGFA Compugraphic typeface outline—the same faces used by the Type Director font generator—to whatever size you like during a Windows print session. The DeskJet 500 Scalable Printer Driver also generates Windows screen fonts, but you must create these in advance at the particular sizes you expect to need. Other scalable font drivers make screen fonts on the fly, but they cost money—this one is free (call 303/353-7650 to get a copy).

Installing the Scalable Printer driver is no more complicated than installing the standard DeskJet driver. You start Control Panel and open the Printers

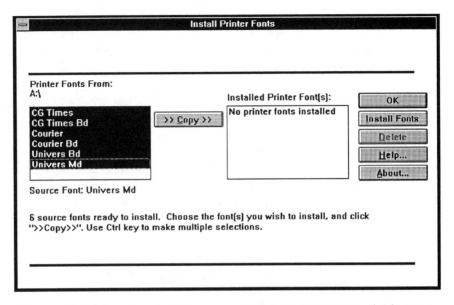

Figure 10-5: *Choosing fonts for use with the DeskJet 500 Scalable Printer Driver.*

dialog, then select Add Printer. Scroll to the bottom of the list of printers to the final choice, "Unlisted printer," and double click.

As the installation process proceeds, you'll be asked to indicate which typefaces you want to install (the driver comes with typeface outlines for plain and bold varieties of CG Times, Univers, and Courier), as shown in Figure 10-5, and where to install the fonts and related files used by the driver. Once the typefaces and support files have been copied to your hard disk, you can generate screen fonts. If you want to change the sizes of the screen fonts to be made, click on the relevant font outline, then select *Edit*, and add or delete font sizes from the text box.

Adobe Type Manager

Adobe Type Manager (ATM) is the preeminent font scaling utility for Windows by reason of its unmatched output quality and its widespread popularity. With ATM, you can print any Type 1 PostScript typeface at any size on your DeskJet—and for most people, type, not graphics, has been

PostScript's main attraction. In other words, ATM turns your DeskJet into an affordable PostScript text printer, giving you access to the hundreds of beautiful PostScript typefaces available from Adobe and numerous other vendors.

ATM works by putting your printer into graphics mode and printing the text characters as graphics. This process is slower than printing with soft fonts, but far more flexible. You don't need screen font files at all—the program creates the screen fonts as you work, storing them only temporarily during your Windows session. ATM does have some limitations: most importantly it only addresses text printing, and offers none of SuperPrint's benefits for graphics. It also requires a fairly large chunk of memory.

Figure 10-6: *The ATM dialog box shows you your in-stalled PostScript fonts and lets you set a few options.*

FaceLift

Another font management option for Windows users is Bitstream's FaceLift. FaceLift performs the same sort of as-you-need-it scaling for both printer and screen fonts as ATM. FaceLift is based on Bitstream's new on-the-fly font-generating system (see Chapter 7), giving it the speed and reduced memory requirements necessary for on-demand printing.

The most significant difference between the two products is simply that FaceLift works only with Bitstream typefaces, while ATM works only with Type 1 Postscript typefaces. Besides that, FaceLift was slightly slower than ATM, but consumes less memory. FaceLift also gives you more free typefaces than you get with ATM, and the selection is more interesting. Finally, FaceLift offers more sophisticated controls, although you usually won't need them.

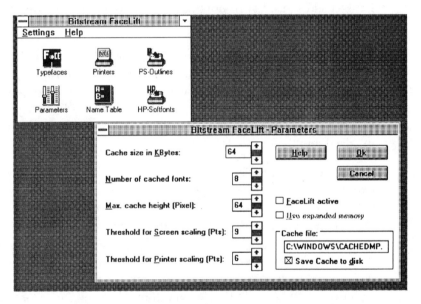

Figure 10-7: *The main FaceLift window, at upper left, gives you access to several groups of program functions; the main controls are in dialog box displayed here.*

SuperPrint

There are printer drivers and then there are *printer drivers*. Zenographics' SuperPrint bestows PostScript-like superpowers on ordinary-mortal printers like the DeskJet, and is well worth considering as a way to improve both text and graphics printing within Windows.

Like ATM and FaceLift, SuperPrint can scale master typeface outlines into fonts of any size for both your printer and your screen as you work.

But what's particularly great about SuperPrint's font scaling feature is that it works with all kinds of industry-standard typeface outlines. The list of compatible formats include Bitstream's Fontware, Adobe's Type 1 PostScript, Agfa Compugraphic's Intellifonts, and The Company's Nimbus Q. In addition, SuperPrint will print ordinary LaserJet soft fonts as well, though only at each font's one original size. And SuperPrint can be faster than either ATM or FaceLift. Whenever possible, Version 2.0 creates and downloads regular DeskJet soft fonts, which print faster than do the graphics-mode characters the other type managers use.

The SuperPrint driver is faster and more capable than the Windows' standard DeskJet driver when it comes to fancy graphics as well. Tapping directly into the place where Windows stores an image of the file to be printed, SuperPrint enlists your PC's processor and memory to carry out PostScript-like image-processing and page-formatting functions. There's no PostScript code actually involved, but the results are comparable.

Compared to the PostScript solutions covered in Chapter 20, SuperPrint has two main advantages. One is speed. SuperPrint churns out pages considerably faster, since it attaches directly to Windows, eliminating the steps of translating graphics and text into PostScript commands and then reinterpreting these commands to create a printed page. It also requires less memory than a PostScript driver. On the other hand, SuperPrint works exclusively with Windows programs, while PostScript software can handle any PostScript-compatible application. Even within Windows, SuperPrint can't handle true PostScript files—including the EPS type that often get embedded in PageMaker documents, for instance. SuperPrint may gain true PostScript-interpreting ability in a future upgrade.

Finally, there's SuperQueue, a print spooling program that's faster than Windows' Print Manager and that lets you create temporary printer files that it can print in a batch later on.

Access: Windows print managers

SuperPrint/$149
Zenographics
4 Executive Circle
Irvine, CA 92714
714/851-6352

FaceLift for Windows/$99
Bitstream, Inc.
Athenaeum House
215 First Street
Cambridge, MA 02142
800/522-3668; 617/497-6222

Adobe Type Manager,
Windows Version/$99
Adobe Systems, Inc.
P.O. Box 7900
Mountain View, CA 94039
415/961-4400

MoreFonts and Publisher's
Powerpak—see Chapter 7

11

Word Processing

∾

Word processing is the one software application all PC users have in common. It's also the one of primary interest to most DeskJet owners. After all, most people buy their DeskJets mainly to make their correspondence, professional papers, and reports look sharper and more visually interesting.

In this chapter, you'll learn how to get the most from the DeskJet using several of the most popular word processors. Depending on the word processor under discussion, you'll find an overview of the program's capabilities and limitations with respect to the DeskJet and instructions on how to set up the program for the DeskJet and access DeskJet fonts and print features as you create your documents. The chapter also includes a look at techniques for merging graphics with word-processed text, and covers programs that let you enter scientific and engineering symbols in your documents.

Profile: WordPerfect

$495/WordPerfect Corp.
288 West Center
Orem, UT 84057
800/321-5906

WordPerfect stands head and shoulders above all other DOS word processors, at least in terms of popularity—everybody seems to use this program. And whatever your opinion of the way WordPerfect works, it's hard to argue with its list of features: excellent typographic control, style sheets, the ability to merge graphics with text, sophisticated macros, mouse support, a menu system, and equation formatting are among the more recent additions.

A new version of WordPerfect designed for Windows was being readied at the time I finished this edition of *DeskJet Unlimited.* I haven't seen the program yet, but setting it up to work with the DeskJet won't require any effort at all—just install Windows properly for the DeskJet (see Chapter 10) and WordPerfect will be automatically set up to work with your printer.

DeskJet Capabilities

WordPerfect now includes drivers for all three DeskJet models, offering support for whatever mix of HP's cartridge and soft fonts you have at your disposal. With a little effort, you can even set up the program to work with soft fonts from suppliers other than HP.

All of WordPerfect 5's typographic and layout features are available for use with the DeskJet—for proof, take a look at the simple layout on the opposite page, printed on a DeskJet straight from WordPerfect. WordPerfect 5.1 corrected the only problem of note with the DeskJet driver in version 5.0—that text printed alongside graphics were malpositioned. If you still have WordPerfect 5.0, or an earlier release, you should definitely upgrade to 5.1.

Setting up WordPerfect for the DeskJet

In WordPerfect 5.1, the process of setting things up for the DeskJet starts during the initial installation of the program. You must use the Install program again to add the DeskJet driver to an existing installed version of WordPerfect

Catalog of Delusions

♦ *Imagines he is gradually swelling, his body becoming larger and larger.*

♦ Illusion that he was a *pump-log*, through which a stream of hot water was playing, and threatening his friend with a wetting.

♦ Illusion that he was an inkstand, and that, as he lay on the bed, the ink might spill over the white counterpane. In the person of an inkstand he opened and shut his brass cover—it had a hinge—shook himself, and both saw and felt the ink splash against his glass sides, and, angry at his friends' incredulity, turned with his face towards the wall, and would not speak a word.

♦ Now he is a huge saw, and darts up and down, while planks fly off on either side of him in utter completeness; and then he is a bottle of soda water, running to and fro; then a huge hippopotamus; then a giraffe.

♦ He seems to himself to be transformed into a vegetable existence, as a huge fern, and to be surrounded by clouds of music and perfume.

♦ His eyelashes became indefinitely prolonged, and began to roll as gold threads upon small ivory wheels, which revolved with great velocity.

♦ He has ludicrous visions of old and wrinkled females, who are found to be composed of knit yarn.

♦ *He fancies he hears numberless bells ringing most sweetly.*

(Excerpts from records of experiments with the homeopathic medicine Cannabis indica as recorded in the 10-volume Encyclopedia of Pure Materia Medica, by Timothy F. Allen, M.D., 1874-1880.)

5.1, or to update your installation with a new version of the DeskJet driver (WordPerfect periodically releases improved versions of its printer drivers).

✂ Tip: Printer driver updates come out fairly frequently. If you bought your copy of WordPerfect some time ago, call the WordPerfect support line to see if a new version of the DeskJet driver has been released since then.

Once you've chosen a printer driver you must then set it up properly for your particular system. One of your main jobs here is to identify the fonts you have so WordPerfect can make them available in your documents.

Setting up a Printer Resource File

A finished WordPerfect printer driver is called a PRS (printer resource) file and is stored on disk with the extension .PRS in your WordPerfect directory. But WordPerfect doesn't come with any ready-made PRS files. Instead, the master printer disks contain source data for many printer drivers stored together in several large files called ALL files. In essence, the process of selecting a printer simply extracts the pertinent information for your printer from an ALL file and saves it as a PRS file in the proper directory. In version 5.1, the ALL files you need are stored in a compressed format on the master floppies, and the only way to access them is with the Install program. To install the DeskJet driver, collect all your WordPerfect disks and driver update disk, if you have one. Run the Install program, which is pretty self-explanatory. If you've previously installed WordPerfect, you can install a new printer driver without re-installing the entire program by choosing option 4 on the main Install menu.

Helps and Hints

After you've confirmed your choice of the DeskJet as your printer, Install next displays a detailed Helps and Hints screen with tips on how best to use the model you've chosen, as shown in Figure 11-1. While you're reading, the program saves the appropriate printer resource file in your WordPerfect directory. (You can also display the Helps and Hints screen during printer setup, the process outlined below.) After you've read the hints, press any key to exit the printer installation procedure.

```
┌────────────────────────────────────────────────────────────────┐
│ Printer Helps and Hints:  HP DeskJet 500                         │
│                                                                  │
│ 7/12/91                                                          │
│ When using landscape fonts, the minimum left margin should be .7"│
│ and the minimum top margin should be .3".                        │
│                                                                  │
│ A 128k or 256k Ram font cartridge is necessary to use soft fonts.│
│ Contact your HP Dealer.                                          │
│                                                                  │
│ Use DeskJet specific fonts; LaserJet fonts are not supported.    │
│                                                                  │
│ Graphics are not supported in landscape.                         │
│                                                                  │
│ To use soft fonts, mark the appropriate group with an asterisk(*)│
│ Each group contains four soft fonts (eg., the Times Roman 8pt has│
│ the 8pt and 4pt as well as the bolded 8pt and 4pt versions of    │
│ that typeface).                                                  │
│                                                                  │
│ HP Line Draw is available with font cartridges 22706A, 22706B,   │
│ and 22706C. ASCII Line draw characters are available with the    │
│ PC-8 character set.                                              │
│                                                                  │
│ When printing envelopes, the minimum left margin should be .63", │
│ right margin should be 1", top margin should be .1" and bottom   │
│ margin should be                                                 │
│                                                                  │
│ Press any key to exit                                            │
└────────────────────────────────────────────────────────────────┘
```

Figure 11-1: *The WordPerfect helps and hints screen offers tips on using your DeskJet to best advantage from within WordPerfect.*

Selecting DeskJet setup options

The setup process continues with a couple of steps in which you configure WordPerfect for specific DeskJet options, including the communications port used to connect to the printer, the paper size you'll be using, and the paper feeder.

Here's how to proceed. Start WordPerfect itself from the DOS prompt. Press (SHIFT)(F7), then choose the Select Printer option by pressing **s**. If necessary, highlight the DeskJet in the printer list. Now press **3** to edit the settings.

At this point, you should be viewing the Select Printer: Edit menu as shown in Figure 11-2. As you can see, the menu offers several setup options for the DeskJet, and displays the current settings for these options at the right of the screen.

Option 1, *Name,* lets you change the name that WordPerfect displays for the printer—feel free to rename the DeskJet at your whim, since doing so doesn't affect the way your printer works.

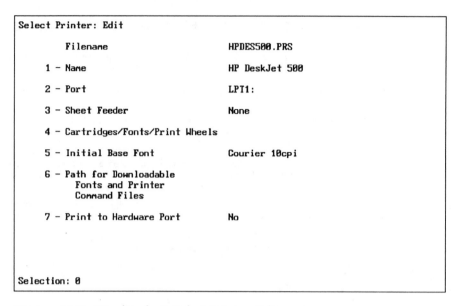

```
Select Printer: Edit

        Filename                    HPDES500.PRS

   1 - Name                         HP DeskJet 500

   2 - Port                         LPT1:

   3 - Sheet Feeder                 None

   4 - Cartridges/Fonts/Print Wheels

   5 - Initial Base Font            Courier 10cpi

   6 - Path for Downloadable
         Fonts and Printer
         Command Files

   7 - Print to Hardware Port       No




Selection: 0
```

Figure 11-2: *WordPerfect's Select Printer: Edit menu*

Option 2, *Port,* allows you to select the printer port to which you've connected the DeskJet. WordPerfect assumes you'll be connecting the DeskJet to LPT1: (parallel port #1), which is by far the most common situation. If you've connected to another port, select the Port option by pressing **2** or **p**. At the bottom of your screen you'll see a list of possible ports. Select the port you'll be using by pressing the appropriate number, and then pressing ⏎.

Option 3 on the Select Printer: Edit menu, *Sheet Feeder,* can be ignored, since an add-on sheet feeder is not available for the DeskJet. Leave it set to "None".

Defining fonts

Now it's time to tell WordPerfect which DeskJet fonts you plan to use with the program.For this purpose, you'll use the next option on the Select Printer: Edit menu, *Cartridges and Fonts.* Press **4** or **c** to select thatoption. You'll see (what else?) a Cartridges and Fonts screen, as shown in Figure 11-3, listing three choices: *Built-in, Cartridges, and Soft Fonts.*

```
Select Printer: Cartridges/Fonts/Print Wheels

Font Category                              Quantity         Available

Built-In
Cartridges                                    2                2
Soft Fonts                                  256 K            256 K




NOTE: Most fonts listed under the Font Category (with the exception of Built-In)
are optional and must be purchased separately from your dealer or manufacturer.
If you have fonts not listed, they may be supported on an additional printer
diskette.  For more information call WP at (801) 225-5000.

If soft fonts are marked '*', you must run the Initialize Printer option in WP
each time you turn on your printer.  Doing so deletes all soft fonts in printer
memory and downloads those marked with '*'.

If soft fonts are not located in the same directory as your printer files, you
must specify a Path for Downloadable Fonts in the Select Printer: Edit menu.

1 Select; 2 Change Quantity; N Name search: 1
```

Figure 11-3: *The Cartridges and Fonts screen*

Selecting cartridge fonts

If you have font cartridges, highlight the *Font Cartridge* choice and type **2** to select the *Change Quantity* option. Type in the number of font cartrdiges you have and press ⏎ (even though you can only use two at a time, you should set up the program so that it can use all your cartridges). Now, with the *Font Cartridge* choice still highlighted, press (F7) to display a list of the font cartridges that WordPerfect supports. Highlight one of the cartridges you have, and then press * to select that cartridge. Repeat this process for each of the font cartridges you'll be using. When you're through marking cartridges, press (F7) to save your work and return to the Cartridges and Fonts screen.

⌒ *Caution:* *The R,T,U,V cartridges only work with the DeskJet Plus or 500, not with the original model. Cartridges labelled for the 500, such as the Dom Casual cartridge, work only in that model.*

Selecting soft fonts

If you'll be using any of the soft fonts sold by HP, the next step is to select them (if you have third party soft fonts, you'll have to do a little custom work as described in the section "Using PTR to customize your DeskJet printer driver" later in this chapter).

The first thing you should do is tell WordPerfect how much RAM cartridge memory you've installed in your DeskJet for soft fonts. At the Cartridges and Fonts screen, scroll down to highlight the *Soft Font* choice. Now press **2** or **q** to select the *Change Quantity* command and type in the total amount of memory in your printer's RAM cartridges. Press ⏎ to complete the command.

✄ *Tip: For maximum soft font flexibility, enter a very large number for soft font memory no matter how much RAM cartridge memory you've actually installed. That way you'll be able to access a large number of soft fonts from within WordPerfect using a single driver. The drawbacks are that you won't be able to use WordPerfect to download the fonts for you with the Initialize Printer command, and you'll have to make sure that you've downloaded the correct fonts before you print.*

Now you're ready to actually select your soft fonts:

1. With the highlight still on the soft fonts option, press **1** or **f**. You're presented with a list of HP soft font disks. Select one of the font sets you own and press 1 again. Now you'll see a list of individual font names as shown in Figure 11-4.

2. Mark each font you have in turn by highlighting the name and typing *. Remember that there are separate fonts for upright and italics printing, and you must select them individually. On the other hand, each font you select will automatically be available in bold and in half-size versions.

3. As you mark fonts, notice that WordPerfect updates the amount of memory remaining at the upper right of your screen, based on how much you originally indicated as the available quantity.

4. If you own more than one soft font set, return to the previous screen by pressing ⏏F7. Repeat steps 1 through 3 for as many soft font sets as you have.

```
Select Printer: Soft Fonts                          Quantity
                                           Total:    512 K
                                       Available:    156 K

HP 22708C                                               Quantity Used

    22708C Helv  8pt                                         28 K
    22708C Helv  8pt Italic                                  28 K
*   22708C Helv  10pt                                        32 K
    22708C Helv  10pt Italic                                 32 K
    22708C Helv  12pt                                        52 K
    22708C Helv  12pt Italic                                 56 K
    22708C Helv  14pt                                        64 K
    22708C Helv  14pt Italic                                 68 K
*   22708C Helv  30pt                                       216 K
    22708C TnsRmn  8pt                                       28 K
    22708C TnsRmn  8pt Italic                                28 K
    22708C TnsRmn  10pt                                      32 K
    22708C TnsRmn  10pt Italic                               32 K
*   22708C TnsRmn  12pt                                      52 K
*   22708C TnsRmn  12pt Italic                               56 K
    22708C TnsRmn  14pt                                      64 K

Mark:  * Present when print job begins              Press Exit to save
                                                  Press Cancel to cancel
```

Figure 11-4: *Selecting soft fonts*

5. Once you've selected and marked all the soft fonts you wish, press (F7) one or more times to save your work and return to the Select Printer: Edit menu.

Defining the initial font

Now that WordPerfect knows which fonts will be available in your DeskJet, you can tell the program which font you want to use as your default. WordPerfect will print your documents using this font unless you specify another font explicitly. The relevant menu selection is *Initial Base Font.*

1. At the Select Printer: Edit menu, type **5** or **f** to choose the Initial Base Font command. You'll see a list of all the DeskJet fonts you've installed so far via the Cartridges and Fonts menu, plus the DeskJet's internal fonts.

2. Scroll down to the font you want to use as your default, and press **1**, **s**, or ***** to choose that font. WordPerfect automatically returns you to the Select Printer: Edit menu.

Telling WordPerfect where your fonts are

Your next step in the font setup process is to tell WordPerfect where you've stored your soft fonts, so that it can find them when it's time to download them. If you'll be using a downloading utility or downloading the fonts yourself, this step is unnecessary.

1. At the Select Printer: Edit menu, choose the *Path for Downloadable Fonts* command by pressing **6** or **d**.

2. The cursor moves up so you can type in the name of the path (disk and directory) where you've placed your soft fonts. If they're stored in the directory named FONTS on hard disk C:, for example, type **c:\fonts**.

3. Press ⏎.

Saving your customized printer resource file

In the vast majority of cases, you can ignore the last option on the Select Printer:Edit menu, Print to Hardware Port. Leave it set to "No." Later, if you can't get the DeskJet to print, you may want to change this setting as a last resort.

Now that you've made all your DeskJet setup choices for printer port, paper handling, and fonts, save your changes permanently as follows:

1. Return to the Select Printer menu by pressing **0**, (F7), or just ⏎.

2. Press **7** or **u** to select the *Update* command. As WordPerfect saves your newly modified DeskJet printer resource file, you'll see the Hints and Helps screen again. When the updating process is complete, return to the Select Printer menu by pressing (F7) twice.

3. Finally, to get WordPerfect to use the new driver, you must explicitly select it. At the Select Printer menu, press **1** or **s** to bring up a screen listing the printers you've installed. If the DeskJet is the only printer you have, it will be the only printer listed here. Scroll to the DeskJet's name in the list of printers, and press ⏎ or **1** to select it. You'll be returned

to the main Print menu. From there, you can go back to your work in WordPerfect by pressing ESC or Exit (F7).

Adding fonts from other vendors

Although the Select Printer command within WordPerfect proper doesn't recognize third-party soft fonts, you can get WordPerfect to work with just about any font. The easiest way out is provided by some soft font vendors, who supply utilities that make the necessary modifications to your DeskJet driver (the printer resource file) for you. Check with your soft font supplier to see if such a utility is available. If not, the ultimate solution is a program called PTR that comes with the WordPerfect package.

Using PTR to customize your DeskJet printer driver

PTR performs many different modifications to your existing printer drivers, and it works with both ALL and PRS files. To add new fonts with PTR, however, you *must* install them into the appropriate ALL file. You then build an updated PRS file by reselecting the DeskJet within WordPerfect with the Select Printer command, and then choosing the new fonts as described in the section "Defining fonts" a few pages back.

The PTR program may not have been copied to your working disk with the other WordPerfect program files when you installed WordPerfect; if not, rerun the Install program and choose the option for installing PTR.

PTR gives you jillions of different choices, some of them quite obscure, but unfortunately, no instructions for the program come with WordPerfect. If you plan to make extensive modifications in your printer driver, you'll definitely want to beg a copy of the *WordPerfect Printer Definition Program Technical Reference* from WordPerfect. On the other hand, all the PTR options options are presented on a reasonably straightforward set of hierarchical menus, and if you're reasonably experienced with computers, you may be able to figure out how to add new soft fonts to your DeskJet driver. To get you started, I've outlined the steps you'll need to follow below.

Tip: *Use* CTRL F3 *to get on-screen help about the particular PTR function you're using.* F3 *by itself displays an overall help screen.*

Start PTR with the name of the DeskJet driver file you're modifying as a parameter on the DOS command line. For example:

PTR WPMS1.ALL⏎

Highlight the DeskJet as your printer and press ⏎to display the main PTR menu, shown in Figure 11-5. Select the Fonts menu choice. Then, under the Soft Fonts heading, select the group of fonts you want to add your new fonts to (the groups that come with the DeskJet driver are named to correspond to HP soft font packages, but you can add new fonts to an existing group and rename it to suit yourself). You'll see a list of the soft fonts already assigned to that group.

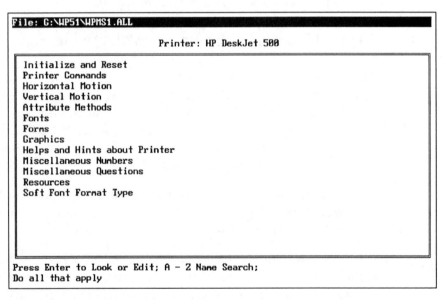

```
File: G:\WP51\WPMS1.ALL

                         Printer: HP DeskJet 500

    Initialize and Reset
    Printer Commands
    Horizontal Motion
    Vertical Motion
    Attribute Methods
    Fonts
    Forms
    Graphics
    Helps and Hints about Printer
    Miscellaneous Numbers
    Miscellaneous Questions
    Resources
    Soft Font Format Type




Press Enter to Look or Edit; A - Z Name Search;
Do all that apply
```

Figure 11-5: The main PTR menu.

Now type **1** to select the Add option. At this point, PTR requires you to choose a template font from the list. It doesn't really matter which font you use for the template, since you can change any aspect of the template in defining your new font. However, the closer your template is to the new font, the less work you'll have to do—so pick a template that is at least the same point size as the font you're adding. (In case you're worrying, the original font on which the template is based is not affected in any way.) To choose a template font, highlight it and press ⏎.

Name your new font. PTR will place the new name in the driver's font list.

Now it's time to define the new font so WordPerfect will know where to find it and how to use it. The new font should be highlighted, so just press ⏎ to start editing its definition. You'll be presented with a lengthy list of font characteristics, each of which opens onto other menus where you can make changes in various specific aspects of the font's definition. Crucial items include point size, character width, default leading, and proportions. Your soft font supplier should have provided you with the information necessary to complete all these menu choices.

One of the font-related menus, *Load and Select Strings*, deserves special mention. In order for WordPerfect to select your new soft font when you use it in a document, and to download it for you if you want it to do so, you'll also need to complete the choices on the menu.

Use the *Load Font* choice if you want WordPerfect to be able to download the new soft font for you when you give the Initialize Printer command, discussed in the section "Downloading soft fonts" below. Type in the download command in this format:

[27]"(*c*x*D" DOWNLOAD("*filename.ext*")[27]"*c5F"

This command consists of three parts: an escape sequence that tells the DeskJet to expect a new font, the command that actually gets WordPerfect to download the font file, and an escape sequence that instructs it to make the font "permanent." (see Chapter 7 for details on the escape sequences used for downloading and a discussion of permanent versus temporary soft fonts). Enter a number between 0 and 32767 for the *x* in the command, using a different number for each font you define. Substitute the filename of your soft font for *filename.ext*. Don't enter the path, since WordPerfect expects all soft fonts to be located in the path you chose during printer setup.

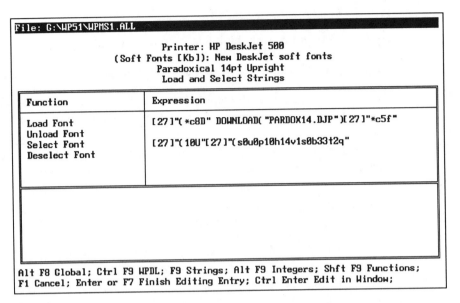

Figure 11-6: *Entering font downloading and selection strings in PTR*

In the *Select Font* choice, enter the PCL string that WordPerfect must send to select that font, as explained in Chapter 22. The string will look something like this (include the quotation marks in the string):

[27]"(1ØU"[27]"(sØuØp10h12v1sØb33t2Q"

You don't need to enter anything in the *Unload Font* or *Deselect Font* choices. Press (F7) to finalize your entry.

When you're through defining the font, return to PTR's main Fonts menu by pressing (F7), and add your next font. When you've added all the soft fonts you want, save your new version of the PRS file and exit the program.

WordPerfect and Fontware

Bitstream's Fontware Installation kit is a sophisticated font generating system with which you can create soft fonts from master typeface outlines in as many different sizes as you like. Bitstream offers a large library of typefaces for both body text and display applications. The consensus opinion is that the quality of Bitstream's DeskJet fonts isn't quite as high as the ones for the LaserJet family. Still, these are excellent fonts.

The WordPerfect Fontware Starter Kit comes with three free typefaces: Charter, Dutch (similar to Times Roman) and Swiss (similar to Helvetica). You can buy as many additional faces as you can fit on your hard disk, or as you can afford, whichever comes first.

The starter kit costs only $29.95, and you can order it by phone at 800/222-9409. In general, though, you'd be better off with FaceLift for WordPerfect, MoreFonts, Glyphix, or another on-the-fly scalable font package (see Chapter 7).

Using DeskJet fonts within a document

WordPerfect gives you a lot of flexibility as to how you pick fonts for the text in your documents. To use the available options wisely, you need to understand the way WordPerfect uses two terms, *initial font* and *base font*.

The initial or default font is the font that WordPerfect will use for all your text unless you tell it otherwise. You defined the initial font when you created and installed your DeskJet printer driver—if you didn't explicitly name an initial font, WordPerfect automatically selected the DeskJet's internal Courier 12 point font for you. The base font is the font that's currently active as you're typing in WordPerfect. Until you choose a new base font, it's the same as the initial font.

Changing the initial font

You can change the initial or default font at any time. Your new choice will remain in effect, even when you exit WordPerfect, until you change it again later. Here are the steps in outline form:

1. Print — Select Printer — Edit — Initial Font

2. Highlight the desired font and press ⏎

3. Exit

Changing to a new font within a document

With WordPerfect's Base Font command, you can assign a new font to any text within a document with the Font command. To use the command, position the cursor where you want the font change to occur, then press (CTRL) (F8), then **4** to select the *Base Font* option. Select the font you want to use from the list that appears on your screen and press (⏎). The new font will remain in effect until your next Base Font command.

⌃ Caution: *You can't apply a new base font to a selected block of text.*

When you press (CTRL)(F8), you're presented with a menu at the bottom of your screen offering five choices, including *Size, Appearance, Normal, Base Font,* and *Print Color.* You can ignore the *Print Color* option, since the DeskJet is strictly a black-on-white machine.

The "base" in the term base font refers to the fact that WordPerfect lets you modify some of the characteristics of the base font without explicitly selecting a whole new font. For example, if the base font is 12-point upright TmsRmn, you can use the Appearance command to switch to an italic version of the font, or the Size command to switch to a "Large" TmsRmn.

These modifications to the base font work OK with the limited fonts on standard dot matrix printers, but they give unpredictable results with printers such as the DeskJet or LaserJet. As you know by now, a DeskJet font is defined quite strictly as a particular typeface at a particular size and with a particular style (italics or upright). When, say, you request a large version of the base font, WordPerfect doesn't actually enlarge the base font. Instead, it looks for a font that's identical to the base font except for point size. You may not get the size you wanted; if no larger font is available, you simply can't print at a larger size. Similarly, while the DeskJet can print most fonts at half-size, that may not be what you have in mind when you ask for a small font with the Size command.

✄ Tip: *In general, it's always a better policy to explicitly select the new font you want with the Base Font command, even if all you want to do is change from an ordinary upright font to an italics version of the same typeface at the same size.*

Your results will be more predictable when you request bold type with the Appearance command, since the DeskJet can transform any font so that it prints in boldface. Still, a genuine bold font looks better. Other options of the Size and Appearance commands will work reliably with any font. These include underlining, redlining, and strikeout on the Appearance menu, and super- and subscript on the Size menu.

Undoing font selections

To remove a font selection, all you have to do is delete the font code, as follows:

1. Select Reveal codes by pressing (ALT) (F3).

2. Cursor to the code for the font change you want to delete.

3. Type (DEL) to delete the font code.

The text following the deleted font code will now be formatted with the same font used for the text that comes earlier in the file.

Changing leading

In Chapter 5, there's a discussion of why it's nice to be able to control leading, or the amount of space between lines of text. Fortunately, WordPerfect can automatically adjust the leading to an appropriate amount based on a line-by-line basis, based on the largest font used in the line. However, you may want to override WordPerfect's leading decision, since additional leading often helps to improve the appearance of a document. Type:

(SHIFT)(F8) **1 4 2**

Now enter the amount of leading you want. If WordPerfect is set to display units in inches instead of typographer's points, you can enter the leading value in points simply by typing a **p** at the end of the number. For example, if you want 15 points of leading, type **15p**. When you press ↵, the program converts the point value into inches. (Note that WordPerfect measures leading from baseline to baseline.)

Adding graphics to your documents

With version 5.0, WordPerfect has added a powerful ability to merge graphics files created in other programs with text to create illustrated documents. Unfortunately, while WordPerfect graphics hemselves print well on the DeskJet, nearby text gets knocked out of position, printing too high or too low.

✄ *Tip:* *If you're planning to print text and graphics on the same page, be sure you have WordPerfect 5.1—earlier versions couldn't position text and graphics properly relative to one another.*

In the process of importing a graphic image, you get all kinds of control over how the image will look—you can specify the location on the page where you want the graphic printed, the size for the printed graphic, whether you want text in the document to wrap around the image, whether you want a caption, whether there should be a box printed around the graphic and how thick it should be, and on and on.

In my view, these fancy new graphics capabilities make WordPerfect a true desktop publishing program, though it isn't as efficient for this purpose as the upscale DTP packages such as Ventura and PageMaker. In Daniel Will-Harris' *WordPerfect 5: Desktop Publishing in Style*, you'll find all you need to know about using WordPerfect for desktop publishing.

Drawing lines and boxes

WordPerfect's new graphics talents extend to letting you draw your own boxes and lines using the standard line drawing characters in the PC's screen character set. A caution is in order here: be sure you use a monospaced typeface such as Courier for these characters. Otherwise you may get broken boxes and lines that don't line up.

Embedding printer commands

If there's ever a time when your WordPerfect DeskJet driver fails you, and some special command is out of your reach, you can get direct access to this printer feature by embedding DeskJet commands directly in your document. Here's how to embed escape sequences and control codes:

1. Place the cursor where you want to embed the command (WordPerfect will send the command to the DeskJet immediately before printing the text to the right of the cursor).

2. Press the following keys in succession:

(SHIFT)(F8) **4 6 2 1**

3. Type in the command you want to send to the DeskJet. You can enter codes between 32 and 126 decimal directly from the keyboard. Enter codes below 32 or above 126 by typing in the numerals within angle brackets (<>). For example, to enter the escape sequence ^{E}s$_c$*r1A type **<27>*r1A**.

4. Press (F7) to complete the command and go back to regular editing.

You can even send a whole series of commands stored in a separate file to the DeskJet from within a document. Create and save the file in WordPerfect, saving it as plain ASCII text in the same directory where you store downloaded fonts (check the Printer Settings menu by typing (SHIFT)(F7), then **S**, then **3** to make sure that the directory is the one selected for downloaded files). Then, to embed the file in another document:

1. Place the cursor where you want to embed the command. The commands in the file will be sent to the DeskJet immediately before the text to the right of the cursor is printed.

2. Press the following keys:

(SHIFT)(F8) **4 6 2 2**

3. Type in the filename.

4. Press (F7) to complete the command and resume regular editing.

Previewing your document

In WordPerfect, you create and edit text in WordPerfect in the screen's standard text mode. That's fine for the text content, but now that WordPerfect is so handy with multiple fonts and graphics, you need a way to see how your document will look in print before you actually print it out. That way, you can see whether your layout settings have produced the intended result, without having to waste time and paper on a futile printout.

WordPerfect's new View Document feature meets this need. If you have a graphics monitor, you can use the command series (SHIFT)(F7), then **6** to bring up an image that closely approximates the way your document will appear in print. You can't change anything in this preview mode, but you can go back and forth between ordinary editing and the preview until everything looks right.

The preview mode displays one or two pages at a time. You can scroll around to see parts of the page image that don't fit on the screen, or change the magnification to zoom in for detail or zoom out for a bird's eye look at your whole page. The major limitation of the preview mode has to do with fonts. No matter what font you use in your document, WordPerfect will substitute a generic serif or sans-serif screen font. Still, even if you can't see what your characters will look like in details, you'll know where they will be placed on the printed page.

Printing your document

To access any of WordPerfect's print features, start by issuing the Print command by pressing (SHIFT)(F7). A full screen menu appears, offering a variety of print options, whose functions are summarized in this section.

Downloading soft fonts

If your document uses soft fonts, you must download these fonts before you can print it. You can do the downloading yourself or use a font management utility such as Backloader (see Chapter 7). Alternatively, you can use WordPerfect's own Initialize Printer command. From the Print menu, press

7 or **i** to select the Initialize Printer command. WordPerfect downloads the soft fonts you chose in your DeskJet driver.

⌒ *Caution:* *Don't use the Initialize Printer command if you've added more soft fonts than your DeskJet can hold at one time to your driver. See the section "Defining fonts" above for a discussion of the pros and cons of doing just that.*

Selecting print options

Before you begin printing, you should make sure you've selected the print options you want for your printout. On the Print menu, you can select the text quality (draft or full quality) and graphics resolution (75 through 300 dpi). You can even shut off graphics printing altogether when you want a quick text draft, or vice versa.

The WordPerfect print spooler

To reduce the amount of time you spend waiting for your documents to print to a minimum, WordPerfect comes with its own print spooler. As described in more detail in Chapter 4, a print spooler provides a temporary parking place on disk or in memory for printer data. The spooler takes over the job of feeding the data from this temporary storage to your DeskJet as fast as the printer can digest it. With the spooler in control of the data transfer, WordPerfect can go on about its business, and you can get back to work. The print spooler continues to monitor the DeskJet, and whenever necessary interrupts WordPerfect just long enough to send the next mouthful of data to the printer.

Whenever you give one of the commands to print a document, you'll see the message **Please wait** at the bottom left of your screen while the document is transferred to the print spooler. When the transfer is complete, you can go back to the main program screen to do more editing while printing continues.

The WordPerfect spooler can accept several print requests, or "jobs," at a time. With the option 4 on the Print menu, Control printer, you can display the jobs that are currently waiting to be printed, cancel a job, or rush a job so that it prints before earlier ones.

⌒ *Caution:* *Although it's possible to cancel the job that's currently being printed, doing so may foul things up enough that you'll have to re-initialize the printer. Also, remember that the DeskJet has a built-in 16K buffer, and will continue to print until that buffer is empty, even after the spooler stops sending new data. In other words, if something is really wrong with the printout, you may have to turn the DeskJet off and then reprint the entire document.*

Printing options

To print the entire document that you're currently working on: From the Print menu, choose the Full Document option by pressing **1** or **f**.

To print a single page, place the cursor anywhere on the page you want to print before using the Print command. When the cursor is located properly, press (SHIFT)(F7) to select the Print command, then press **2** or **p**.

To print a WordPerfect document stored on disk, from the Print menu, press **3** or **d** to choose the Document on Disk command. At the prompt, type in the path and file name for the WordPerfect file you want to print, and press (⏎).

Profile: Microsoft Word

$450/Microsoft Corp.
16011 N.E. 36th Way
Redmond, WA 98073
206/882-8080

Way back in the early days of PC computing, Microsoft Word anticipated the present popularity of two pieces of equipment: the mouse and the laser printer. Word was also the first major word processor with style sheets. A style sheet is a collection of "styles," each of which determines everything about the way a paragraph of text looks with a single command. Styles encompass such formatting attributes as indentation, line spacing, justification, font, and so on. For example, you might define one style for headings as a 30-point bold font centered on the page. Another style for body text paragraphs might be a 12-point regular-weight font with 14 points of leading, 1" margins, and a first line indentation of ½".

Over the years, Word has added a slew of features, including a macro capability and the ability to merge graphics with your text. In Word 5.0, the Print preView function that lets you see how your pages will look before you print them is now part of the main Word program, instead of a separate Windows application. And with Version 5.5, Microsoft changed the whole look-and-feel of the program, giving it a Windows-like pull-down menu structure.

And of course there's Word for Windows, by far the most successful word Windows processor. Aside from file compatibility with the DOS version of Word, Word for Windows is a much different program. Significant points of departure are its easy-to-use graphical editing controls, a more sophisticated macro language based on BASIC, and the ability to edit your document as it will look in print, with some limitations. For DeskJet ownwers, there's not much to worry about with Word for Windows—once you've installed the Windows DeskJet driver as outlined in Chapter 10, Word for Windows will automatically be able to print properly to your DeskJet. For that reason, we'll focus on using the printer with the DOS version of word.

Word and the DeskJet

As far as the DeskJet goes, Word 5 does a fair to good job. Version 5.5 comes with six predefined drivers for the DeskJet, two for the internal fonts only, the other four supporting different combinations of HP cartridge and soft fonts. All the drivers allow you to print envelopes as well as ordinary paper, and to select graphics resolutions from 75 to 300 dots per inch.

Setting up for the DeskJet

Word's printer drivers are stored in PRD files (PRD stands for PrinteR Driver, I guess), with accompanying DAT files specifying soft fonts for downloading. In version 5.5, you can select the DeskJet as your printer during installation of the program, so that the necessary PRD files get copied to your hard disk along with program itself.

To set up the program to work with your DeskJet, all you have to do is make sure that the correct PRD is active. If not, you can install it while you are working in Word itself. In version 5.5, all you have to do is select the correct PRD from the Printer Setup dialog box on the File menu as shown in Figure 11-7.

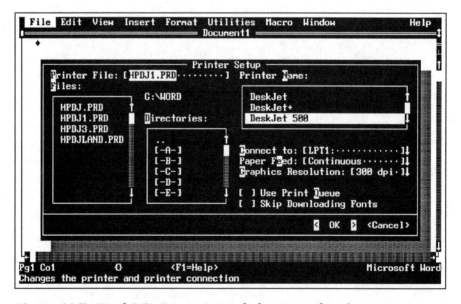

Figure 11-7: *Word 5.5's Printer Setup dialog. You select the PRD you want to use in the box on the left.*

In version 5.0, you choose *Print,* then *Options* to display the menu shown in Figure 11-8. With the *Printer* field highlighted, press (F1) to display the available PRD files in the current directory. Move the highlight to the *Model* field. Again, press (F1), and choose the "model" of the DeskJet you have. In the standard PRDs included with Word, there are two model names: *HP Deskjet (No Cartridges),* which supports the internal fonts only, and *HP Deskjet* (cartridges*),* with the letter names of the supported cartridges listed in the parentheses. Check to make sure that the printer port selection in the *Setup* field is correct. Then press (↵) to confirm your choices.

```
holds that in choosing the "similar" medicine, the
practitioner must take into account all of the patient's
current symptoms, sensations, and physical findings, whether
or they are thought to be associated with the chief
complaint, and even if they don't seem to have pathological
signficance. The underlying assumption of the homeopathic
methodology is that symptoms are adaptive responses of the
organism to stress or infection. Utilizing a medicine that
mimics the symptoms of the sick person can therefore aid the
body's inherent defenses, ultimately leading to an improved
healing response.

The third fundamental homeopathic principle is that the
chosen medicine must be administered in extremely dilute

PRINT OPTIONS printer: HPDESK1            setup: LPT1:
         model: HP DeskJet (No Cartridges)    graphics resolution: 300 dpi
         copies: 1                            draft: Yes(No)
         hidden text: Yes(No)                 summary sheet: Yes(No)
         range:(All)Selection Pages           page numbers:
         widow/orphan control:(Yes)No         queued: Yes(No)
         paper feed: Continuous               duplex: Yes(No)
Enter printer name or press F1 to select from list
Pg1 Co1              {¶}                            Microsoft Word
```

Figure 11-8: Setting up your PRD choices in Word 5.0.

Modifying your DeskJet PRD

✂ *Tip: If you're planning to use soft fonts with Word, save yourself a lot of trouble and buy them from a vendor who includes a utility that will make the necessary PRD changes for you.*

To customize Word's DeskJet driver for your own set of soft fonts and any other special requirements you have, you must run one or both of two utility programs that come on your Utilities disks, MergePRD and MakePRD.

Instructions for using both programs are found in the *Printer Information for Microsoft Word* manual that comes with Word. So that you know what you're up against, we'll cover some of the fundamentals here.

Using MergePRD

MergePRD lets you combine fonts from several PRD files to create a single PRD file that supports all the fonts you have. You can also use this utility to delete fonts you don't have or don't use from a PRD file and to update a customized Word 4.0 PRD file.

When you start MergePRD, you begin by telling the program which PRD files you want to work with. This done, other menu choices let you see the fonts available in the existing PRDs, and select the fonts you want in your new merged PRD. To select a font for inclusion in your new PRD, you must type its number as displayed on the screen. You then name your new file, save it on disk, and exit the program.

Using MakePRD

If your PRD file needs more extensive customization—specifically if you want to add new soft fonts—you need the MakePRD program. MakePRD converts the information in the current PRD file from computerese (binary) format into readable (though inscrutable) text. You load this text file into Word, where you make whatever changes you see fit, and then convert the text with your modifications back to PRD format. Figure 11-9 offers a sample of what you'll be up against.

With MakePRD, you can specify new soft fonts for use in Word, and describe them in detail so Word can use them properly. To complete this process, you'll need a considerable amount of technical information about your fonts from the font vendor. You can also redefine which printed characters correspond to which characters on the screen.

As you can guess, the fact that you can freely edit the text of the PRD file makes this an error-prone process. Essentially, you're writing a computer program. Just as in BASIC or C, one little typing error in a crucial location can disable the whole program. Be absolutely sure to save a copy of your

```
┌─────────────────────────────────────────────────────────────┐
│▐AutoSkipTop:1 UnprintableTop:384                             │
│ AutoSkipLeft:1 UnprintableLeft:360                           │
│ UnprintableBottom:491 UnprintableRight:360                   │
│ DownloadFlag:0                                               │
│ GraphicsNotSupported:NIL                                     │
│ FontsNotSupported:2 3 4 5 56 57 58 59                        │
│ BinsSupported:0 1 4                                          │
│ IniFile:NIL                                                  │
│ ModelName:HP DeskJet (No Cartridges)                         │
│                                                              │
│ InhibitCIT:0 InhibitRevLF:0                                  │
│ LinedrawAutoMap:0 LinedrawNoShade:0                          │
│ LinedrawFlag:0 LinedrawFont:0 LinedrawAdjust:0               │
│ ColorMod:0 ColorFlags:0 DuplexFlag:0 OrientationFlag:0       │
│ AutoSkipTop:1 UnprintableTop:384                             │
│ AutoSkipLeft:1 UnprintableLeft:360                           │
│ UnprintableBottom:491 UnprintableRight:360                   │
│ DownloadFlag:0                                               │
│ GraphicsNotSupported:NIL                                     │
│                                          ═DSKJET.DRV═        │
├─────────────────────────────────────────────────────────────┤
│COMMAND: Copy Delete Format Gallery Help Insert Jump Library  │
│         Options Print Quit Replace Search Transfer Undo Window│
│Edit document or press Esc to use menu                        │
│Pg1 Co1          {}                        Microsoft Word     │
└─────────────────────────────────────────────────────────────┘
```

Figure 11-9: *This excerpt from the standard DeskJet PRD file should convince you that customizing a PRD is not for the faint of heart.*

original PRD before you start, follow the instructions carefully, and check over your work before you convert the file back to PRD format.

Downloading soft fonts from within Word

Word has a built-in downloading capability. To take advantage of this feature, however, you must create a gawdawful binary DAT file containing the names of the fonts that can be downloaded along with numeric descriptions. Don't bother with DAT files unless they come with your soft fonts or unless you're a true-blue programmer—stick with a downloading utility instead, or do the downloading yourself with DOS commands (Chapter 7).

Changing fonts in a Word document

To format text in your file with a new font, you begin by highlighting the block of text you want printed in the new font.

If you're using 5.5, you open the Format menu; in 5.0, you press (ESC) to activate the Command menu, then choose *Format*. In either version, choose *Character* next.

Highlight the *Font Name* option, and press (ALT)-down arrow (in 5.5) or (F1) (in 5.0) to see the list of available font choices. Select the one you want, then press (⏎).

The alternative to this direct approach is to use style sheets. Define a style that includes the desired font along with the other formatting characteristics you want. Then, after you've typed your text, you can apply the style's entire collection of formatting characteristics, including your font choice, to any paragraph in your file. To assign a style to a paragraph, position the cursor in the paragraph, use the command sequence Format—Style—Paragraph, and select the particular style you want.

Profile: WordStar Release 6

$495/WordStar International, Inc.
201 Alameda del Prado
Novata, CA 94949
415/382-8000

Venerable old WordStar struggles on, still distinguished by the touch-typing efficiency of its control key commands. Though it poses no threat to WordPerfect's and Word's dominance of the word processing market, WordStar is their equal in features and performance. Release 6 is a thoroughly modern beast, with *de rigueur* pull-down menus, style sheets, the ability to merge graphics, a host of first-class utilities—and support for today's printers with their multitudes of fonts. And WordStar's page preview function is superior to WordPerfect's because it lets you see facsimiles of the actual fonts you'll be printing, not just generic stick characters.

♪ **Note:** *WordStar gained its ability to merge graphics with text by incorporating a version of Inset, a utility you can use with other word processors. Inset is described later in this chapter.*

WordStar works well with a DeskJet, and the developers have finely tuned its DeskJet driver to some of the technical idiosyncracies of your printer. Unfortunately, installing your own soft fonts is considerably harder than it should be—but it can be done.

WordStar printer drivers are stored in Printer Description Files (PDFs). Its DeskJet PDFs cover the HP cartridge and soft fonts. You can customize your DeskJet PDF for the particular collection of fonts you own, or even create several different PDFs, each with its own set of fonts.

If you own a version of WordStar prior to 5.5, you'd be well advised to upgrade to version 6 if you want to get the best possible results from your DeskJet. According to the technical people at WordStar, version 5.5 benefitted from changes in the way the program as a whole works with many printers, including improvements in paper handling and character positioning. If you don't have the newest release of the program, you won't be able to take advantage of these upgrades.

Customizing WordStar for the DeskJet

If you didn't install the DeskJet driver when you first installed WordStar, you'll have to do so now, a simple process. WordStar 6 also makes it possible, after a fashion, to add third-party soft fonts to your DeskJet driver. The instructions for these procedures are found in a slim pamphlet that accompanies the main program manual, although you'll need the procedures outlined here for success withthird-party fonts.

The following steps summarize the procedure for installing the WordStar DeskJet driver. However, if you need to install new soft fonts, go on to the section "Adding soft fonts" below before continuing with) the installation procedure.

1. Run the program WINSTALL, which you should have already installed on your hard disk (otherwise, it's on the Installation/Customization floppy).

2. At the opening menu, if you just want to select from fonts already available, or make other modifications to the driver not related to fonts, choose *Modify or install a printer (PRCHANGE)..*

3. You should now be at the Installed Printer Menu. If you're modifying an existing DeskJet driver, highlight the name of the PDF file you want to change and press ⏎. If you're creating a new DeskJet PDF, type in the name of the PDF file you wish to create—call your PDF "DESKJET"

unless you can think of a better name. When you press ⏎, the install program will produce a list of available printer types. Choose HP DeskJets, then your DeskJet model from the next list, on the Printer Selection Menu.

4. You can now choose or modify the selections for printer port, print controls, and available fonts.

5. As far as fonts are concerned, the *Add or delete font groups* option lets you select which of the fonts that are theoretically available for the DeskJet you actually want to place in this PDF. If you choose this option, you'll see a list of the currently installed fonts in your PDF. Type **Y** to change them. You'll now be able to pick from a menu listing DeskJet internal fonts, cartridge fonts, and so on. Don't choose the "Add fonts from custom database option unless you've already created the custom database, as described in the next section.

6. When you're through making changes, go back to the Installed Printer Menu. You'll be asked if you want the PDF you've just created to be the default. There, you can create or modify another PDF, or exit back to WINSTALL by pressing (F10).

Adding soft fonts

Before you can add new soft fonts to your DeskJet PDFs, you must first install the fonts into a special database that WordStar uses to keep track of character spacing information. The problem here is that WordStar doesn't recognize third-party DeskJet soft fonts. However, there is a way you can work around this limitation. The trick is to start with LaserJet soft fonts while you're creating the WordStar font database, then switch to DeskJet soft fonts for actual use with your printer. In other words, you have to have both LaserJet and DeskJet versions of your fonts to make this work.

The easiest way to meet this requirement is with the Type Director or MoreFonts programs, since both let you generate near-identical LaserJet and DeskJet fonts. Another way is to start with LaserJet fonts from any source, then use the LJ2DESK utility covered in Chapter 7 to convert them to DeskJet fonts.

Assuming you've secured a way to create LaserJet/DeskJet font pairs, here's how to proceed:

1. Start by making both versions of the fonts, if you don't already have them. Remember that the DeskJet doesn't accept fonts any larger than about 30 points, so don't make big LaserJet fonts. Place the LaserJet versions in the directory where you eventually want to store your DeskJet fonts, and put the DeskJet versions in a different directory for now. The two versions of each font should have exactly the same name.

2. Run WINSTALL, and at the opening menu, choose *Add third-party laser fonts (LSRFONTS)*. Then choose *HP LaserJet and compatible fonts*.

3. Follow the instructions on the screen to add the fonts to a new WordStar font database. After you identify the directory where your LaserJet soft fonts are stored, the LSRFONTS installation program will list the fonts in that directory for you. You can then pick the ones you want in this particular font database. You'll need technical information from the font manufacturer to complete the process correctly. You can press (F1) for help at any time. When you're through choosing fonts, you press F10 to add them to the database (you can name them something like "DeskJet Group 1" during the process).

4. When you're finished installing the new soft fonts, go back to the WINSTALL main menu. To add the new fonts to a DeskJet PDF, select *Modify or install a printer (PRCHANGE)*, and continue with steps 3 through 6 in the section "Customizing WordStar for the DeskJet" above. When you get to step 5, choose the "Add fonts from custom database" option and select as many of the fonts you've installed as the PDF can hold (PDF files can be as large as 32K).

5. As you exit the font selection screen, you'll be asked whether you want to create screen fonts for use with WordStar's page preview mode. Type **y** it you want screen fonts; if you type **n**, you'll get generic fonts when you use page preview.

6. Now it's time to get rid of the LaserJet fonts and replace them with identically named DeskJet fonts. That completes the process.

Changing Printer Definition Files

If you like, you can create multiple PDFs for your DeskJet, each customized for a particular situation. The default PDF is automatically assigned to all your documents. Each time you create a new PDF you're given the opportunity to designate it as the default, and you can select a new default PDF from the WINSTALL Set Basic Editing Defaults Menu whenever you like. You can also change the PDF on a document-by-document basis. Press (CTRL) **P?** and choose the new PDF. Then press (CTRL) **QU** to reformat the document with the new PDF.

Using fonts within a WordStar document

To change fonts within your file, move the cursor to the place where you want the new font to start, then press (CTRL) **P=** or select *Choose font* from the Style menu. You'll see a list of the available fonts in the current PDF. Highlight the one you want and press (↵). The font you selected will now be in effect from the cursor location to the next font change, or to the end of the file.

For even quicker font changes, you can set up two default fonts in advance with the WSCHANGE program, and then switch back and forth between them by pressing (CTRL) **PA** for the first font, (CTRL) **PN** for the second.

Embedding printer commands

WordStar offers several related methods for embedding your own printer escape sequences and control codes directly in your files.

1. To enter a command on a one-time basis, press (CTRL) **P!**. At the prompt that appears, enter control codes and the escape character by typing a carat (∧) followed by the character associated with the code, as shown in the table of control codes in Chapter 22. For example, you'd enter the escape character by typing ∧]. You can type in ordinary characters directly. To include a carat in the command, enter **%∧**, and to enter a percent sign, type **%%**.

Alternatively, you can enter any code in hexadecimal notation by preceding the hex characters with **%x**. To enter the escape character this way, you'd type **%x1b**.

2. You can also define four reuseable print commands and insert them as often as you need them anywhere in your document. Besides cutting down on your typing at the outset, this is a great help if you want to experiment with different values in an escape sequence—just change the definition of the command, and the corresponding escape sequence changes everywhere in your document.

Use the WordStar dot commands **.xq**, **.xw**, **.xe**, and **.xr** to define the corresponding reuseable print commands, (CTRL) **PQ**, (CTRL) **PW**, (CTRL) **PE**, and (CTRL) **PR**. The dot command must be placed in your document above the point where you first use the corresponding print command. Type the dot command followed by the print command you want to define, expressed in hexadecimal notation. You can type a maximum of 24 hexadecimal characters.

For example, to define the (CTRL) **PE** command so that it selects the legal character set, you'd set up the **.xe** dot command for the escape sequence E_{s_C}(1U by typing **.xe 1B 28 31 55**. Then, to insert the command you've defined in your file, just position your cursor where you want the command to take effect, and press (CTRL) **PE**. You can redefine these dot commands as often as you like in a document.

3. You can also create default definitions for the **.xq**, **.xw**, **.xe**, and **.xr** dot commands using the PRCHANGE setup program. Using PRCHANGE, you can have separate definitions for each PDF (see above), and the printer commands can be longer than 24 characters.

Amí Professional

The first popular word processor for Windows was Amí, whose name is supposed to make you think warm, friendly thoughts about the program. Whether or not you resonate in the expected fashion, Amí Professional, the upgraded version now being sold by Lotus, is a top notch word processor that you should consider if you have the computer power necessary to run

Windows. When it comes to printing, Amí's reliance on Windows makes using it with your DeskJet a breeze.

For now, Amí is Word for Windows only serious challenger, since WordPerfect's Windows version is still on the horizon. Reviewers are split about 50-50 between Amí and Word for Windows, but all agree that Amí is a class act. Amí does a better job the WinWord at letting you edit and lay out your text on a mockup of your document as it will appear in print. You'll see each text character at its correct relative size and with all its attributes such as italics, boldface, and underlining. Your margins and indents, the breaks between lines of text, and any text columns occur on screen just where they will the printed page. You can see exactly what you're doing as you place charts and illustrations wherever you like. Amí excels in other areas as well, including its extensive list of text editing commands.

Like any high-end word processor or desktop publishing program, Amí has style sheets, letting you control all aspects of the overall page layout and the format of individual paragraphs with a click or two of the mouse. There's also an automatic headers and footers feature. A thesaurus, mail merge, drawing tools, and a feature for formatting tables automatically are also included.

PC-Write

My favorite word processor is PC-Write. This program has three big advantages: it's shareware, and inexpensive when you register; it has just about every text editing command you could ever want; and above all, it's amazingly fast. You can move from screen to screen or top to bottom of the file instantaneously, something that no other top-name word processor can claim.

Notwithstanding these strengths, PC-Write has one major weakness, and it's an important one for DeskJet owners: the program makes it too hard to format your pages for printing. It's not that you don't have control; in fact, PC-Write offers a dizzying array of formatting options. The problem is that you have to type in formatting choices into your document as strange little codes, rather than by just selecting your layout settings from a menu. There are no style sheets to ease the burden, either. What's more, PC-Write lacks the more advanced desktop publishing features that are showing up in WordPerfect and Word. You can't place pictures into a document, for instance.

Installing the program for the DeskJet is easy, since PC-Write has an automated printer installation routine and the DeskJet is one of the menu choices. During installation, you can select fonts from most of the HP font cartridges and soft font packages. The program even comes with a batch file that downloads soft fonts for you. If you want to use fonts that aren't already supported by the printer installation program, you'll have to rely on Quiksoft's technical support personnel to guide you through the process. Unless, that is, you buy Elfring's DeskJet soft fonts (Chapter 7)—they come with a PC-Write driver.

Merging graphics with your text

Given the DeskJet's talents with both text and graphics, it would be nice to be able to mix both types of information together on a single page.

Of course, the most direct route to text and graphics integration is with a true desktop publishing program. But the DTP approach is overkill for many people, who may only want to spruce up a report with an occasional chart or add a little levity to a letter with a cartoon. Besides, even if you can justify buying and learning a full-scale desktop publisher like PageMaker or Ventura, it takes too much time to switch out of your word processor when all you really need is a company logo on your letterhead.

The ideal solution would allow you to stay within your word processor, so you can concentrate on editing text, but would let you bring in graphics as needed with a minimum of hassle. For owners of WordPerfect, Microsoft Word, and WordStar, among others, that day has arrived. All of these products now sport built-in graphics features that let you select pictures stored in disk files for inclusion in your document. All allow you to size and position the images fairly easily. And once you've imported the graphics, you can switch to a special preview mode that displays a close facsimile of how your finished document will look when printed, graphics and all.

For those of you who use other word processors, the situation isn't nearly as straightfoward. The simplest way to get a graphic and some text to share the same page is to run the paper through the DeskJet twice. In your word processor, hit the ⏎ key enough times to leave a gap for the graphic, then print your file. Put the page back in the paper tray face up, and then fire up your graphics program and print your graphic.

This technique might work in a pinch, but it's a guaranteed time-waster. Plan on making several attempts before you figure out how to space everything so that the picture doesn't sit right on top of your text.

Inset to the rescue

A much better way to go is with Inset, a utility designed just for this purpose. Inset helps ease the process of positioning your text and graphics so they don't conflict, and then handles the printing chores so that both print on a single pass of the page through the DeskJet.

To use Inset, you just type in the name of the graphics file between a pair of special "tag" characters in your word processor document, wherever you want the graphic to be printed. If the image is stored in a file called BALLOON in the INSET directory, for instance, the tag might look like this: [c:\inset\balloon]. Following the tag name, you must still leave some blank lines so that the image doesn't print on top of your text.

Inset is a memory resident program that you load before you start your word processor, popping up when you press a hotkey combination. At this point, you can call on various Inset menu choices. You can see the graphic you want to print and view its relative size and position on the page. You can resize the image at will, rotate it, or place a border around it. Inset actually includes a complete paint program, so you can edit the graphic itself or create new ones from scratch.

Access: Word processing utilities

Inset/$149
Inset Systems
12 Mill Plain Road
Danbury, CT 06811
203/794-0396

Word processor drivers /free
For Multimate, DisplayWrite,
Word, and WordPerfect
Hewlett-Packard
303/353-7650

12

Desktop Publishing

∾

Desktop publishing, the hottest personal computer fad in the mid-1980s, is now an established technology that has irrevocably transformed the way we get communicate in print. From established publishing houses and public relations firms to go-it-alone novelists and eccentric yellow journalists, companies and individuals alike have been turning away in droves from traditional manual pasteup methods and towards personal computers and desktop publishing software. Armed with these tools, they're creating printed documents of every imaginable description: books, manuals, flyers, brochures, magazines; documents with multiple columns, illustrated documents, documents that combine a multitude of fonts.

Desktop publishing on the DeskJet

The DeskJet is your economy-fare ticket to the marvels of high-quality desktop publishing. With a DeskJet, anyone with a little patience can turn out documents that look as good as what you get from any of the popular desktop laser printers, including those ballyhooed PostScript machines. Take the pages you print on your DeskJet down to a professional printshop, and you can transform them into newsletters, flyers, or even books that hold their own in the looks department against all comers. All you need is the right software.

You doubt my claims? I draw your attention to the sample printed on the opposite page. It may not be a model of classic design, but it shows how the DeskJet can handle complex layouts combining a variety of text and graphics elements. It's reproduced directly from an actual DeskJet printout made from Ventura Publisher with the help of Publisher's Powerpak, a utility described later in the chapter.

That's not to say that the DeskJet is the best printer around for desktop publishing. But by far its most serious limitation compared to more expensive laser printers is simply that it's slower.

Do you need a desktop publishing program?

Before you buy a program that carries the "desktop publishing" label, it makes sense to consider whether you need one—your word processor may be all the desktop publishing software you need. Nowadays, top-notch word processors have so much in common with desktop publishing programs that it's hard to tell the two genres apart. Word processors like WordPerfect or Microsoft word now let you take advantage of the cornucopia of fonts you can use with printers like the DeskJet. Just like desktop publishing programs, they can easily import graphics into textual documents. And while their formatting talents won't satisfy a professional book or magazine designer, they can readily produce fairly complicated layouts such as multiple columns. Word processors have the big advantage of letting you do all your work, from outlining your ideas to printing your final copy, using a single program.

Naturalist's Journal

Beagle Blowings

—C. Darwin

I have not as yet noticed by far the most remarkbable feature in the natural history of this archipelago; it is, that the different islands to a considerable extent are inhabited by a different set of beings.

My attention was first called to this fact by the Vice-Governor, Mr. Lawson, declaring that the tortoises differed from the different islands, and that he could with certainty tell from which island any one was brought. I did not for some time pay sufficient attention to this statement, and I had already partially

At sail in the Archipelago

mingled together the collections from two of the islands. I never dreamed that islands, about 50 or 60 miles apart, and most them in sight of each other, formed of precisely the same rocks, placed under a quite similar climate, rising to a nearly equal height, would have been differently tenanted; but we shall soon see that this is the case. It is the fate of most voyagers, no sooner to discover what is most interesting in any locality, than they are hurried from it; but I ought, perhaps, to be thankful that I obtained sufficient materials to establish this most remarkable fact in the distribution of organic beings.

Bugs of Gold

—E. A. Poe

The winters in the latitude of Sullivan's Island are seldom very severe, and in the fall of the year it is a rare event indeed when a fire is considered necessary. About the middle of October, 18__, there occurred, however, a day of remarkable chilliness. Just before sunset I scambled my way through the evergreens to the hut of my friend, who I had not visited for several weeks—my residence being, at that time, in Charleston, a distance of nine miles from the island, while the facilities of passage and re-passage were very far behind those of

Still, there's one place where most word processing programs really fall down: the way they represent your document on the screen. Instead of letting you work directly with an image of the document that looks almost exactly as it will appear in print, most word processors still make you switch back and forth between an editing mode, in which you see the text in, and a "print preview" mode, in which you see an on-screen facsimile of your document. The problem is that you can't edit that screen facsimile. Instead, you must go back to the text mode to make corrections. It's time consuming and frustrating to flip back and forth between the preview mode and your text while you try to figure out how to get the layout to look right.

WYSIWYG: Seeing the document you're formatting

Desktop publishing programs eliminate that bottleneck. The single most significant innovation of the modern desktop publishing era is the ability to lay out your newsletter, book, or what have you by manipulating an on-screen mockup of the document. This screen version of the document looks exactly like the final printed version, within the limits of your monitor's resolution. You can see each character of your text just as it will actually be printed. If a page contains a graphical image, you see the image alongside the text, just where it will appear in print.

But you you're not limited to looking at the page on your screen—you can also edit its layout as well as its text. This approach has obvious majoradvantages. As you make changes in the layout, you see the results immediately, and can decide right then whether you like them. If you make a mistake, you know it, and can make the necessary adjustments without waiting for a printout. For this reason, today's desktop publishing programs are far better for page layout than any conventional word processor. If you want to put together layouts of any complexity, or even if you just change layouts frequently, do yourself a favor and buy a desktop publishing program.

How desktop publishing programs work

Several common themes run through most of the desktop publishing programs. For one thing, their basic mission is to assemble files that come from a variety of sources into complete documents. To serve this purpose, all DTP programs can import a number of file types.

In Ventura and some other programs, the process of importing a file starts when you define a *frame* to hold the file. Whether or not you can see the outline on your screen, a frame is a two-dimensional rectangle into which you "pour" a passage of text, a picture, or in some programs, a table. In some programs, each entire page is treated as a frame, into which you can place text, graphics, or other frames. Each frame exists semi-independently from the rest of the document, in that you can change its size or move it around on the page or from page to page at will. Graphics images are confined to a single frame, while a passage of text that is too long for one frame can flow to another, and then another.

PageMaker, by contrast, relies on a "pasteboard" metaphor, in which you simply place text and graphics units directly on the page, without defining frames for them first.

Style sheets are another feature common to most page layout programs. A style sheet is a collection of preset formatting options ("styles" or "tags") that you can apply as a group all at once to a given document element. In a program with a stylesheet feature, for example, you might define a style for headlines, calling for the text to be printed in the center of the page in a 30-point Helv font, with half an inch of space below the headline. Once you've created the style, a quick mouse click or two can attach it to a line of ordinary looking text, and a big centered headline jumps out at you immediately.

Most desktop publishing programs also give you tools for creating simple line graphics, such as straight and diagonal lines, rectangles, and ovals, with or without shading. With these tools, you can create basic borders and highlights, without having to import a new file for each little line or box you want in your document.

Because of the almost geographic nature of page layout, it helps to be able to move from one part of the screen page to any other very quickly. For this reason, every desktop publishing requires a mouse.

Since most desktop publishing programs only give you rudimentary text-editing features, it's easier to type in your text in a word processor, then fire up the DTP software and import the text file. This extra step is a bother, but once you complete it, your document is "live" on the screen, and you can proceed with laying it out very efficiently. If necessary, you can make minor changes in the text directly, without having to flip to a preview mode time and again. Also, since the DTP program handles the layout for you, you can get by with a word processor that has fewer frills and costs less.

✄ *Tip:* *Once you decide to go with a desktop publishing program for page layout, many of the features of the big-name word processors become irrelevant. What you really need is a fast text editing program with lots of powerful editing commands that will save your words in a format the desktop publishing software can import. PC-Write, QEdit, and VDE are good choices. If you work with Ventura, there are two text editors specifically designed for your needs: VPEditor (my preference) and Venedit.*

Choosing a desktop publishing program

Once you decide to go the desktop publishing route you'll be faced with a myriad of software choices. Available DTP programs span a wide range of price and features. To figure out which page layout software is best for you, start by asking yourself how far you're likely to carry your involvement with desktop publishing. If you're at all serious about it, or think you might eventually be, the only two programs to consider are Ventura Publisher and PageMaker. One of these top-flight programs should satisfy all your page layout requirements.

On the other hand, Ventura and PageMaker are expensive, and they can take a long time to learn. If you don't expect to do professional-level desktop publishing but do want the advantages of WYSIWYG formatting, buy either a Windows-based word processor such as Amí, Microsoft Word for Windows, or WordStar Legacy, or get a good-quality, low-end WYSIWYG desktop publishing package, like Publish-It! or First Publisher.

Ventura versus PageMaker

The choice between Ventura and PageMaker is becoming more and more difficult as each product matures. Originally, and with some justification,

PageMaker was considered as better for short documents such as flyers and newsletters, while Ventura won in long structured documents such as books and manuals.

The problem is that each program is adding features that previously were the exclusive province of its competitor. PageMaker, for example, can now make indexes and tables of contents automatically, and it allows you to tie multiple files together into book-length documents. For its part, brand new Ventura utilities are adding sophisticated color capabilities to that program.

When it comes to printer support, there's little to distinguish the two programs. Since the first edition of this book was written, Ventura has been released in a Windows version, so that it's now competing on PageMaker's own turf. Ventura for Windows relies on exactly the same standard Windows printer driver that PageMaker uses. As far as DeskJet owners are concerned, then, both programs make equally good use of the DeskJet's features.

The story is different when it comes to the original GEM-based version of Ventura. With the snowballing popularity of Windows and the imminent release of Ventura 4 for Windows, Ventura for GEM seems to be waning in popularity. Still, it's widely used, and it's an excellent piece of software. The problem for DeskJet owners is the simple fact that Ventura does not come with a driver for the DeskJet. Although there are ways to get Ventura to work with a DeskJet, they involve extra work and extra expense.

Desktop publishing on a budget

If you don't want to pay through the nose for Ventura or PageMaker, don't think you'll be stuck with ugly documents that people will turn up their noses at. With one of the entry-level desktop publishing programs you can churn out lovely output that looks just as good as if you composed it with one of the big-league programs. Unless you attempt a really complicated layout, only a publishing professional will know the difference. Budge DTP programs that work well with the DeskJet include PFS:First Publisher, Publish-It!, Avagio, and Express Publisher. Note that none of these packages are Windows programs.

Special purpose DTP software

Database publishing: dbPublisher is the first program dedicated to desktop publishing of database files. It's an expensive and complicated beast, but extremely powerful. Instead of buying a separate program for database publishing database files, you can buy add-ons for both Ventura and PageMaker that format the files for the destination desktop publishing package. While complex, dbPublisher for Ventura gives you complete control over the format of your database reports in Ventura, allowing you to dress up information from multiple files in a variety of different database formats. VPData, a much easier to use utility, handles mail merge-type importing of data from dBase files into Ventura. For PageMaker, PageAhead software (206/441-0340) markets a similar utility.

Mathematical equations: Currently, the only popular desktop publishing program that lets you add complex mathematical equations to your documents is Ventura Publisher with the Professional Extension. If you're not ready to spend that much money, you can format math equations with the Windows program MathType, and then import them as graphics into most any word processor or desktop publishing program.

Access: Specialty desktop publishing software

dbPublisher/$695
dbPublisher for Ventura/$249
Digital Composition Systems
1715 W. Northern Ave.
Phoenix, AZ 85201
800/527-2506; 602/870-7667

VPData/$149
Aristosoft
1650 Centre Point Dr.
Milpitas, CA 95035
800/338-2629; 408/946-2747

MathType/$149
Design Science, Inc.
4028 Broadway
Long Beach, CA 90803
213/433-0685

Profile: Ventura Publisher

$895/Xerox Corp.
Ventura Software, Inc.
15175 Innovation Drive
San Diego, CA 92128
800/822-8221

Ventura Publisher is one of the most marvelous software programs ever devised. With Ventura, a PC, and a compatible printer, you can make short work of your most complex layout tasks. The catch for DeskJet owners is that innocent-sounding phrase "compatible printer." But we'll get to that painful subject in a moment. First, let's tick off the highlights of Ventura's features list, which is as long as two or three of your arms:

- Ventura is unsurpassed for longer documents. It automatically creates as many pages as are necessary to hold the document's text. It can combine multiple smaller "chapters" into longer complete manuscripts. It can automatically number chapters, pages, lists, figures, footnotes, and so on, and can generate tables of contents and indexes automatically as well. Graphics images can be attached to particular passages of text; when a document revision changes the layout of the text, the attached graphics automatically move in concert with the text.

- The program has a comprehensive, superbly designed style sheet system for instantaneous text reformatting. Yet although features such as this excel at structured documents with repeating elements such as headers, it's also flexible enough to handle free-form layouts with aplomb and ease.

- Ventura imports text and graphics files from almost every major word processing and graphics program, so there's rarely a problem in assembling documents from whatever component files you're starting with. In the process of importing text, Ventura leaves intact the character formats in the original document, such as bold, italics, underlining, so you don't have to add them again. Even better, Ventura preserves the original files as separate entities in their original formats. This way, even after you've imported a text or graphics file into Ventura, you can make changes to the file using the program that originally created it. The next time you load Ventura, the edited version of the file automatically becomes part of the Ventura document.

- Ventura lets you move and size layout elements quickly and easily with the mouse, or with perfect accuracy by typing in numeric coordinates. If you need a precisely aligned graphic, the by-the-numbers approach actually gets you there much faster than the mouse does—but many DTP programs provide only the mouse method. Ventura has an excellent set of simple line-graphic tools. You can draw lines, rectangles, and ovals.

- Ventura can generate tables automatically, produce sophisticated mathematical equations with a minimum of hassle, and access a 2-megabyte hyphenation dictionary for near-perfect hyphenation.

- Ventura is available in DOS/GEM, Windows, and OS/2 versions, as well as Macintosh one. The DOS/GEM version has one major advantage: it is extremely fast for a large program running in graphics mode—fast enough that it's practical to use it on a standard PC or XT. I'd still suggest an AT-class computer or better, however.

Version 4 of Ventura for Windows, scheduled for release in late 1991, corrects some of the most glaring deficiencies that have long plagued the program. It adds a full search-and-replace feature, a spelling checker, and perhaps most important and Undo/Redo command that lets you recover gracefully from your mistakes. Whether and when the GEM version will receive a similar upgrade, I don't know.

Ventura and the DeskJet

For DeskJet owners who want to use the GEM version of Ventura, there's one terribly nasty fly in the ointment. To date, Ventura's talented programmers haven't come up with a driver for the DeskJet (if you're hazy on what a driver is, see Chapter 3 for a quick review). It can't be that Ventura only works with page-oriented printers like the LaserJet or PostScript machine—the program turns out quality pages on other line-by-line printers like the Epson series. Whatever the explanation, DeskJet owners have to face the fact that Ventura for GEM has ignored them.

You have two solutions. The obvious one is to use Ventura for Windows instead, which can print to the DeskJet just fine using the standard Windows driver for your printer. If you prize the speed of the GEM version, however, you may want to consider another answer.

Using GEM Ventura with a DeskJet: PostScript

To get the best possible printouts from the GEM version of Ventura on a DeskJet, you need one of the PostScript interpreter software packages covered in Chapter 20. To use one of these products, you install Ventura as if you had a real PostScript printer. When it's time to print, you trick Ventura into feeding its printer output into the PostScript interpreter. The interpreter converts the printer data into instructions the DeskJet can understand, and sends them on to your printer. Though the process is slow, the results are excellent. A DeskJet driven from Ventura by one of these PostScript interpreters even does a standard LaserJet one better, by printing Encapsulated PostScript files.

Publisher's Powerpak and LaserTwin

Another eminently workable alternative is Publisher's Powerpak from Atech Software. This product provides Ventura printer drivers for over 200 printers that Ventura itself doesn't directly support, including the DeskJet, along with a font generator that scales master typeface outlines to any size supported by Ventura as you print. Powerpak is covered in Chapter 7. The sample Ventura newsletter reproduced earlier in this chapter was printed on a DeskJet using Publisher's Powerpak.

A similar solution is LaserTwin, the LaserJet emulation utility profiled in Chapter 4. With LaserTwin, you configure Ventura to print to a LaserJet, and the program converts Ventura's output into DeskJet format. The results are just as good as if you'd printed your document on a real LaserJet.

There are several drawbacks common to all these alternatives for getting Ventura to work with a DeskJet. The first is speed—the process of making Ventura's ordinary output palatable for the DeskJet takes time. Another problem is that none of these programs can digest fonts in any of the standard formats. That means you'll be limited to the fonts the vendor provides.

Specifically, you can't use any of these products with normal DeskJet fonts, nor, in the PostScript interpreters' case, with standard PostScript fonts either.

Adding new fonts

Since the only way to use GEM Ventura with a DeskJet is via a third-party software package (Publisher's PowerPak, LaserTwin, or one of the PostScript interpreters) you have to rely on the type of fonts used by that package. Publisher's Powerpak requires proprietary fonts available only from Atech, while LaserTwin and the PostScript products use standard fonts (LaserJet and PostScript respectively).

Profile: PageMaker

$795/Aldus Corp
411 First Ave. S. #200
Seattle, WA 98104
206/622-5500

PageMaker is the program most closely associated with desktop publishing—in fact Aldus president Paul Brainerd is responsible for coining the term. Although PageMaker's PC version looks and works almost identically to the groundbreaking Macintosh version, it hasn't the enjoyed the same market dominance, what with Ventura's overwhelming popularity. Nonetheless, it's a great piece of software that does its intended job well.

PageMaker's name is apt, because the program's strength lies in its ability to lay out individual pages. The screen looks much like a real pasteup table, with icons for various commands designed to resemble a graphics artist's tools as much as possible. The pasteup metaphor is functional as well as cosmetic, since you assemble text and graphics onto a screen page much as you would on paper. Unlike Ventura and most other DTP programs, PageMaker doesn't ask you to draw frames for your text and graphics before you import them. Instead, you "paste" each element onto the page directly where it will go.

PageMaker readily imports text and graphics in all the common formats. Features for modifying and printing imported graphics make PageMaker your best choice if you plan to work extensively with color or scanned images.

best choice if you plan to work extensively with color or scanned images. There's a drawback to PageMaker's approach to imported files, however. The program merges the contents of imported files into one central document, instead of maintaining each file as a separate entity. Once PageMaker has imported a file, any changes you make to the original with another program won't show up in the PageMaker document. There is a function for re-exporting text, however.

Although PageMaker doesn't offer quite the depth of typographic control you get in Ventura, it offers enough to keep most desktop publishers occupied and happy. You can control leading, kerning, letter spacing, and word spacing, and create hanging and nested indents. You also get a variety of simple drawing tools for adding lines, rectangles, and ovals to your documents. Unique features include the ability to print documents larger than a single piece of paper, by printing each page in sections that you then paste together; an on-screen pasteboard, an area in which you can park text or graphics temporarily; and the ability to position graphics so that they straddle adjacent pages.

With versions 3 and 4, PageMaker has also acquired some features essential for producing long documents. It can now automatically generate as many new pages as are needed to fit the document's text. Equally important, PageMaker owners enjoy a well-implemented style sheet feature for much quicker text formatting. The program can build tables of contents and indexes automatically, and you can pull together multiple individual files into book-length documents.

Using PageMaker with the DeskJet

Since PageMaker runs in the Windows environment, it works with the standard Windows DeskJet driver. Once you've installed Windows for the DeskJet, you can print any PageMaker document, with the exception of ones that contain imported Encapsulated PostScript files. PageMaker comes with a free copy of Adobe Type Manager (see Chapter 10), allowing you to print any PostScript font in PageMaker, or any Windows program for that matter.

13

Graphics Software

One of the best things about the multi-talented DeskJet is that it prints high-resolution graphics just as effortlessly as it does text. As usual, all you need is some good software.

Graphics software covers the gamut, from crude low-budget wonders to expensive feature-laden packages that suit the needs of the professional graphics artist. Somewhere in that range, you should be able to find a program that's just what you need to express your visual creativity.

Printing graphics

If computer art for art's sake is your passion, you can print your masterpieces directly from the program in which you create them. In this case, you'll need to be sure that the graphics software you select works well with the DeskJet.

More often, though, your pictures will end up as illustrations in a larger document that you put together with a desktop publishing program. If this is how you plan to use graphics, your concerns will be to ensure that your art files transfer easily to the desktop publishing program, and that the latter program is DeskJet-compatible. These days, you don't need to worry much. All the major graphics programs create files that can be readily imported by the big-name desktop publishing programs. And, with the notorious exception of Ventura's GEM version, all the desktop publishing programs work with the DeskJet.

Paint versus draw programs

A great divide separates two fundamentally different types of graphics software. On one side of the gulf are the "paint" programs, on the other the "draw" programs. The distinction between the two is rooted in the method each type of program uses to represent images within your computer, but this technical difference has important artistic repercussions.

Paint programs get their name from the way they let you apply colors and patterns to your screen much as if you were spreading paint onto a canvas. With complete abandon—within the boundaries of your screen—you can roll on a swath of deep purple here, splash some spots of hot pink there, and drip tiny droplets of gold (of course, all of these colors would show up as different shades of grey when printed on the DeskJet). And don't let the name fool you. You *can* draw—lines, boxes, circles, what have you—with a paint program, just as easily as you can with a draw program.

The key point is that a paint program lets you directly control the placement of every individual dot that makes up the picture. Of course, if you're using a wide "brush" to slather on your colors, you may not take advantage of this dot-by-dot control. But it's still true that you are directly responsible for where the paint ends up in your picture. As a result, an image created in a paint program can be beautifully detailed—even to the point that it starts to look like a real painting, depending on the resolution of your program, screen, and printer.

That brings up the subject of graphics resolution vis-a-vis the DeskJet. The DeskJet's top resolution, of course, is a high 300 dots per linear inch—that's enough dots for some stunningly sharp pictures. Unfortunately, in many paint programs, the maximum resolution you can achieve is limited to the resolution of your screen. Even on a VGA monitor, that's only 640x480 dots for the entire screen, a far lower resolution than the DeskJet's. As a result, the graphics you create in these programs tend to look rough and jagged when printed. However, you can buy paint programs that let you create 300 dpi pictures by enlarging the image on screen—of course, you can only work with part of the picture at a time with this method.

Working at 300 dpi, a paint program lets you create far more richly detailed pictures than a draw program. But even the high-resolution paint programs have some drawbacks. Talking technical for a moment, paint programs render pictures in bitmapped form (see Chapter 3), where each dot of the image is stored in the computer's memory. That consumes a tremendous amount of memory and hard disk space for pictures of any size. In addition, if you try to enlarge or reduce the picture to fit a particular space, the quality of the image may deteriorate. That's because the program has to add and subtract dots where it thinks it should, and its guesses may not be very good.

One important use of paint programs is in editing scanned images. A digital scanner works much like a photocopy machine, passing a beam of light over an image on paper and converting the reflection into a pattern of dots. Instead of printing the dot pattern or bitmap on a new piece of paper, however, the scanner simply stores it in a file on your hard disk. At this point, you can incorporate the scanned image into a document in your desktop publishing or word processing program. For example, you might want to scan in your signature, and merge it into a form letter you're sending out.

Though you can use your scanned image files without modification, bringing them into a paint program first for editing is often a good idea. You may well find you need to remove stray dots, lighten overly dark areas, and do other touch-up work. If you like, you can add shading, or even go hog wild and make the scanned image part of a larger painting.

Paint programs that work well with the DeskJet include HotShot Graphics, ColorRIX, and, of course, all the members of the PC Paintbrush family.

Draw programs work much like paint programs in some ways, but quite differently in others. As you'd expect by the name, draw programs do a great job at drawing lines. But even here, they make work somewhat differently than you'd expect. In a paint program, you just draw your lines, and every spot on the picture that the mouse pointer touches becomes a dot in your picture. The line doesn't exist as a separate entity, and if you wish to change it in any way, you have to erase the old dots and draw in new ones.

In a draw program, the software translates your mouse movements into a mathematical description of the line you trace. It stores this description as a separate object unto itself, rather than as a series of individual dots. Now, if you want to change the line as a whole, you can, by shrinking it, stretching it, moving it as a whole from place to place, or—in the case of the more advanced drawing programs—by reshaping the contour of the line with precision control.

Draw programs handle all the elements in a picture, whether they are lines, triangles, circles, or boxes, in this way, treating them as independent objects stored as mathematical descriptions in the program's memory. These descriptions are converted into dots for display on your screen, or when the picture gets printed.

This *object-oriented* or *vector* approach to graphics has many implications for your artwork. The most important advantage is that it allows the program to automatically adjust things so that the drawing prints at the highest possible resolution on whatever printer you own, independently of the image you see on the screen. This means that you can work on your drawing at actual size even on a relatively low-resolution monitor, and still get excellent quality when you print. All the program has to do is retranslate all those mathematical descriptions into a new dot pattern matching the printer's resolution.

In like manner, you can freely resize any object in the picture, or the entire picture, without any degradation of quality—again, the program just recalculates the objects. Another positive is that these mathematical descriptions consume far less memory and disk space than do the dot-by-dot paint graphics.

On the downside, you don't have anywhere near the control over details of color and shading as you do in a paint program. Draw programs do let you color the lines themselves, of course. But though you can apply colors and shades to empty parts of the picture, you can only do so within boundaries specifically defined by lines. You simply can't daub on a little color here and there. As a result, images created in draw programs can consist of very complex shapes, but they have simple, poster-like color schemes, lacking the life-like realism that's possible with paint programs.

These days, most of the action in PC artwork is on the draw side of the great graphics divide. The advantages of precision control over line contour, and the ability to print at the highest possible resolution are just too great for most artists to ignore. Besides, the simpler color and shading of draw-type images actually works better than the complexity of the paint type variety for the kinds of illustrations most people use.

At this writing, at least five professional-quality draw packages are jockeying for your attention, and there are still several less expensive intermediate-level programs that are good for occasional use. All work well with the DeskJet. Note, though, that some of the most advanced features of the draw programs rely heavily on the PostScript language, which shines when it comes to object-oriented graphics. Since the DeskJet isn't a PostScript printer, you'll be unable to use these features. But as you'll see in Chapter 20, it's possible to add PostScript capability to your DeskJet.

Graphics design in black and white

Being able to print graphics in black and white only means you must be careful to strive for simplicity in the images you create. Although many graphics programs can simulate shades of gray by varying the density of black dots they print, it's often difficult to distinguish between those gray shades. For this reason, images printed on a DeskJet can be muddy looking. Unless you really know what you're doing, stick to larger, solid shapes and simple lines. For great advice on using black and white effectively in computer graphics design, get *The Gray Book,* by Michael Gosney, et al. It's $22.95 from Ventana Press, 919/942-0220.

Profile: PC Paintbrush

$99.95 (for PC Paintbrush IV)/**ZSoft**
450 FranklinRd., Suite 100
Marietta, GA 30067
404/428-0008

In the divided world of PC graphics programs, PC Paintbrush is still the leader of the paint pack. The PC Paintbrush file format for paint-type graphics, PCX, has become firmly established as far and away the most widely used bitmapped format on IBM-compatible microcomputers.

Over the last few years the original PC Paintbrush program has evolved into a whole family of Paintbrushes. There have been too many versions of the program for me to keep them straight without my crib notes, but all of them share the basic strengths: comprehensive graphics editing tools, good performance, and support for just about any type of screen, mouse, and printer you can name, including the DeskJet.

The screen tools common to all versions of PC Paintbrush let you paint swatches of colors or patterns with a brush, draw lines, boxes, and circles,

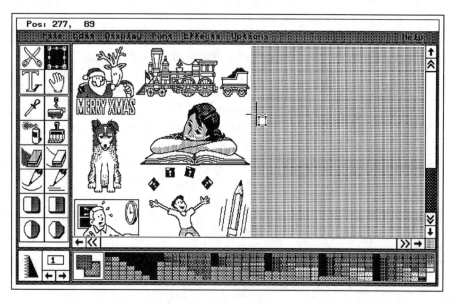

Figure 13-1: *PC Paintbrush IV. Compared to earlier versions, it offers improved gray-scale editing, enhanced type handling, and better on-line help.*

cut, copy, and paste parts of you picture, and type text. A "spray can" tool lets you apply color or paint lightly, in a sort of a mist effect, without obscuring the entire background—this is a great way to lighten up parts of a scanned image that are too dark. The program gives you access to loads of different colors and patterns, and you can create your own if the pre-defined ones aren't enough.

The latest generation of Paintbrushes include two DOS-based programs, the lower-end PC Paintbrush IV and PC Paintbrush IV+, and a Windows version of the top-of-the-line Publisher's Paintbrush. Both of the DOS Paintbrusheshave the ability to import TIFF files (the kind created by most scanners) as well as PCX files, Paintbrushes own format. Both offer gray-scale editing for enhancing black-and-white images and other sophisticated special effects such as blending, smudging, and tiling. Type handling capabilities have also been significantly improved, and you can now use outline fonts created in Publisher's Type Foundry, a sister product, in either program.

The biggest difference between PC Paintbrush IV and PC Paintbrush IV+ is the size of the images each program allows. In ordinary Paintbrush IV, you're limited to whatever you can fit into the standard DOS memory space of 640K. Paintbrush IV+, by contrast, can park portions of your pictures in extended or expanded memory, or on your hard disk, letting you create much larger pictures. In addition, the + version lets you control your scanner directly from within the program, so you don't have to leave your work when you want to scan. The old version of Paintbrush+ could import Lotus 1-2-3 charts in the .PIC format, but this feature has been dropped.

All versions of PC Paintbrush work fine with the DeskJet. The non-Windows editions come with their own DeskJet drivers, which allow you to choose between draft quality (150 dpi resolution) or high quality (300 dpi) printing modes.

Painting in Windows

If you own Windows 3, you already have a decent paint program, Windows Paint. This program was actually written by ZSoft, makers of PC Paintbrush, and it works much like its DOS counterparts. Publisher's Paintbrush for Windows, the new chief of ZSoft's paint clan, has all kinds of sophisticated features which you probably won't need for use with the DeskJet.

High-end draw programs

Once upon a time, the PC took aa back seat to the Macintosh when it comes to high-quality graphics. Now, however, PC drawing tools equal or better anything available for the Mac. Any of the professional-quality drawing programs covered here can be used to produce artwork that rivals the creations of a traditional graphics artist, yet can be printed on your DeskJet.

The real key to the quality of a high-end draw program is the method it uses to let you place lines very accurately, and then modify the lines after you've drawn them. In their inner workings, all these upscale illustration programs use an efficient method of representing lines mathematically; lines defined by this method are called *Bezier curves.* To form the outline of a Bezier curve, you only need to know where a few points on the curve are located: the points where the line starts and stops, and the points where the curve changes direction, known variously as the *anchor points, handles,* or *nodes.* On the screen, the anchor points appear as big squares or rectangles directly on the path of the curve.

At each direction-changing anchor point, you must also know the angle of deflection, and how far the curve extends in that direction. These characteristics are represented on screen by the length and direction of dashed lines which extend out on either side of the anchor points and end in *control points.*

Once you've defined the anchor points and the control points, the program just connects the anchors with a smooth curve. Of course, you never see the formulas involved. Instead, you simply draw on the screen. Some programs let you draw freehand; after you've drawn a line, the program converts it to a Bezier, calculating where the anchor points and control points should go. In other programs, you place the anchor points by hand, one at a time. This method may sound less intuitive than the freehand approach, but it can actually be more precise and quicker. To modify the shape of the line, you can move the anchor point itself, or manipulate the control points to lengthen or shorten the deflection lines or change their angles. Figure 13-2 shows how this process looks in Artline.

All this sounds quite complicated, and it does take awhile to get the hang of these bizarre Beziers. But if you keep at it, you'll soon find that working with

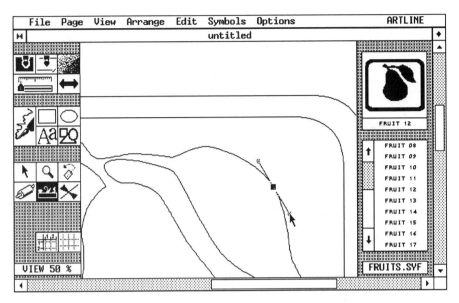

Figure 13-2: *This screen from the first version of Artline shows how the high-end illustration programs work. The small dark box on the curve of the pear's lefa is an* anchor point, *while the little lines extending from either side of the anchor end in* control points.

Bezier curves becomes a fairly intuitive process, and it definitely lets you place curves exactly where you want them to go.

Because so many images are already available in bitmapped, paint-type files, an *autotrace* feature is common to many of the illustration programs. Autotracing converts the outlines of the bitmap into Bezier curves, allowing you to print the image at the highest resolution your printer can produce, and to edit it with the other drawing tools provided by the software.

Since they're targeted at professional graphics artists, most of these illustration programs have strong tools for manipulating text. That way, you can compose an entire brochure or flyer in one program, without resorting to manual pasteup or even a desktop publishing product.

The emphasis is on jazzy headlines and captions, not long stretches of copy. Typically, you can use a wide assortment of fonts, and you can dress them up with all kinds of fancy special effects. For instance, you can fill the characters with patterns or colors, create bold outlines around them, rotate, stretch, or squeeze them, or array them along a curve. In three of the programs, you can even edit the character outlines just as if they were ordinary graphics, adding ornate embellishments, or enlarging the first character in a logo for emphasis.

Choosing an illustration package

With the exception of Artline, all the professional illustration packages are designed for Microsoft Windows. Artline is based on GEM, sort of a pared down Windows workalike. Both Windows and GEM assume primary responsibility for interacting with your printer, relieving the actual program you're using from this burden. This being the case, the results you can expect when printing your graphics on the DeskJet from any of these illustration packages depend mostly on the quality of the DeskJet driver that comes with the environment (Windows or GEM).

These programs are expensive, so you won't want to buy one until you're sure it's right for you—so which one is best? There's a short answer and a long answer.

Corel Draw

Like everybody and her sister, I choose Corel Draw as my hands-down favorite among today's crop of upscale drawing programs. Corel Draw has just about every graphics feature you could imagine, and a whole bunch more beyond that. And Corel Draw is the fastest of the Windows-based illustration packages, almost as responsive as GEM-based Artline.

Corel Draw's core drawing features are second to none. The program responds quickly and accurately as you draw your Bezier curves freehand, giving you a better sense of control over the placement of your lines than in most of the competition. Even more important, there's a complete set of functions for editing the Beziers, and they work. In addition, you get tools for drawing ovals and rectangles in a single step, and you can resize, rotate, or skew the objects in your drawing with the mouse or with numeric precision. Draw also sports a decent built-in autotrace feature for converting

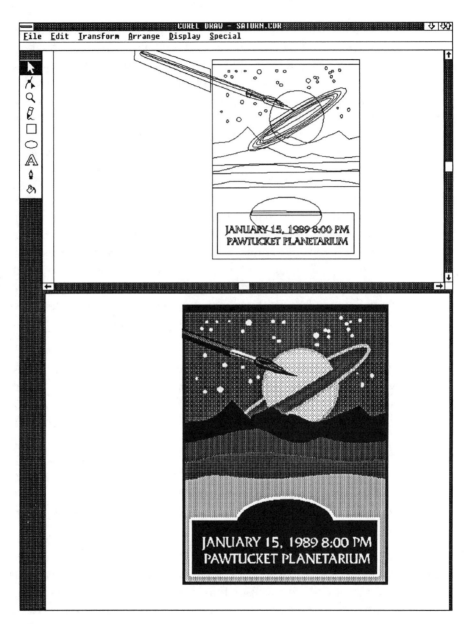

Figure 13-3: *A screen from Corel Draw, taken from a full-page monitor. You draw with the outlines in the top window, and see the results as they'll print in the preview window below.*

most of the competition. Even more important, there's a complete set of functions for editing the Beziers, and they work. In addition, you get tools for drawing ovals and rectangles in a single step, and you can resize, rotate, or skew the objects in your drawing with the mouse or with numeric precision. A new special effects menu has been added, for perspective and block letter effects, among others. Draw sports a decent built-in autotrace feature for converting bitmap images into Corel's draw-type graphics, but it also comes with a separate, extremely capable autotracing program.

Corel's prowess with text is nothing short of phenomenal. The program comes with a whole slew of built-in typefaces—150 of them or more—many of which are near-identical copies of popular PostScript originals sold by Adobe Systems. You're restricted to using typefaces in the Corel format, but as a reward you get to print them in any size on any printer that works with the program, the DeskJet included. Purchase Corel Draw, and you've instantly acquired an entire library of typefaces. What's more, you can tell the program to convert the type outlines into graphics objects, and then edit them just as you would any other shape in your picture for really classy text effects.

As if that weren't enough, the package includes a new that takes outline typefaces in most of the major formats, including PostScript and Fontware,and converts them into Corel Draw's own format. Once the conversion is made, you can modify the text with any of Corel Draw's text features. What's more, you can run the conversion in the other direction, creating your own font characters in Corel, then converting them or any existing Corel typeface into a Type 1 PostScript typeface that will work with Adobe Type Manager, a font scaler for Windows (Chapter 10). For easy integration with other programs, Corel Draw imports and exports many different graphics file formats.

Print quality is better in version 2 by virtue of improvements in font scaling and in the halftone gray shades that the program generates. To top it off, all these capabilities are wrapped up in a screen package that's attractive and easy to use. The major drawing tools have been combined into an efficient, uncluttered icon bar, while ordinary menus give you access to less commonly used commands for printing and fine tuning.

Designer

Micrografx' Designer was the first PC illustration package, and the program has won a lot of converts over the last couple of years. Designer boasts many strengths, including a wide range of excellent drawing tools, strong import-export capabilities, and the best built-in autotrace function I've used. Designer was the first drawing package that let you set up drawings with independent *layers*. You can turn the display of a given layer on or off as necessary, making it much easier to work with complex, richly textured illustrations. On the convenience side, it's the only program that lets you customize the screen palette of tools so that it contains icons for the commands you use most often.

The current version of Designer, 3.1, has vastly improved text capabilities, though they still come up short against those of Corel. You can scale any Fontware or URW typeface to any size, and you can convert the characters into graphics for freeform editing as necessary. All this works equally well with PostScript fonts if you have ATM installed. And there's now a feature

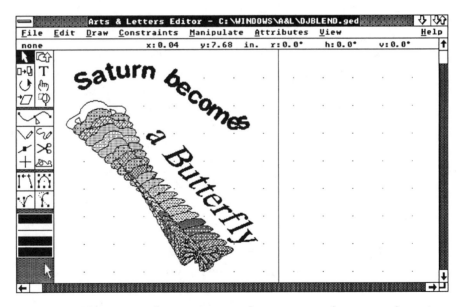

Figure 13-4: *Amazingly, Arts&Letters lets you transform one shape into another through a series of gradual intermediates. You can also fit text to any shape, as shown crudely with the words "Saturn becomes" above.*

that automatically fits text to a curved line. Like Arts & Letters, the program can blend one shape into another in a series of gradual shape-changing steps.

Arts & Letters

The Arts & Letters Editor is often touted as the program of choice for those who aren't skilled graphics artists themselves, since the program comes with more free clip art images than any of the other illustration packages. But ignore the clip art altogether, and you'll find that Arts & Letters stands on its own as an excellent drawing package with features not yet available in the competition. Many of its special strengths lie in color handling, which doesn't do you much good if you print only on the DeskJet. But A&L has other distinguishing features as well. No other program offers as many different ways to limit which lines go where in advance, helping ensure that your results are as you expect them. Finally, no other drawing package has A&L's built-in charting capability—you can make ordinary bar graphs, or stack up pictures of eggs when you want to show how much they cost in Wisconsin.

Like Corel's Envelope command, the "warp tool" allows you to bend, stretch, and twist any shape in your drawing, making perspective and other special effects extremely easy to implement. Like Designer, A&L gives you the ability to edit the outlines of any Type 1 PostScript font, without going through a cumbersome conversion process, as long as you have ATM installed. And just because Arts & Letters has lots of clip art doesn't mean it has the clip art you want. My advice is to shop for your clip art and your drawing program separately. Of course, if it turns out that you like what you see in the Arts & Letters clip art catalog, and that you're just as happy with the features of the Arts & Letters editor, this program would make a great choice.

Artline

Feature for feature, DRI's Artline doesn't quite measure up to the other programs in the list, but don't count Artline out until you've looked it over closely.

Based on the same lean GEM environment that gave Ventura its reputation for speed, Artline runs quickly enough for practical use on a standard PC or

XT, a feat none of its competitors can manage. Artline's fundamental drawing tools work reliably. Version 2 lets you draw freehand, but I find that Artline's point-by-point method of placing curves permits makes it easier to draw accurately in this program than in any of its competitors. And that, of course, makes it quicker. Also new in version 2, Artline's automatic trace tool is unique in that it lets you trace parts of a bitmap image at a time, interrupting the process to adjust your settings for best effect. The biggest problem I've encountered is that you can't have more than 128 points (anchor and control points) in a single curve, a limit that you can easily reach when you're doing complex artwork.

Access: Professional Illustration Software

Arts & Letters Graphics Editor/$695
Computer support Corporation
15926 Midway road
Dallas, TX 75244
214/661-8960

Corel Draw/$595
Corel Systems Corp.
1600 Carling Ave.
Ottowa, Ontario
K1Z 8R7 Canada
613/728-8200

GEM Artline/$495
Digital Research, Inc.
Box DRI
Monterey, CA 93942
408/649-3896

Micrografx Designer $695
Micrografx, Inc.
1303 Arapaho Rd.
Richardson, TX 75081
800/272-3729; 214/234-1769

14

Charting Software

∾

For the workaday business professional, the most important graphics are the ones that relate to the bottom line. Sure, a drab report on fourth quarter shoe sales looks a little snappier when adorned with a cute clip-art picture of a shoehorn. What you really need, though, is a compact, high-impact, easy-to-understand chart summarizing the sales trends graphically. That way, those who read your report can understand the essence of your message at a glance; they'll have a much easier time deciding how much leather to buy.

Because the DeskJet prints charts with just as much clarity as it does text, it makes a superb printer for managers, scientists, teachers, or anyone who has to put together reports and papers that are rich in graphical information content. Of course, you'll need the appropriate charting software. To create charts most efficiently, you want software that can read your numbers directly and automatically turn them into bars, pie chunks, or lines of the correct size and shape. The ideal charting software will let you pick from a wide variety of chart types, and will automate the process of adding labels, legends and titles. More, it will let you embellish the chart with graphics, text, and boxes and arrows anywhere you like. And as long as you're asking for the moon, why not wish for a program that makes the whole process easy?

Charts in reports

When you're ready to add a finished pie chart or bar graph to a textual document, you have two choices. The quickest and simplest alternative is to print out the chart on a separate page, directly from the software you used to create it. You then just insert that page where it belongs in your report.

If you want to get fancier, you can integrate your charts with the text of your report into a single complete document. When your chart is on the same page as the text that describes it, your readers will have no trouble relating the two. To use this strategy, you need a desktop publishing program that can read both your text and your charts. Of course, designing an integrated report takes more time than simply printing your charts on separate pages.

Charting with your spreadsheet

Some people forego separate business graphics software, preferring to rely on the charting features of their spreadsheet instead. After all, if you use spreadsheet software to generate the data represented on the chart, it makes a lot of sense to create the chart itself in that same program. Otherwise, you're forced to export your data from the spreadsheet, start up the charting program, import the data—and then commence work on the chart. If your luck really goes sour, you'll realize you set up the data the wrong way to begin with, and you'll have to go back to the spreadsheet and start all over. Even if your charting program has "hot links" to the spreadsheet file, so that changes in the data are automatically reflected in the corresponding chart, you must still return to the spreadsheet to make the changes in the first place.

Nowadays all the major spreadsheet programs include charting modules of their own, most of which give you an acceptable range of options and produce excellent printed output. The 3 in Lotus 1-2-3 stands for graphics, meaning basic charts suitable for typical business applications; in Releases 2.3 and 3.1+, 1-2-3 charts are more sophisticated than they were in prior versions. Excel, Quattro Pro, and WingZ deserve high marks for their charting abilities. In fact, a complete drawing program for embellishing your charts is built right into Quattro Pro, giving it presentation graphics tools that are in the same league as those of the full-fledged charting programs discussed in this chapter.

However, even Quattro lacks some of the more sophisticated features of the top-notch charting packages such as Freelance Plus, Harvard Graphics, or Charisma. And if you don't have a spreadsheet program, but need a way to make basic charts, low-cost graphics packages such as Graph-in-a-Box, PFS:First Graphics, or Pixie (a Windows program). should do the trick. And for scientific graphs, look at Axum. All these programs work well with DeskJet.

PFS:First Graphics

If you're looking for a simple and relatively inexpensive charting program, the best non-Windows alternative is PFS:First Graphics. First Graphics offers 15 different types of charts to work with. The list includes a number of chart types that aren't available in other DOS-based programs in this price range, such as high-low-close, trend, and overlapped bar. You can add a 3-dimensional effect to your charts, a feature not provided on the other inexpensive DOS charting programs. Five fonts are included, and you can scale these to 100 different sizes, again a far wider range than the competition permits.

First Graphics directly reads Lotus 1-2-3 files, so you don't have to translate them into ASCII format first. You can still import ASCII data too, of course. The program is easy to use and relatively fast at displaying graphs on the screen. Overall, First Graphics is an excellent low-cost way to get started with business graphics.

Pixie

For quick charts in Windows try Pixie, a dandy little graphing program with a difference. Pixie's contribution to software evolution is the concept of "live" chartmaking. Other charting programs make you start with raw numbers, and show you your finished chart only after you've chosen all sorts of options from menus and dialog boxes. Since you don't actually see the effect of each design decision until the final chart appears, it's easy to make mistakes that force you to go back and try again.

Pixie takes a different tack. The program presents you with a generic version of the type of chart you want to generate. You then manipulate this template on the screen with the mouse until it shows off your own data in the way the best communicates your message. The process is much more intuitive than the traditional dialog box routine, and the direct feedback you get at each step along the way gives you a much greater sense of control. On the downside, Pixie is a fairly limited program, with far fewer customization options than the Harvards and Freelances. Also, while Pixie's template approach is easier to learn, some people claim that the traditional charting methods are faster once you're used to them.

Access: Charting Software

Charisma/$495
Micrografx, Inc.
1303 E. Arapaho Rd.
Richardson, TX 75082
800/272-3729
214/234-1769

PFS: First Graphics/$149
Spinnaker Software
800/826-0706; 617/494-1200

Harvard Graphics /$495
Software Publishing Corp.
1901 Landings Dr.
Mountain View, CA 94309
415/962-8910

Freelance Plus/$495
Lotus Development Corp.
55 Cambridge Parkway
Cambridge, MA 02142
617/577-8500

Presentation Team/$495
Digital Research, Inc.
P.O. Box DRI
Monterey, CA 93942
800/443-4200

Pixie/$195
Zenographics
19752 MacArthur Blvd.
Irvine, CA 92715
714/851-6352

15

Spreadsheets

It used to be that a printed spreadsheet looked about as interesting as the white pages of your phone book. All that changed with the introduction of Microsoft's Excel, the first major spreadsheet program to wed desktop-publishing design capabilities to PC number-crunching. Nowadays, all the major spreadsheet packages include features that let you select fonts, add boxes and lines, print charts and spreadsheets on the same page, and create more sophisticated charts in general.

The twin assumptions behind this rush to better output quality are sound. First, when facts and figures look good, the important points jump out at the reader. Second, slick-looking printouts are simply more impressive. Whether or not it's fair, the people you want to influence are likely to take you and your numbers more seriously when your report looks professionally published instead of banged out on a typewriter.

The DeskJet is an excellent spreadsheet printer. It serves equally well for quick draft copies for your own use and for polished final reports for your clients or superiors. Of course, the DeskJet isn't fast enough if you need to print lots of very long spreadsheets. However, most printed reports summarize large amounts of data in a few pages, and that's an application for which the DeskJet is ideal.

Basics of spreadsheet printer control

Back in the old days—a couple of years ago—most spreadsheets offered precious little in the way of print formatting commands. In 1-2-3, for example, about all you could control was the position of characters in a cell: flush left, centered, or flush right. However, if you were dedicated to better formatting control, there was a way to get it. Most programs had a Setup String command that allowed you to type in an escape sequence which the program send to your printer immediately before printing the spreadsheet itself. In addition, you could embed escape sequences directly within your spreadsheets. If you wanted to print a certain cell in boldface, for instance, you could type in the necessary escape sequence directly into that cell in front of its data.

Today's presentation-quality spreadsheet programs are making most of this painful printer programming unnecessary. With Excel, with Quattro Pro, and with the latest versions of 1-2-3, you can switch fonts or type styles simply by marking a range of cells and choosing a menu command. Nevertheless, if you ever need to send out a DeskJet command that your spreadsheet program won't issue for you, you can still use the old method.

⌒ *Caution:* *Excel does not permit you to enter escape sequences yourself.*

The technique is essentially the same in every major spreadsheet program. To enter a printer command at the prompt for the setup string, you type in the initial escape sequence or control code in decimal notation, preceding the code digits with a backslash (\). You then type the remaining characters of the command from the keyboard. For example, to enter the escape sequence for boldface printing, $^E s_c$(s3B, you would type in **\027(s3B**. You use the same method to enter escape sequences with a cell, but you must precede the escape sequence or control code with a special character, typically one or two vertical bars (|).

Profile: Lotus 1-2-3

$495, 2.3; $595, 3.1+/Lotus Development Corp
55 Cambridge Parkway
Cambridge, MA 02142
617/577-8500

Lotus 1-2-3 is the best-selling computer program of all time, and was largely responsible for the early popularity of the IBM PC. The current versions are Releases 2.3 and 3.1+, with a Windows version right around the corner. Both products feature a built-in mode that lets you format the appearance of numbers, legends, and charts at the same time you enter and edit the data themselves—you can forget about the cumbersome preview systems of past versions. Release 2.3 gives you a healthy selection of high-quality Bitstream fonts to give your reports a slick, typeset look. And all these features work perfectly on the DeskJet—drivers are included for all three DeskJet models. Release 3.1+ has similar printing talents, plus some sophisticated analysis features not found in Release 2.3.

Both versions include a background printing capability, allowing you to send a spreadsheet to your printer and then quickly return to your work.

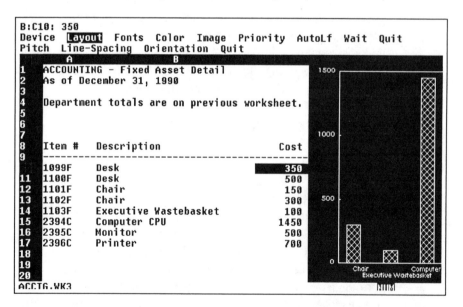

Figure 15-1: *1-2-3 Release 3 lets you control many print features with the menus shown here. You can see a graph and worksheet side by side as you work, and print a graph and worksheet range on the same page.*

Background printing is another name for print spooling, a technique we covered back in Chapter 4. Earlier versions of 1-2-3 did not have the background printing feature.

Though the "WYSIWYG" modes offer excellent quality for your finished reports, there'll be plenty of times when speed matters more than good looks. In these situations, you'll use the standard 1-2-3 display, without all the fancy formatting. Still, you'll need a way to control some basic printer features. 1-2-3 provides some simple controls such as margin settings on menus and dialogs. When these aren't enough, you can also send printer commands to your DeskJet yourself. You have to type them in as escape sequences as outlined previously. To place an escape sequence in your worksheet, you must place it in an empty cell on an empty row. The cell must in the leftmost column of the portion of the worksheet you'll be printing. Precede the command by two vertical bars (|) (you won't see the first bar on your screen).

⌒ **Caution:** *You cannot embed printer commands in 1-2-3 Release 1A.*

Release 3.1+ is a bit more savvy, allowing you to control more print characteristics from a series of simple menus. Specifically, the menus let you set margins, page length, fonts (including boldface and italic type), pitch, line spacing, and page orientation from the menus. You can still use the old system of embedding the commands in your spreadsheet, but you shouldn't combine both methods in the same document.

1-2-3 printer utilities

If you're looking for a way to control your DeskJet more easily from within 1-2-3 for fast, text-mode printouts, look into DeskSet and the Worksheet Utilities. DeskSet is specifically designed to for the DeskJet and 1-2-3, allowing you to visually select margins, line length, headers and footers, and letting you select and download fonts from a pop-up menu. You can print any range of cells without cumbersome macros simply by highlighting the cells and hitting a key. DeskSet's publisher, Intex, also offers a DeskJet font cartridge specifically designed for use with spreadsheets. It includes 68 fonts in sizes from 3.5 to 28 points in both landscape and portrait orientations.

The Worksheet Utilities include PrintSet, a handy tool for creating reuseable libraries of print settings and escape codes. Instead of typing in escape code gibberish cell by cell, you can select from predefined escape codes, singly or in sets, by plain-English description from a scrolling menu. Other components of the package add a formula editor, a search and replace function, and an autosave feature to 1-2-3.

P.D.Queue is an add-in print spooler tailored to 1-2-3 Release 2.*x*. Now that the current versions of 1-2-3 come with their own background print capability, P.D.Queue is probably unnecessary once you upgrade to 2.3—but it does provide fancier control over your print jobs than you'll get with the stock 1-2-3 program.

Access: 1-2-3 Printer Accessories

Worksheet Utilities/$99.95
P.D.Queue/$89.95
Funk Software
222 Third St.
Cambridge MA 02142
800/822-3865; 617/497-6339

DeskSet $95
DeskJet spreadsheet font
cartridge/$179
Intex Solutions, Inc.
161 Highland Ave.,
Needham, MA 02194
617/449-6222

Profile: Quattro Pro

$495/Borland International
1800 Green Hills Rd.
Scotts Valley, CA 95066
408/438-5300

Borland's Quattro Pro is a blunderbuss spreadsheet program that combines a wealth of advanced analysis tools with knock-their-socks-off printed output. Version 3.0 even includes a WYSIWYG mode that lets you work with your formatted spreadsheet on the screen as it will look in print. And it delivers the goods in the confines of ordinary DOS memory—you can build large spreadsheets even if you don't have oodles of expanded memory.

Quattro Pro works superbly with the DeskJet. The chart on the opposite page was printed on a DeskJet Plus, and, while hardly a model of great graphics design, should give you some idea of Quattro Pro can do. The program comes with a slew of high-quality Bitstream fonts (see Figure 15-2) so both spreadsheets and graphs can have typeset-quality text (you can forget about those little stick-like characters of yesterday's spreadsheet). Quattro doesn't download the fonts to your printer, but instead translates them into graphics, whether it's printing a spreadsheet, a chart, or both. In fact, because it prints

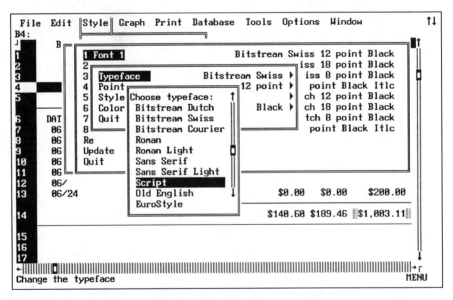

Figure 15-2: *Selecting a typeface with Quattro Pro's menus*

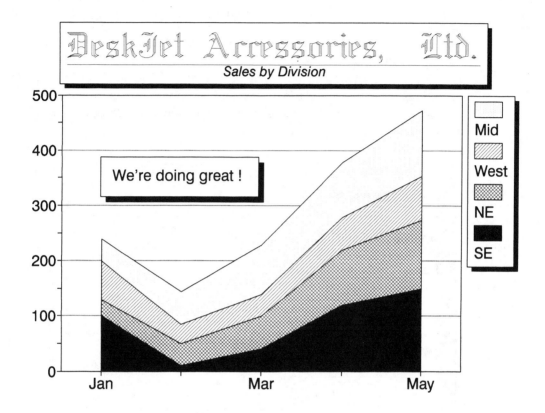

all final-quality output in graphics mode, Quattro can rotate any spreadsheet or chart, complete with all its text, into the "sideways" landscape. If you want a sideways spreadsheet printed in 8-point Old English, you've got it.

For faster spreadsheet output, you can print in a draft mode that uses the DeskJet's text fonts. In this case, you can use the method outlined in the section "Basics of spreadsheet printer control" above to insert escape sequences with the Setup String command, as shown in Figure 15-3, or in individual cells. When embedding an escape sequence in a cell, precede the whole thing with a vertical bar character (|).

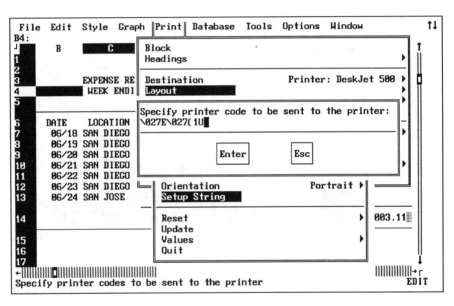

Figure 15-3: *Typing in a printer setup string in Quattro Pro. Use the menu sequence Print—Layout—Setup String to display this window.*

Excel

Excel was the first Windows spreadsheet, and it's still the most popular by far. Version 3 eliminates some of the restrictions on printed output of its predecessors, allowing you to freely mix fonts and to combine spreadsheets and charts on the same page. As a Windows program, Excel can take advantage of all of the DeskJet's features your Windows printer driver gives you access to. See Chapter 9 for the details on Windows and the DeskJet.

Date	Expense	Amount	Vendor
1/1/91	overhead	$1,000	A.B. Properties
1/5/91	overhead	$566	Ace Power & Light
1/5/91	overhead	$600	Wheelin's Gas Co.
1/5/91	overhead	$200	Ralph J Cook Garbage
1/5/91	overhead	$440	City of Franklin
1/6/91	inventory	$16,000	SW Wholesale
1/5/91	salary	$1,000	Mary Fuller
1/5/91	salary	$1,270	Carol Stansen
1/5/91	salary	$945	Jim Parsons
1/5/91	salary	$700	Karen Bush
1/5/91	salary	$1,000	James Gregory
1/5/91	salary	$1,160	Lisa La Flemme
1/5/91	salary	$2,000	Andy Lubert
1/15/91	overhead	$5,000	AR Office
1/15/91	salary	$1,000	Mary Fuller

Figure 15-4: Excel 3.0 imposes few limitations on spreadsheet output format.

Supercalc 5

Supercalc is another top-notch spreadsheet package. It packs a features list comparable to that of 1-2-3 Release 3.0 into DOS's 640K memory space, which means you can use it effectively on a standard PC or XT. The sophistication of Supercalc 5's printouts is only a notch below what you can produce with with Quattro Professional or the 1-2-3 add-ins, with a variety of striking chart formats available from a comprehensive menu system.

In SuperCalc, you control the layout of printed spreadsheets via the Output Options menu, which lets you choose margins, set line width and page length, select page orientation, and set up headers and footers. SuperCalc supports the DeskJet for these basic features, but only the built-in and cartridge fonts can be directly accessed from the program. However, if you're facile with escape sequences, you can insert them freely in your spreadsheets and reports. As in Lotus 1-2-3, you can type in keyboard characters directly and enter non-keyboard control characters by typing the character's 3-digit ASCII code preceded by a backslash (\Ø27 for ^{E}s$_C$, for example). Unlike 1-2-3, however, SuperCalc also lets you enter non-keyboard by typing the equivalent ASCII keyboard sequence from the control code chart in Chapter 22. For example, you can enter ^{E}s$_C$ by typing Ctrl-[or a form feed character by typing Ctrl-L. Printer commands can be up to 240 characters long.

You can enter printer commands in three different places in a SuperCalc spreadsheet. To define a command that will be sent at the beginning of the print session, enter it at the *Setup* choice on the Output Options menu. You can also embed printer commands wherever you need them in the spreadsheet itself. Place the command in an otherwise empty row in the first column that will be included in the printout. As in 1-2-3, you must precede the command with two vertical bars. So, to turn on boldface printing, enter ‖\Ø27(s3B in the cell, pressing ⏎ to finalize the entry.

Finally, if you want to change printer setup for the headers or footers, you can enter printer commands directly within the header. In this case, you must precede the command with a vertical bar and two colons (| ::) and follow it with two colons and vertical bar. So, to print a header in boldface, you would enter the escape sequence in this format:

| ::\Ø27(s3B:: |

The two colons on either side of the command are necessary because SuperCalc uses a vertical bar by itself to indicate placement (right, center, or left) of the header or footer text. So, to print only the center portion of a header in boldface, the complete header entry would look something like this:

October 24, 1991‖::\Ø27(s3B:: | Report Title |::\Ø27(sØB::‖Page 1

Access: Spreadsheets

Supercalc 5.0/$495
Computer Associates
1240 McKay Drive
San Jose, CA 95131
408/432-1727

Excel for Windows, 3.0/$495
Microsoft Corp
16011 NE 36th Way
Redmond, WA 97017
206/882-8080

16

Database Software

∾

The DeskJet isn't fast enough for high-volume database printing, but it's an excellent printer for the kind of several-page summary reports that managers most often generate. In fact, the DeskJet has one advantage over its faster cousins in the LaserJet family when it comes to printing database reports. Its built-in ability to scale fonts to half their normal size means that you can print the internal Courier font at 6 points high and 20 characters per inch, for a readable 160 characters per line and 90 or so lines per page.

Current database management systems offer a lot of control over where your data appears on the page, but little or none over the appearance of the printed data itself—er, themselves. If you want to dress up a report with bold or italic type or even a few different fonts, you'll have to send the necessary escape sequences to the DeskJet yourself. (see Chapter 22 for a complete discussion of all the DeskJet commands you can use). Fortunately, however, most database software makes it relatively easy to accomplish this task.

✂ Tip: *If you do plan to change fonts within a report, remember that most database software uses a row/column system rather than absolute measurements such as inches or points to determine where to print each item. If you change fonts, and especially if you switch to a proportionally spaced font, you'll throw your margins and your column alignment out of whack unless you're very careful. It's safer to use font changes only for titles and other headings. If you stick with one monospaced font for the body of your report you can still add emphasis to important data with italics and boldface.*

Profile: dBase

$895 /Ashton-Tate
20101 Hamilton Ave.
Torrance, CA 90502
213/329-8000

While the dBase programming language remains a widespread database standard, Ashton-Tate's dBase product has fallen on hard times. dBase IV's initial release was bug-ridden and slow, and the company is struggling to generate interest in the update, version 1.1. Many dBase developers continue to use dBase III Plus, or have switched to a dBase-compatible database product such as AlphaFour or FoxPro. Others have jumped ship altogether for competing products such as Paradox, which I'll discuss in the next profile.

Printing in dBase

Whether you're working from the dot prompt or writing a program, all versions of dBase let you output information using the ? command, the ?? command, and the @..SAY.. command. Output from any of these commands goes only to the screen until you explicitly direct it to your printer by giving the command SET PRINT ON, or, in dBase IV, SET DEVICE TO PRINTER.

To use one of the output commands to print normal alphanumeric characters, you just enter the characters between a pair of single or double quotation marks. For example, the command **? "Call me Ishmael."** will print *Call me Ishmael.* on your page.

The difference between the three output commands is as follows: the ? command sends a carriage return and line feed before printing its output, so that the output appears at the left margin of a new line. By contrast, the ?? command outputs to the current cursor position. With @..SAY, you can specify exactly where you want the output to appear on the page in rows and columns. To print *Call me Ishmael* on the 10th row at the 12th column, you would give the command **@ 10,12 SAY "Call me Ishmael."**

After you're through printing, issue the command SET PRINT OFF or SET DEVICE TO SCREEN.

Using your own escape sequences

The only way to achieve full control over the DeskJet from dBase is to send the necessary escape sequences and control codes yourself using any of the dBase output commands (?, ??, or @..SAY..). You can't type the escape character or the other control codes from your keyboard, but you can use the CHR() function to enter the corresponding ASCII code instead. For example, escape character would be CHR(27), while the form feed character would be CHR(12).

To complete an escape sequence, you add a + after the CHR(27), then the remainder of the characters between quotes. So, to ouput the complete escape sequence that turns on boldface printing, you'd enter the command:

? CHR(27) + '(s3B'

dBase IV offers a new ??? command meant specifically for sending commands to your printer. With this command you output any of the non-keyboard control code characters by typing a predefined name between curly braces. These names should be easier to remember than the corresponding ASCII codes. For example, to send the above escape sequence with the ??? command, you would enter **??? "{ESC}(s3B"**. Since this command automatically sends its output to the printer you don't have to give the SET DEVICE TO PRINTER command first. Of course, since you're certainly going to be printing text immediately, you'll have to issue the SET command anyway if you want to see the output on paper.

Using variables for printer commands

With the dBase STORE command, you can define any escape sequence as a reuseable, easy-to-remember variable. That way, you only need to type in the escape sequence once. In the remainder of the current dBase session or program, you can use the variable in output commands as often as you like. dBase will substitute the full escape sequence and send it on to your printer.

For example, if you to print certain portions of a report in boldface, you could define two variables, one for bold type, one to restore ordinary weight type, as follows:

```
STORE "CHR(27) + '(s3B'" TO DJBOLD
STORE "CHR(27) + '(s1B'" TO DJBOLDOFF
```

Note that the entire escape sequence is enclosed in double quotes, and that the part of the sequence made up of keyboard characters is in single quotes. Follow this format when entering any escape sequence.

Then, to print a title in bold, followed by a piece of data in ordinary type, you'd enter the following lines:

```
SET PRINT ON
? &DJBOLD
? "Report Title"
? &DJBOLDOFF
? "First report field"
```

Note that the variables must always be preceded by the & character. Otherwise, the program would print the actual characters you typed between the double quotes of your escape sequences—you'd see *CHR(27) + '(3B'* in your report.

You can further automate your printer control by storing the variable definitions in a disk file for later use. Name all the variables with the same first few characters, the obvious choice being *DJ* as in the examples. Then use the SAVE..ALL LIKE command follows to collect them in a file called DJCMDS:

```
SAVE TO DJCMDS ALL LIKE DJ*
```

When you want to recall the definition file, use the command **RESTORE FROM DJCMDS ADDITIVE**. You'll then again be able to send printer commands via expressions such as **? &DJBOLD**.

⌒ **Caution:** *Be sure to include the ADDITIVE clause when reading in variable definitions stored in a disk file. ADDITIVE merges the variable definitions from the file with whatever variables are already defined. If you enter the RESTORE command without ADDITIVE, you'll lose all your current variables.*

Creating printer control programs

Another way to automate the sending of escape sequences from dBase is to create a miniature dBase program for each sequence. For example, you might create a program file named DJBOLD.PRG containing the lines:

```
SET PRINT ON
? CHR(27) + '(s3B'
SET PRINT OFF
```

Then, to switch the DeskJet to boldface printing, you would run the program by entering the command **DO DJBOLD** at the dot prompt.

Printing reports: basics

The Create Report menu system in dBase III Plus makes it easy to print reports. However, although the menus let you set basic formatting characteristics such as the margins, the number of characters per line, and the number of lines per page, but you can't directly select fonts or control spacing of individual report fields. For ultimate control of your report's appearance, you must write your own report-printing program, placing the desired printer commands where you want them in the program.

As a compromise, however, you can include printer commands at the beginning of a report with one of two methods. Escape sequences may be embedded in the report when you specify the fields to be printed at particular locations. For example, if you wanted to print the contents of the LASTNAME field from your database file in boldface, you would enter **CHR(27) + '(s3B'**

+ FIELD1. With this technique, however, you can't use the variable system described earlier to minimize your typing.

The second approach lets you send a printer command immediately before the report itself is printed. With this method, you define the basic layout of the report via the Create Report menu options, then save the report definition. Next, you create a simple dBase program that sends as many printer commands as you like and then prints the report. For example, if your report file is named SALES90, you might write the following program to print the entire report in boldface type:

RESTORE FROM DJCMDS ADDITIVE

SET PRINT ON	recalls the escape sequence variables you defined and saved earlier.
?? &DJBOLD	djbold is a variable for the escape sequence for bold type
REPORT TO PRINT FORM SALES90	this command prints the report
SET PRINT ON	
?? &DJBOLDOFF	djboldoff represents the escape sequence to restore normal weight type

Using dBase IV printer drivers

dBase IV was the first version of dBase to include printer drivers. These simple modules give you a little better control over various aspects of your printouts such as the orientation, font pitch, graphics resolution, and character style (bold, italics, or underlined).

Consult your dBase manual and disks for information about the set of drivers that came with your copy of dBase. If your version includes specific drivers for the DeskJet, be sure to install them; if not, use the generic LaserJet drivers, which will work for most, if not all, print features. You choose printer drivers using the *Printers* option in the DBSETUP program when you initially install dBase or any time thereafter.

You can select up to four separate printer drivers—one might print in landscape mode, another in portrait mode, for example. Once the drivers are in place and you're running dBase, you can switch between them from the dot prompt with the _prdriver function. To activate a driver named HPDJ.PR2, you would issue the command

_priver = "HPDJ.PR2"

As you can see, you need to know the filename of each driver you plan to use with this command.

Profile: Paradox

$725/Borland International
1800 Green Hills Rd.
Scotts Valley, CA 95066
408/438-5300

Among heavyweight relational database management systems for the PC, one of the top contenders is Borland's Paradox. Although Paradox doesn't come with a predefined DeskJet driver, there are several ways to enter escape sequences and other printer commands in your database printouts.

Whatever combination of these methods you use, enter the commands as follows: for control codes and the escape character numbered lower than 32 decimal in the ASCII code, type in the ASCII code value as a three-character string of numerals preceded by a backslash. So, to enter the escape character, type **\027**. Other characters in the command can be typed in directly from the keyboard.

To select the default printer setup for an entire printout, use Paradox's Custom Configuration Program. Access the Reports menu, then select the *Setups* option. You'll be shown a table of the printer setups already defined. Each setup includes the name of the printer, the printer port to which it is connected, and a Setup String field for the commands that Paradox will send to your printer at the start of each print job. To create customized printer setups for your DeskJet you can edit existing setups or create as many new ones as you like. Just type in your commands in the *Setup String* field using the backslash-ASCII code method described above to enter the escape character and other non-keyboard characters.

To select a default printer setup, enter an asterisk at the end of its name in the Setups table. Thus, if you want Paradox to print your reports in landscape orientation and in condensed 20-pitch type by default, the complete entry for this setup would look like this:

Name	Port	Setup String
DJ-LandscapeCond*	LPT1	\027E\027&l10\027(s20H

You can also control the format of a particular group of fields within a report by creating a pair of special fields containing your the printer commands. Define the basic layout for your report first. When you have all the fields where you want them—and only then—use the command sequence Field — Place — Calculated to create a new field immediately to the left of the field whose format you want to change. At the *Expression:* prompt for the field, type a quotation mark, then enter your escape sequence, and then type a second quote mark. When you press ⏎ to complete the "calculated" field, the command string will appear in your report, shoving the adjacent field to the right. But though your report layout will now look misaligned on the screen, it will print just fine, since the characters in the printer command don't actually print. Insert a second printer command field into the report where you want to switch back to your regular print settings. There's no way to simply cancel the commands you sent in the previous calculated field; instead, you must enter from scratch all the commands necesasry to restore the previous printer setup.

⌐ *Caution: If you use any command that changes the spacing increments, be sure to switch back to the defaults before the end of a line in your report. Otherwise, you'll get varying margins.*

Defining printer commands ahead of time

If you use one or more text formatting commands regularly in your Paradox reports, you don't have to type them in character by character every time—you can have Paradox do it for you. This trick takes advantage of Paradox' ability to link tables (database files) by blank fields. Start by creating a new table named DESKJET. The table must consist of only one row. The first field should be named something like *PrinterLink,* and should be left completely empty. Define as many additional fields as you need for the printer commands you'll be using, and in each field type in an escape sequence and name the field to correspond to the function of the command. For instance *BoldOn, BoldOff,* and so on.

At the very end of the table you wish to print, create a new field also named PrinterLink (or whatever you named the first field in your DESKJET table). Link the report table to the DESKJET table. Now, go on to design your report. After the data fields are laid out, use the Place command to add fields from the DESKJET table wherever you want to introduce a printer command.

Printing graphs

You can print Paradox graphs on the DeskJet by configuring the program for the LaserJet Series II. The only problem you may encounter involves positioning of the graphs when you print them in Paradox's landscape mode.

When Paradox prints a landscape page, it doesn't actually switch the printer into landscape mode. That's good, because the DeskJet can't print graphics in landscape. Instead, Paradox itself stands the chart on end, and sends the resulting rotated dot-by-dot image to the DeskJet in normal portrait mode.

Since the DeskJet responds to exactly the same graphics commands as does the LaserJet, a chart looks the same when printed by either printer. The problem is that its position is shifted slightly to the right (on a landscape-oriendted page). If your chart is especially long along the horizontal axis, its right side may even show up on a second page. That's because the DeskJet has a larger unprintable areas at the top and especially at the bottom of a vertically-oriented page then does the LaserJet. When you print the rotated chart, the top of the page becomes its left margin, which will be located at a slightly more rightward position than with a LaserJet. And there'll be less room for the chart at the right margin. You'll have to restrict yourself to slightly fewer data elements in order to print some types of charts successfully on a single page.

17

Forms, Labels, and Faxes

∾

In this chapter, we'll look at some of the most common, mundane printing chores businesses must face: the production of forms, mailing labels, and fax printouts.

Forms on the DeskJet

Every business needs forms. Forms for invoices, forms for requisitions, forms for bills of lading. Retail shops need inventory forms, employers need time sheets, medical offices need forms for medical histories and insurance billing. And everyone needs tax forms.

With a computer and a high-resolution printer like the DeskJet, you no longer have to rely on (and wait for) a professional printing service to produce forms that are custom-tailored to your needs. It's fairly easy to create forms using a general-purpose desktop publishing program, a simple drawing package, or even a word processor equipped drawing tools such as WordPerfect. After all, forms mainly consist of boxes, lines, and text, simple elements that you can produce in hundreds of programs. If you design many forms, however, your work will be considerably easier if you turn to a specialized forms software package.

The forms software market has expanded dramatically over the past several years. Gone forever are the days when you were forced to design forms via a trial-and-error cycle of entering codes onto a text-mode display and then printing out a draft to see if you got it right. Instead, in all the leading packages, you work with an accurate full-screen facsimile of the printed form using a mouse, just as in a drawing or desktop publishing program. You're also provided with special tools for adding evenly spaced lines, duplicating fields and aligning boxes and other elements of the form, making the work faster than it would be in a general-purpose program. What's more, you can import graphics and place them wherever you like on the form.

But forms software isn't just for designing forms, it's also intended to let you fill them out on your screen, and to keep the information in them organized in database fashion. To fill out a form on the screen, you usually use a separate smaller program to open the form file. When you've typed in all the information, you can save the completed form on disk as a new file, or print it out if you need a paper copy. When you lay out the form, you're able to designate the order in which fields are to be filled in, specify default entries or constraints (for instance, that a field must contain a number between 10 and 100), and create fields whose entries are automatically calculated from other fields.

Some forms packages also provide strong database features. You can import a database file to print its records on your forms, or export the data you've entered in your screen forms to a database file. In FormBase's case, in fact, you can even use the program as a standalone relational database manager, sorting and searching for data across multiple files.

The DeskJet as a forms printer

You wouldn't think of using the DeskJet to print a large supply of forms all at once—the printer is just too slow for that. On the other hand, the DeskJet is excellent for forms design. You can produce a master copy of your form on the DeskJet, then take it to a copy shop or professional printer for economical duplication. In addition, the DeskJet is serviceable for forms that you print as you fill them out.

PerFORM

PerFORM is arguably the best of the modern forms generation programs. PerFORM PRO, the high-end product, runs as a Windows program for form design. That gives you the ability to simultaneously run other programs to exchange data as you work. But it comes with a software module for filling out the forms you've created either in Windows or in GEM, which is fast enough for acceptable performance on older PCs.

PerFORM reads and writes dBase files and can append new records to them. Not only that, it can generate the dBase index files (NDX files) necessary if you want to get at your data fast. If you're graphically oriented, you'll appreciate the fact that PerFORM imports a good variety of graphic file formats. The program also includes a barcode printing feature. A sample form printed on the DeskJet by PerFORM is shown on page 251.

Printing mailing labels

Mailing labels pose an everyday printing challenge. Though the DeskJet is too slow for volume label-printing chores, you can certainly rely on it for turning out smaller numbers of good-looking labels from time to time.

⌢ *Caution:* *While the DeskJet does a creditable job of printing labels, the printer was not designed for this purpose. Specifically, Hewlett-Packard does not recommend the DeskJet for label printing.*

On the off chance you haven't seen them before, printable labels are made of heavy paper with an adhesive on one side applied to a peelable backing. The labels are available in several different precut sizes, and they come on both single sheets and continuous fanfolded sheets with pin-feed sprocket holes.

The most widely used kind of label stock is intended for photocopy machines. But this isn't the type to use with the DeskJet— get the kind for laser printers instead. Whereas copiers can print all the way out to the edges of the paper, the DeskJet, like laser printers, can't. Since copier labels have no margins, your alignment will be off if you print them with a DeskJet. Laser label stock has the necessary margins.

Another problem with copier labels is that the stock isn't flexible enough and tends to jam in the tight printer path of a laser printer or the DeskJet. By contrast, laser label stock is specifically designed for greater flexibility. (Laser labels also require a different adhesive to resist the high temperatures inside the laser printer—this isn't necessary for the cool-running DeskJet.)

Even with laser labels, there's one problem you can't overcome, at least at the moment. It has to do with the water-soluble ink the DeskJet uses. On the slick surface common to all label stock, the ink tends to spread out irregularly, blurring the normally razor-sharp characters. The text is still legible, but it's not as attractive as it should be.

The biggest name in printable labels is Avery. They offer several different sizes of mailing labels, as well as diskette labels for both 5¼" and 3½" floppies. They even have a technical support line you can call (see the tip

TIME SHEET

PERIOD END	MONTH	DAY	YEAR	PERSONNEL #				NAME	DIV

FOR INTERNAL USE ONLY

Description of Work	TIME DISTRIBUTION FOR PERIOD															Total Hours
	1	2	3	4	5	6	7	8	9	10	11	12	13	14	15	
	16	17	18	19	20	21	22	23	24	25	26	27	28	29	30	31
Excused From Office																
Holiday																
Personal Illness - Approved																
Total Hours (incl. overtime)																
Overtime																

Total Hours

List of Expenses and Dollar Value (attach receipts)			
Description	$	Description	$
		Total Expenses	

Overtime Approved By	Time Report Audited

PAGE   OF

Created using PerFORM from Delrina Technology Inc.

below). By the way, Avery says that it's actively working to develop a label paper that will give good results with the DeskJet.

✂ *Tip: Avery is a good source of information about how to print mailing labels using your PC. When you buy a package of Avery laser printer labels, you get a small booklet with tips on printing labels from popular PC and Macintosh programs, including 1-2-3, Microsoft Word, WordPerfect, and dBase. For help over the telephone with label printing, call Avery's support line at* **818/792-8489**.

Mailing label software

While few application programs sport envelope-printing functions, many tackle mailing labels. Any general-purpose database program worth its salt has a built-in routine for printing all the standard mailing label formats that should work well with the DeskJet, assuming you're happy with the internal Courier font.

Still, the label printing functions of database programs are hardly intuitive. If you really want to minimize the hassle of label printing, turn to a utility specifically designed for the job. Many mailing label-printing programs are available as shareware. You might also look into Labels Unlimited, which specifically supports the DeskJet with a selection of scalable Compugraphic fonts ($79.95, Power Up Software, 800/233-1479).

LaserLabel

LaserLabel is a brainchild of Paul Mayer, the same developer who created the GrabPlus envelope printing utility covered in Chapter 18. With its no-nonsense quality and low price, LaserLabel represents a great choice for basic mailing label printing.

As you'd expect, LaserLabel works hand-in-hand with the GrabPlus database, GrabDB. You choose the addresses you want to print from the database by specifying one of the tags you assigned when setting up your address collection (see the profile on GrabPlus a few pages back for details). LaserLabel culls the database file for the addresses marked with the matching tag, and sorts them at print time by last name or by ZIP code.

LaserLabel has a good selection of practical options for controlling the alignment and appearance of the printed labels. It's set up in advance for three popular Avery mailing label sizes, and you just pick the size you have from a simple menu. In a really classy touch, LaserLabel lets you print the first line of the label address in one font, and the rest of the label in another. It will even automatically send the DeskJet commands (escape sequences) that select the fonts you want in these two roles.

The DeskJet is one of the choices on the printer menu, and the program even comes with a set of DeskJet soft fonts and a prefab batch file for downloading them.

Printing faxes

You can use your DeskJet as half of a fax machine if you buy a fax modem board for your PC. Most PC fax software can intercept incoming faxes and turn them into graphics files that you can then print on the DeskJet. If the software that comes with your fax board doesn't measure up, consider Winfax Pro. As the name suggests, this utility runs within Windows where it functions like a printer driver.

When you receive a fax, Winfax takes care of pulling in the data and assembling it into a reproduction of the original image. Winfax also works in the reverse direction, for sending faxes. All you have to do is activate the Winfax driver and then print as you normally would. Winfax steps in, turning the print data into the language of fax, and sending it on its way.

Access: Software for forms, labels, and faxes

PerFORM PRO/$495
Winfax PRO/$119
Delrina Technology
15495 Los Gatos Blvd., #8
Los Gatos, CA 95032
800/268-6082

LaserLabel/$49.95 (with Grab+)
ZPAY Payroll Systems, Inc.
2526 69th Avenue South
St. Petersburg, FL 33712
800/468-4188; 813/866-8233

Special Topics

18

Printing Envelopes

When you go to the trouble of printing your letters with a typeset-quality font, you probably don't want to stuff them into hand-scrawled envelopes. With the DeskJet, you won't have to—unlike most computer printers, the DeskJet comes with a capable envelope-feeder built right in.

Once you know how to load envelopes and learn a few software tricks, you'll find it easy to make your envelopes look just as good as the letters inside. Before we get started with the how-to details, though, you should be aware of two limitations you'll face. The first is one of size. The built-in envelope feeder isn't adjustable, and only accepts regular business size (#10) envelopes. The second catch reflects the DeskJet's intended function as a low-volume personal printer: you have to feed in the envelopes one at a time.

Loading envelopes

The mechanics of feeding an envelope into your printer are simple:

1. Take off the output tray's dark translucent plastic cover.

2. If there's any paper in the output tray, remove it. You'll now be able to see the envelope guides, the two plastic wings attached to either wall of the output tray on the portion that fits into the printer. The guides nearly touch the floor of the output tray, leaving a slit for the envelope.

3. Put the envelope into the guides with its top toward the printer and its address side down, or flap side up, if you prefer. You'll have to bend the envelope a bit to get it past the flippers and down on the floor of the output tray.

4. Keep the *right* side of the envelope flush with the wall of the output tray on that side as you gently push the envelope into the printer as far as you can, until it's stopped by the feeder rollers.

5. Your envelope is now in position, ready for the DeskJet to load it the rest of the way into the paper feed path. The printer will carry out its part of the envelope loading sequence when one of two things happen: either you press the envelope load keys on the keypad, or the DeskJet receives an envelope load software command from your computer.

The correct method for activating the DeskJet's envelope loader depends on the software you're using to print the envelope.

If your software doesn't send the envelope load command for you, you'll need to activate the envelope feeder using the DeskJet's keypad. Press the UP and DOWN keys on the keypad (the two leftmost keys in the back row) simultaneously.

⌒ **Caution:** *If your software sends the envelope command for you, you should not press the envelope keys—if you do, the software will try to load a second envelope, and the one you just fed in will come out unprinted.*

Printing the envelope

Loading an envelope into the DeskJet is simple—a more daunting challenge can be to print the addresses in the right places. Of course, if your word processor comes with its own envelope printing function, it should be able to do the job for you. WordPerfect 5.0, Nota Bene, PFS:Professional Write, and Q&A all have at least adequate envelope printing features. If your word processor lacks such features, or if you want to print envelopes without loading the word processor, read on.

The lowest-budget and least complicated envelope printing solution relies on an ordinary text file you create ahead of time with your word processor. The idea is to use this file as a template for envelope addressing. You place your return address and a dummy recipient address in the template file, positioning each address in the file so that they print in the right places. Then, when you need to print an envelope, you just load a copy of the file into your word processor and type the real recipient's address over the dummy. After you've loaded the envelope itself into the DeskJet (with the procedure outlined earlier in the chapter), you print.

This sounds simple enough, but the tricky part is positioning the text in your template file so that the addresses print where they're supposed to. Of course, the basic idea is to start near the top of the file close to the left margin for the return address, skip down a few lines, and then space over so that the dummy recipient address is somewhere in the middle of the screen. But since the size of the characters, spaces, and lines that you print don't match the ones on your screen, you can't use a ruler to check the spacing on the monitor against a real envelope.

While a little trial and error will quickly produce the results you're after, I've found the following recipe to work well for the DeskJet's internal 12-point, 10-pitch Courier font.

Creating an envelope template file

1. Load your word processor, then set the left margin to 0. The right margin can be anything over 75.

2. Start with the cursor at the very first position in the file (the top left corner).

3. Type in your return address, if any, pressing ⏎ at the end of each line. Align the left border of each line with the one above it.

4. If your return address is only 3 lines long, press ⏎ again. If you don't want a return address at all, press ⏎ 4 times.

5. Press ⏎ 6 more times.

6. Space or tab over to the 33rd column. Type the first line of your dummy recipient address. (By positioning the line with spaces or tabs, not by resetting your margins, you don't have to worry about having a DeskJet driver to get proper spacing.)

7. Type the remaining lines of the dummy address, aligning the left borders of all the lines.

8. Save your envelope template file—call it something like ENV.DOC.

Printing an envelope with the template file

When you want to print an envelope:

1. Place an envelope in the envelope guides as described above.

2. Press the envelope keys on the keypad at the same time to load the envelope (these are the two leftmost keys in the back keypad row).

3. If it's not already selected, select the DeskJet's internal 10-pitch point Courier font by pressing the Font button on the keypad until the adjacent indicator light is lit.

4. Create a new file in your word processor.

5. Without moving the cursor, import the ENV.DOC file into your new file (by importing the template into a new file, rather than opening ENV.DOC itself, you ensure that you won't accidentally change the copy of ENV.DOC on disk).

6. Type your recipient's address over the template's dummy address, without changing the placement of the lines.

7. Print the file. If the envelope doesn't emerge after printing stops, press the FF button on the keypad.

8. If you plan to print the same envelope again, you might want to save the new file under another name.

Adding DeskJet commands to your envelope template

If you'd prefer, you can include the DeskJet commands for loading the envelope and for switching to the correct font in your envelope template file so you don't have to press the keypad buttons. If your word processor has a good DeskJet driver, it may have its own commands for envelope loading and for switching to the right font. Otherwise, you'll need to type in a few escape sequences, so the word processor must allow you to embed printer commands with non-keyboard characters in your files.

If you take the escape sequence route, enter the sequences on the top line of the template file immediately in front of the first part of the return address. For example, to reset the printer, select load an envelope, then select the 10-pitch, 12-point Courier font, the top line of your file would look like this:

$^{E}s_{C}E^{E}s_{C}$&l3h$^{E}s_{C}$(1ØU$^{E}s_{C}$(spsb1Øh12v3T*Return address*

This line includes the several escape sequences just mentioned, plus the first line of the return address.

Using batch files to print envelopes

A slightly more elegant method of printing envelopes is to write a short DOS batch file to automate the process. With this approach, you print the envelope directly from DOS, not from within your word processor. (If you need a refresher course on the basics of creating batch files, see Chapter 9 or your DOS manual).

You'll need to create three files for your complete envelope printing set: a file to set up the printer properly and to print your return address; the batch file that lets you enter the recipient's address, or reads it from a file, and then prints it; and a file to eject the envelope from the printer.

Figure 18-1 on the opposite page shows the three files, set up to print the envelope in 12-point Courier. Create the files using a word processor that lets you enter non-keyboard characters, and store them as plain, unformatted ASCII text files. Create and save each of the files separately, naming them as indicated here. In the first file, the first escape sequence series resets the printer, feeds an envelope, sets the top and left margins to 0, then selects the font. You can enter additional return addresses as needed. The second escape sequence below the return address sets the left margin to 33.

Printing envelopes with ENVDJ.BAT

Once you've saved your three envelope printing files, you're ready to start printing envelopes. At some point in the process, of course, you have to enter the recipient's address. You can do this in one of two ways: by typing it in during the printing process, or by specifying a file that contains it.

To enter the address during the printing process:

1. Switch to the disk drive and directory where ENVDJ.BAT is stored. From the DOS command line, type

    envdj⏎

2. You'll see the following message on the screen:

    Type in the envelope's address,
    pressing [Enter] after each line.
    Press F6 when the address is complete.
    Press Ctrl-Break to quit without printing.

Type in the address, correcting any mistakes as you go with the backspace key. Once you press ⏎ to start a new line, you can't go back to the previous line. When the address is complete, press **F6**. In a moment or two, the DeskJet will load your envelope and start printing.

File 1: Name: ENV1.DJ

$^{E}s_C$E$^{E}s_C$&l3h$^{E}s_C$(1ØU$^{E}s_C$(spsb1Øh12v3T*Return address name*
Street address
City, State, ZIP
$^{E}s_C$&a33L$^{E}s_C$&a11R

File 2: ENVDJ.BAT

```
echo off
cls
if "%1"=="" goto screen
rem If a file name was entered, will print envelope address from file
if not exist %1 goto exit
copy env1.dj+%1+env2.DJ lpt1
goto exit

echo The file you requested is not available.
echo Check the filename and try again. goto exit

:screen
rem If no file name was entered,  type in address on screen
echo
echo
echo Type in the envelope's address,
echo pressing [Enter] after each line.
echo Press F6 when the address is complete.
echo Press Ctrl-Break to quit without printing.
copy env1.dj+con+env2.dj lpt1

:exit
```

File 3: ENV2.DJ

♀

Figure 18-1: *Your three envelope printing files should contain the lines shown above. The ♀ in file 3, ENV2.DJ, represents the form feed control code, ASCII value 12 decimal.*

To print an address stored in a file

Although it's often handy to address envelopes on the fly, it would be nice not to have to retype an address every time you print it. That's why ENVDJ.BAT can print addresses stored in disk files. Even if you're never going to send another letter, once you've typed an address into your word processor at the beginning of a letter, for example, it would be nice not to have to type it again. In most word processors, you can mark a block of text and export the block to a file of its own.

1. Switch to the disk drive and directory where ENVDJ.BAT is stored.

2. At the DOS prompt, type

envdj bob.ltr ⏎

Be sure to include the pathname for your address file, if it's different than the current path. For example, if you're in the DJ directory on drive C:, and the file bob.ltr is stored in the LETTERS directory on drive B:, you'd type

envdj b:\letters\bob.ltr ⏎

3. ENVDJ.BAT takes over at this point and prints the envelope, assuming it finds your file.

Envelope printing software

While templates and batch files work well, the easiest way to print envelopes is with a utility specifically designed for the task. This particular software category has gone from non-existent a few years ago to overcrowded today, and there are now a bewildering multitude of envelope printing programs to choose from. Fortunately, one inexpensive utility stands out from the pack.

Profile: GrabPlus	**$49.95** (with LaserLabel)/**ZPAY Payroll Systems** *2526 69th Avenue South* *St. Petersburg, FL 33712* *800/468-4188; 813/866-8233*

GrabPlus is an exceptionally powerful, exceptionally flexible envelope printing program, yet it's one of the least expensive.

As the name tried to suggest, GrabPlus runs as a memory resident program (TSR) that will "grab" addresses directly from the screen and print them on an envelope while you're running another program. (Like all TSR functions that read the screen, this feature only works with programs running in text mode; some word processors often (Microsoft Word) or always (Ami) use graphics mode instead.)

To use GrabPlus, you position the address you want to print somewhere on the screen and then pop up the utility. You'll see a highlighted block which you can move around with the cursor keys until it covers your address. Once you've got the highlight into position, another key press prints the envelope. Or you can edit the address first, and then print it.

Those are the basics, but GrabPlus does a lot more:

- You can adjust the size of the highlighted address block in both dimensions.

- The program will print either of two return addresses, or none at all, as you decide.

- It works with either of the two standard size envelopes automatically, and you can adjust the printing positions of the return and recipient addresses to accomodate oddball sizes as well, within limits.

- You don't have to grab addresses from the screen. Instead, you can simply type in the address you want in a little window, and print that.

- You can use any DeskJet font you like for your addresses—in fact, you can use a separate font for the top line

- You can run GrabPlus in a swap-to-disk mode that requires only 6K of system RAM when the program isn't active, or in a faster full-strength memory resident mode requiring about 60K, or as a non-memory resident ordinary DOS application for typed-in addresses. A separate configuration program lets you select defaults for all the above options and others.

The latest release of GrabPlus includes a Windows version of the program that can print envelopes while you are in the middle of using any other Windows programs. You can choose fonts and add graphical logos to your envelopes from self-explanatory menus.

In addition to the pop-up envelope printer itself, the GrabPlus package includes a separate database program for storing and retrieving your frequently-used envelope addresses. You can enter addresses into the database either by typing them in on a simple screen, or by importing them from an outside file.

In the process, you can assign up to five "tags" to each address to help you track related addresses. Let's say you run a record store for collectors servicing several distinct interest groups. You might tag the addresses of your Rockabilly customers with an "R", the Do-wop customers with a "D", and the Old-timey customers with an "O." Then, when you want to send all the Do-wop customers a special mailing advertising a new shipment of obscure recordings by streetcorner groups, you just have GrabDB search your database for the D-tagged addresses.

GrabDB will also search the database file for individual names. Either way, when you find an address you want to print, GrabDB taps GrabPlus and out comes the envelope. But GrabDB has an automatic address formatting feature that goes GrabPlus one better. At the touch of a function key, you can choose any one of these three address formats. GrabDB can also export addresses to other programs such as mail-mergers or other databases. Again, you can use the tag system to export only the addresses that fall into a certain category.

19

Printing Screenshots

∾

It's often handy to print what you see on the screen. In a pinch, screen snapshots or "screenshots" make great quick-and-dirty reminders and crib sheets. Maybe you're due at a meeting and you want to make a fast copy of a single paragraph or a bar chart from a longer file. Maybe you've just received a short memo in your electronic mailbox, and you'd like to print it out without saving it on disk first.

But while printing a screenshot may save you a little time in situations like these, you could print the same information using a more conventional approach (such as the Print command in your word processor). What screenshots can do that other printing methods can't is give you an illustration of what the entire screen looks like, not just your file. When you need a way to document how a piece of software works and looks on the screen—its menus, dialog boxes, prompts, and so on—screenshots are far quicker and more accurate than freehand sketches and much cheaper than a professional typesetter or graphics artist.

It's easy to guess who needs this capability most: people who write or publish software manuals and software reviews. But even if you're in another line of work, there may well come a time when you'll want to print some software screens. You've probably experienced the frustration of trying to talk a computer novice through a maze of commands and menus. Print a few key screens that your apprentices can refer to as they work, and everything will seem much clearer to them. Among experienced users, a judiciously chosen screen shot can replace a long-winded technical explanation of how a spreadsheet macro works, or how you achieved a fancy desktop publishing layout.

Printing screens versus saving screen files

There are two routes to obtaining printed screenshots: printing the screen directly, while you're viewing it, and recording the screen image as a disk file to be printed later. The first approach has the advantage that you get your results immediately, you don't waste time and disk space saving and then printing a file. The primary drawback is that you can't incorporate the screen image into another document. If you save the screenshot as a file, you can merge it with text and other graphics in a word processor or desktop publishing program—perfect if you're illustrating a report, or writing a commercial software manual, or even putting together your own home-grown tutorial.

Text screens versus graphics screens

Just like the DeskJet, your PC has two main ways of displaying information. In text modes, you can only display a standard set of characters, and only in predetermined rows and columns on the screen. What's really going on is that each character has its own ASCII code, and special circuits in the PC automatically translate each code into a preset pattern of screen dots.

To print a screenshot of a text screen, all you have to to do is send the ASCII codes of the characters on the screen to the DeskJet. Likewise, if you're capturing the screenshot in a file, the file is mainly just a record of the screen ASCII codes. Fortunately for PC owners, the DeskJet's standard character set matches the character set you see on the screen. So, whether you print directly or from a stored file, you don't have to do anything special to set up the printer for screenshot printing. Because text mode screenshots consist of ASCII codes instead of the actual dots on the screen, you can print them in any font you like. In the case of stored files, you may even be able to edit them in your word processor.

When your display is in a graphics mode, by contrast, each and every dot you see—even a dot that's part of a text character—has to be placed independently on the screen by the PC's main microprocessor. In this case, without ASCII codes to fall back on, printing the screenshot entails sending every individual dot to the DeskJet. Similarly, graphics screenshot files consist of dot-by-dot bitmaps of the image.

Since you're not locked into the DeskJet's built-in preformed text characters, it's possible to squish, stretch, or otherwise manipulate the screen image before you print it. On the other hand, switching to another font doesn't do anything for text in the screenshot, since you're printing it in graphics mode.

Using DOS to print screenshots

The simplest way to get a printout of what you see on the screen is with the DOS "print screen" key. If your PC screen is in a text mode, just press Shift-Prt Sc, and your computer will immediately start sending all the ASCII characters on the screen to your DeskJet.

Though the print screen function works fairly well for ordinary text screens, it has many limitations. For one thing, the DeskJet can't print some PC screen characters. Yes, it's true that the little happy faces and musical notes you see on some screens are represented in the DeskJet's PC-8 character set. But unless the DeskJet receives a special command first—and DOS doesn't send it—the printer interprets these low-numbered ASCII codes as control codes instead of printable text. With DOS 5.0, however, you can print graphics screens on the DeskJet with the Shift-Prt Sc command. You must first load the graphics driver with the command

graphics deskjet

at the DOS prompt.

Another problem with DOS' screen printer is that there's no option for "printing" the screens to a disk file, so you can't incorporate the screen images into other documents. Worse yet, many programs disable the print screen function.

Using screen capture software

For printing all but the simplest text screens, a memory resident screen "capture" utility is far preferable to DOS. A good capture utility will handle both text and graphics modes, and will reproduce either type of screen accurately on the DeskJet.

To use a screen capture program, you start the utility and then run your application software. When you see a screen that you want to capture, you press a special hotkey to activate the capture function. At this point, you can either print the screen directly, or store the screen image in a disk file. Depending on the utility, you may be able to edit your screenshot files before you print them, or translate them into other file formats.

Choosing a screen capture utility

As a look at the Access box will convince you, screen capture utilities have proliferated over the past few years. Here are my recommendations: for both DOS and Windows graphics screens, Collage Plus is the best program I've found for screen capture. It requires little memory, it's very quick, it puts out good-looking images, and it can save screens in a variety of PCX and TIFF formats. Collage Plus also does a fine job with text screens, but if you want to be able to edit them, get HotShot Graphics.

But what do I know? If you want to do your own comparisons of screen capture utilities, some of the criteria you should consider when deciding on a capture program are listed below.

✂ *Tip: If you capture screens extensively, it's a very good idea to buy two or more screenshot utilities. I've repeatedly had the experience of being unable to capture a screen with one utility—apparently because of some obscure incompatibility between the two programs—but having success when I switched to a different screen capture routine.*

Video mode compatibility: A basic requirement is that your screen capture utility should work in the video modes you use to display your screens. If you want to record all the fine detail on your 1600 x 1200 ultra high-resolution monitor, a capture utility that tops out at VGA resolution (640 x 480) won't do. You can safely assume that every capture utility supports the Big Four graphics video modes: CGA, Hercules, EGA, and VGA. Obviously, if the program captures text screens, it will also work in the 25-line monochrome adapter (MDA) mode. On the other hand, support for the extended text modes of the EGA (43 lines) and VGA (50 lines) isn't universal. If you use one of these text modes or an uncommon graphics mode, make sure the utility you buy can capture its screens.

DeskJet compatibility: When choosing a screen capture utility, it may or may not matter whether the utility works directly with the DeskJet. Of course, if you want to use the utility itself to print the screenshots, it should have a DeskJet-specific driver, or at least a LaserJet driver that works well with the DeskJet. On the other hand, if you're planning to merge the screenshots into a larger document with a word processor or desktop publishing program, your want a utility that saves the screen files in a format understood by the destination program.

File format: If you're planning to merge screenshots into other documents, it's helpful if the capture program saves the screen files in a format your graphics program, word processor, or desktop publishing program can read directly. Otherwise, you'll have to run the non-standard screen files through a conversion process to produce a useable format.

Several utilities save screen files in PC Paintbrush .PCX format, the most widly used PC graphics format—the list includes GrafPlus, PCXGrab, and the Frieze utility that comes with PC Paintbrush itself. Obviously, this is ideal if you want to edit your screenshots with PC Paintbrush. But it's also good if you're using WordPerfect or any of the major desktop publishing programs, including Ventura and PageMaker, which can accept .PCX files.

Capture programs that generate non-standard screenshot files are always part of a larger software package that includes format conversion functions. Converting from one format to another consumes both time and disk space, but at least you end up with a screenshot file you can use. HiJaak is primarily marketed as a file-conversion program, with screen capture thrown in to boot. HotShot Graphics' format conversion options are a little less extensive, but the program also offers a full graphics editor and a graphics database, and has special features for working with text screens.

Memory requirements: Since these screen capture utilities are memory resident, they consume memory that your main application program may need. It won't do you much good to load your screen capture program and find that there's no room left to run the program whose screens you want to capture. GrafPlus and WordPerfect's Grab are the most frugal of the pack, weighing in at around 15K. They're followed by Hotshot Grab at 23K, pcxGrab and Pizazz Plus at around 35K. The most voracious capture program is HiJaak, which eats up more than 45K of your system RAM. (All of these figures are approximate, and depend on the type of display adapter in your computer.)

Editing capabilities: The simplest capture utilities just capture screens. Others let you modify the resulting images to one degree or another. GrafPlus, for example, lets you change the size of the image, crop it, change the aspect ratio, or reverse the screen colors (black to white and vice versa). Cropping lets you use only a particular portion of the screen image. Because screen dots (pixels) are rectangular while the dots the DeskJet prints are square, printed screenshots often look vertically squashed. By adjusting the aspect ratio (the ratio of height to width) you can correct for this proportion problem. And while many monitors display bright characters against a dark background, people expect to see dark characters on a white background in printed text—which is why the ability to reverse the colors or shades in the screenshot can come in handy.

More extensive editing capabilities are supplied in Hotshot Graphics and PC Paintbrush, the full-scale paint-style graphics packages of which Hotshot

Grab and Frieze are respectively a part. Both Hotshot Graphics and PC Paintbrush treat your screenshots like any other graphic, allowing you to add new lines, shapes, colors, and text, and to copy or delete any portion of the image.

♪ ***Note:*** *WordPerfect includes a utility called Grab which saves files in WordPerfect's .WPG graphics format, so you don't have to buy a separate product or worry about file format compatibility. However, such freebies don't have the range of options available with the capture packages sold separately.*

Hotshot Graphics

Hotshot Graphics started life as a screen capture utility, but it's grown into a complete screen image/graphics package. In addition to a pair of screen capture utilities, Hotshot Graphics capabilities include full-scale image editing, file format conversion, and a simple filing system for your image files. No DeskJet driver is provided, but the LaserJet driver substitutes adequately.

Hotshot Grab, the screen capture part of the package, takes only about 23K of RAM, supports a good variety of video display systems, and has worked reliably for me. Unlike GrafPlus, Hotshot Grab doesn't let you print your screenshots directly. Instead, you type in a filename for the screenshot you want to store into a little window. A second little window then pops up where you can enter a detailed description of the image. When that's done, Grab stores the file.

Hotshot has two separate editing modes for your screenshots, one for text images, the other for graphics. In the graphics department, Hotshot's paint-type (bit-mapped) editing features rival those of PC Paintbrush. You can draw shapes and lines, paint colored swatches, inverse existing colors, and type graphics text. In fact, you're not limited to editing files you've captured with Grab—you can edit .PCX and .IMG files from other programs, or even paint new graphics from scratch. And you can interconvert captured screens and other graphics files between the .PCX, .IMG, TIFF, WordPerfect .WPG, MacPaint, and EPS formats, among others.

But Hotshot's most unique capabilities have to do with editing text-based screenshots. To emphasize particular portions of the screen image, you can highlight any area with colors or inverse video, or draw borders or boxes around it. You can type new characters or delete old ones, and you can insert special characters such as male and female symbols from a pop-up table. You can even move or copy blocks of the text image from one location to another.

Though Hotshot offers an excellent collection of features, I have to mention some of its weak points. My biggest gripe is that Hotshot tends to print very slowly. I've found it more efficient to transfer images to a program such as Ventura Publisher and print them there. Another problem is that the keystrokes you have to use for some functions aren't very intuitive, and the menu system is a bit on the clunky side. In the graphics editor, the menus respond too slowly. Despite these weaknesses, I recommend that you consider Hotshot Graphics seriously if you're interested in a one-product solution to your basic PC screen image and graphics needs.

Creating screenshots in Windows

Taking snapshots of your Windows screens used to be tricky, but Windows itself now has a built-in screen capture routine that usually actually works. If the built-in routine isn't enough, several Windows-specific screen capture utilities offer more options.

✂ Tip: If you're going to be printing your screen shots on the DeskJet, they're going to be in black and white. For better looking printouts, use the Windows Control Panel to select black and white shades for your screen before you capture.

To capture the current screen, placing it on the Windows clipboard, just press Prt Sc. If this procedure doesn't work (usually, this means you have an older keyboard), try pressing Alt-Prt Sc or Shift-Prt Sc.

If you're running Windows in 386 Enhanced mode, you can also capture only the currently active window. To do this, activate the window you want to capture and press Alt-Prt Sc. Again, if nothing happens, try Shift-Prt Sc as well.

For higher-quality screenshot files, and for more options on which parts of the screen to capture, turn to Tiffany Plus, Collage Plus, or Do-DOT. Tiffany gives you a choice of black and white or color capture, saving in a variety of flavors of TIFF and PCX file formats. TIFFANY works with any Windows-compatible monitor, so no special printer information is required. The problem with this program is that it's so slow—you can wear holes in your fingertips waiting for the capture to be completed.

Collage Plus, my overall favorite, now comes with a Windows screen capture program. This lets you save any region of the screen very readily—more easily than you can in Tiffany—and it also gives you considerably faster performance than does Tiffany. Do-DOT is perhaps primarily a graphics translation program, allowing you to convert one type of file to another, preserving the picture it contains. But Do-DOT also includes an excellent screen capture routine, and the resulting file can be saved in many more formats than either of the other programs can manage. These include a variety of FAX formats, so that theoretically you could easily transfer a captured image over the fax lines.

Merging screenshots in word processor documents

WordPerfect, Microsoft Word, WordStar, and Amí can all integrate graphics such as screenshots into text documents. If you favor another word processor without this capability, you can still place graphics into your text via the Inset utility, covered in Chapter 11.

Access: Screen Capture Utilities

Collage Plus/$89
Inner Media, Inc.
60 Plain Road
Hollis, NH 03049
800/962-2949; 603/465-3216

HiJaak /$149
Inset Systems, Inc.
12 Mill Plain Rd.
Danbury, CT 06811
203/775-5866

pcxGrab (included in PCX Programmer's Toolkit)/$195
Genus Microprogramming
11315 Meadow Lake
Houston, TX 77077
800/227-0918; 713/870-0737

HotShot Graphics/$249
HotShot Grab/$99
Symsoft
Call Box 5
Incline Village, NV 89450
702/832-4300

Tiffany Plus/$89
Anderson Consulting & Software
P.O. Box 40
North Bonneville, WA 98639
800/733-9633

Frieze (included in PC Paintbrush)
ZSoft
450 Franklin Rd, Suite 100
Marietta, GA 30067
404/428-0008

GrafPlus $49.95
Jewell Technologies, Inc.
4740 44th Ave. SW #203
Seattle, WA 98116
206/937-1081

Pizazz Plus/$149
Application Techniques
10 Lomar Park Drive
Pepperell, MA 01463
800/433-5201; 508/433-5201

The Graphics Link Plus/$149
HSC Software
1661 Lincoln Blvd., Suite 101
Santa Monica, CA 90404
213/392-8441

20

Pretty in PostScript

∾

Chalk it up to the perverse human impulse that drives us to rise to impossible challenges just because they're there. Despite major technical obstacles, at least three companies have succeeded in creating PC software that turns your $500 DeskJet into an excellent imitation of a PostScript printer.

The DeskJet already prints high quality text and graphics—why should you bother with PostScript? It depends entirely on how much you covet the sophisticated typographical control and amazing special effects that Post-Script makes possible, and that the DeskJet can't hope to produce without help. Though the PostScript language has its critics and its challengers, it remains the only vehicle for advanced printing features that even begins to qualify as a standard in the personal computer industry. In fact, almost every high-quality graphics or desktop publishing program achieves its best output with a PostScript printer.

✂ *Tip:*   *If you want to use the GEM version of Ventura with your DeskJet, a PostScript interpreter or emulation program is one of the few ways to do it. To date, the folks at Xerox have yet to deliver a DeskJet driver, and none appears to be on the horizon. But all three PostScript interpreters covered in this chapter do an excellent job with Ventura printouts.*

GoScript from LaserGo, Freedom of Press from CAI, and UltraScript from QMS all deftly manage the metamorphic feat of turning the DeskJet into a PostScript workalike. Before we do, an examination of some basics relevant to all three is in order.

How does it work?

Inside every PC printer, including the DeskJet, lurks a specialized electronic intelligence. In the DeskJet's case, HP has provided a built-in computer with impressive smarts. The DeskJet's microprocessor can handle the complexities of translating incoming ASCII characters and graphics data into dots on the printed page, and of carrying out commands such as "set a 1" left margin," or "move to the middle of the page and then start printing." But in comparsion to a PostScript printer, the DeskJet is a relatively simple device.

That's because the PostScript language itself is so complex. A PostScript file consists of a long series of software commands specifying every aspect of the page to be printed in intricate detail. In PostScript, most printed shapes, including text characters, are represented as mathematically-described objects rather than as collections of dots (see Chapters 3 and 13 for more on the types of PC graphics). In addition to the descriptions of individual objects, many PostScript files also include complex instructions that tell the printer how to perform repeated tasks that are unique to that file. In other words, a PostScript file is truly a computer program, comparable to a program written in C or BASIC.

The PostScript printer must digest the objects and programming instructions it receives and translate them into a simple bitmap image of which dots are to be printed where. The printer constructs the bitmap for one entire page at a time, prints that page, and then moves on to the calculations for the next page.

To handle all this complexity, a PostScript printer needs a full-scale microprocessor of the same caliber, or better, as the one in a fast AT-compatible. The printer must also be permanently equipped with a highly sophisticated program of its own for interpreting the incoming PostScript files. And it must be endowed with large amounts of memory for storing the programs it receives, and for "composing" the final image of each page. These additional components explain why a PostScript machine costs so much more than an otherwise comparable laser printer such as the LaserJet. Although a LaserJet also composes and prints a page at a time, it does so by simply assembling the bitmap data it receives from the computer and its font files into a larger, page-sized bitmap.

On the other hand, once a PostScript printer has finished with its page description computations, all it does is print a pattern of dots, just like a standard LaserJet. Recognizing that the printer's only indispensable job is to place ink on the page, PostScript interpreter programs allow your PC to take back responsibility for PostScript-specific printing chores: interpreting the PostScript file, and converting the resulting commands into a final bitmap of the page to be printed. After all, the PC contains a sophisticated microprocessor, and it has the necessary memory; add a program that can interpret and execute the PostScript code, and your PC should theoretically be able to duplicate the PostScript printer's page composition abilities.

Working entirely with your system's own resources, the interpreter program interprets the PostScript code and performs the calculations, storing the final bitmap temporarily in RAM or on your hard disk. It then feeds the bitmap data to your printer a line at a time.

To the DeskJet, there's nothing to distinguish the incoming graphics data from the data it would receive from a non-PostScript program. The DeskJet knows how to print dots, and dots are all it is asked to print—all the printer sees are streams of numbers representing the dots it is to lay down, along with a few simple commands.

How well does it work?

While the idea of using a PC to duplicate a PostScript printer's computational functions is sound in concept, the complexities of PostScript make it an ambitious project. Nevertheless, several persistent programmers seem to have carried it off.

All three of the interpreter packages profiled below do an excellent job of producing PostScript printouts on the DeskJet. They can all reproduce the fancy special effects at which PostScript excels—greyscale shading, graduated fills of graphical shapes, scaled and rotated text—on the DeskJet. The opposite page shows three PostScript files printed by GoScript on the DeskJet (the musical example was created with Passport Designs' Score, a music printing program).

But it's so slow...

If you've ever used a PostScript laser printer, there is one major difference you'll notice when you print PostScript files on the DeskJet. To state it baldly, the DeskJet is a slow PostScript printer.

You can blame the DeskJet's leisurely performance partly on the fact that the printer just isn't as fast as a laser machine when it comes to actually putting dots on the page. Leaving PostScript out of the picture for a second, the DeskJet takes much longer to print a page of graphics that its older cousin the LaserJet requires.

Still, your PC and the interpreter packages have to take some of the blame for the slowdown. Your PC is just not as quick at turning PostScript code into bitmap images as a specialized PostScript printer is. After all, the computer inside a PostScript machine is optimized for the specific sorts of image-related calculations it must perform, so it has an innate advantage over any general-purpose PC. Installing a math coprocessor in your computer will improve the speed of any of the PostScript emulation products considerably.

Trouble with Type 1 fonts

One other stumbling block the interpreter packages have had to face has to do with text. Type 1 PostScript typefaces from Adobe Systems give the highest

*W*hy is it no one ever sent me yet
One perfect limousine, do you suppose?
Ah no, it's always just my luck to get
One perfect rose.
                    —Dorothy Parker

quality in print, but they're stored in an encrypted format that is hard to digest. To date, Freedom of the Press is the only one of the three programs that has solved the problem fully. You can set your application software to use Type 1 typefaces just as you would if you were printing to a real PostScript printer. UltraScript can make use of Type 1 fonts, but only indirectly; you have to convert them to a special proprietary format first. So far GoScript is still unable to process Type 1 typefaces, but a major upgrade that removes that limitation is right around the corner.

These limitations are worth noting, but they hardly detract from the minor miracle the PostScript interpreters accomplish. For about $1000 at street prices, you can buy both a DeskJet and PostScript interpreter software. Assuming your PC already has enough memory to run the interpreter program, that's all you'll have to pay for a PostScript system that can equal the output quality of printers costing thousands of dollars more. That ought to make you feel pretty good about waiting that extra minute or three for your PostScript pages to pop out.

PostScript emulation roundup: GoScript, Freedom of Press, UltraScript

All three of the competing PostScript emulators achieve roughly equivalent quality on the DeskJet, and all three turn out finished pages at about the same speed. Still, there are important differences to note among them.

One concerns printing convenience. Printing with GoScript or the non-Windows versions of Freedom of Press requires a two-step process. First, you must get your application program to save its PostScript printer output as a file on disk instead of sending it directly to the printer. Next, you exit the application program and start the PostScript emulator. This system works, but it's hardly ideal. If you find anything in your printout that needs correcting, you must restart your application software and go through the whole cycle again.

Using UltraScript or the new Windows version of Freedom of Press is far simpler. To use either of these products, you just tell the application software that you want to print to a PostScript printer, just as if you'd actually attached a LaserWriter or other PostScript machine to your PC instead of the lowly

DeskJet. Then, when you print a file, the UltraScript interpreter commandeers the PostScript code generated by your software before it ever gets to the printer port and translates it into DeskJet instructions.

Another important consideration in choosing a PostScript emulation package is how much memory it requires in your PC. Although all the products work best with plenty of additional memory (2 megabytes or more is ideal), GoScript and Freedom of Press aren't too demanding, and will perform acceptably in a 640K machine. UltraScript needs 800K of extended memory (actually, UltraScript itself can run in a 640K by itself, but in this situation you can't print directly from your application software).

UltraScript includes the most typefaces, 47 in the Plus version compared to 35 in Freedom of Press and GoScript Plus. Currently, only Freedom of Press supports color printers such as HP's PaintJet, so it's a good choice if you own such a printer as well as the DeskJet. On the other hand, would be PostScript programmers should note that Freedom of Press lacks the interactive Post-Script mode provided by both GoScript and UltraScript. In the interactive

---

Access: PostScript Interpreter Software

GoScript $195
GoScript Plus $395
Lasergo, Inc.
9235 Trade Place, Suite A
San Diego, CA 92126
619/450-4600

UltraScript pc $195
UltraScript pc Plus $445
QMS, Inc.
One Magnum Pass
Mobile, AL 36618
205/633-4300

Freedom of Press/$495
Freedom of Press Light/$98
Custom Applications, Inc.
900 Technology Park Dr., Bldg B
Billerica, MA 01821
800/873-4367; 508/667-8585

mode, you can send PostScript commands to the program and receive an immediate, informative response when you make a programming error.

Pricing is comparable for the top-of-the line versions of all three products. However, Freedom of Press Light is the only one of the bunch that's truly affordable, and it still has all the really important capabilities, including Type 1 support. At the moment, it's the best choice for price-conscious DeskJet users.

21

Printing with the Macintosh

∾

While it's hardly a match made in heaven, the union of the DeskJet and an Apple Macintosh can grow into an amiable, productive relationship. The DeskJet certainly has some important limitations compared to printers designed specifically for the Mac, but with a little effort and the right software, you can get the the printer to produce both text and graphics from just about any Mac program, with good to excellent results.

The most likely reason you'd want to arrange this marriage is that you happen to wind up with both machines through some serendipitous combination of circumstances. In many companies, PCs and Macintoshs share the same offices, each computer valued for its own strengths. This being the case, the growing popularity of the DeskJet makes it increasingly likely that Mac users will find themselves in an office where the DeskJet is the only printer in the vicinity.

On the other hand, you shouldn't go out and intentionally buy a regular DeskJet just for use with a Mac. A far better choice would be HP's DeskWriter, a revamped DeskJet designed specifically for the Macintosh.

Hybrid capabilities

When your Mac-DeskJet hybrid system is properly configured, you'll be able to print both text and graphics from most application programs. But don't be surprised if you run into occasional problems or quirks with particular programs—there are too many variables for everything to work right every time.

Graphics: The simplest kind of Macintosh graphics files are based directly on the bitmapped images you see on the screen—MacPaint files are the classic example. The DeskJet can handle this type of graphic quite capably. The Macintosh screen displays 72 dots per inch, which is almost exactly one-fourth of the 300 dpi the DeskJet can print. To print a MacPaint graphic, the DeskJet lays down a four-by-four solid block of dots for each black dot in the original, thus rendering the image at 75 dpi. The slight discrepancy between the screen and printed resolutions means that the graphic comes out a bit reduced on paper, about 96% of the original's size (since there are slightly more dots per inch, each 16-dot block printed by the DeskJet is slightly smaller than the corresponding screen pixel).

Many other Macintosh graphics programs are designed to work with the 300-dpi Apple LaserWriter. Since the DeskJet prints at 300 dpi as well, it can reproduce these graphics flawlessly. The exception, of course, is PostScript graphics, which you just can't print on a DeskJet. PostScript-based programs such as Adobe Illustrator and Aldus Freehand are incompatible with the DeskJet.

Text: depending on the utility software you buy, you may have several options for printing Macintosh text on your DeskJet. The first method simply places the DeskJet in graphics mode and prints a dot-for-dot reproduction of the characters you see on your screen. At its best, this approach gives you reasonably readable text—at a resolution of 75 dots per inch, the outlines of the characters will be noticeably jagged. This is method is also much slower than printing in true text mode.

MacPrint, one of the best Mac-to-DeskJet utilities, uses a modified version of this approach to get far better resolution. By shrinking larger versions of the same fonts you see on the Mac's screen, MacPrint can use the DeskJet's graphics mode to print 150 or 300 dpi text. Results with this method look great, but it's even slower than printing the same-size screen fonts (see the profile on MacPrint for more details).

To get the best combination of quality and speed you need a way to access the DeskJet's own fonts from the Macintosh. It's not difficult for a DeskJet driver to put the DeskJet in text mode and simply send the sequence of characters in your file. Theoretically, the driver can select any DeskJet font you wish to use for the task.

The fly in the ointment is that your Mac's regular screen fonts don't correspond to the DeskJet's fonts. As a result, the spacing between the characters you print and those on the screen doesn't match. Justifying your text is out of the question, unless you're using a monospaced typeface like Courier. Again, MacPrint offers a solution, by supplying Macintosh screen versions of the common DeskJet fonts.

⌒ *Caution: Macintosh PostScript fonts, of course, won't print on the DeskJet.*

How to mix Apples and DeskJets

As with any computer/printer pairing, you have both hardware and software considerations to worry about when you try to print on the DeskJet from the Macintosh.

Connecting the hardware

The hardware part of the equation is actually very straightforward, as long as you're trying to use the DeskJet with a single Macintosh, and not on a network. The Mac's printer port is of the serial variety, and the DeskJet has a built-in serial port, so all you need is a serial cable with the proper connectors on either end.

Before you actually connect the cable, though, you should first set the DeskJet to communicate at its fastest possible serial speed, 19,200 bits per second (baud). As you may know, the Mac can talk considerably faster, but the DeskJet sets the limits here. At any rate, making this change doubles the DeskJet's default speed, and will make printing much faster.

To set the DeskJet to the new speed, you need to change the position of one of the little function (DIP) switches located on the lower front of the printer, a little to the right of center. Here's how:

1. Make sure the printer is off.

2. Scrounge up a small flatblade screwdriver, the tinier the better. In a pinch, a dinner knife, ball point pen, or similar instrument will suffice.

3. There are two banks of switches recessed behind cutouts in the DeskJet's plastic housing. Stand the printer on its rear end so you can see the switches and locate Bank B, the one on the right.

4. Assuming no one has changed the switch settings since your DeskJet left the factory, all of the switches will be pointing towards you (downward when the printer is sitting flat). Your job is to flip the fifth switch in Bank B so that it points away from you (or up with the printer in its normal position). Use the screwdriver to do the job, making sure you don't disturb any of the other switches.

Now go ahead and can connect the Mac to the DeskJet with the appropriate cable.

Network connections

The DeskJet can't be connected directly to an AppleTalk network, since it doesn't understand AppleTalk messages. However, you can buy special translating devices that convert AppleTalk into the DeskJet's lingo.

Using printer drivers

When it comes to the software part of the Mac-DeskJet connection, the major challenge is to find a good utility designed for the job. The core of any such utility is a DeskJet driver that you place in your Mac's system folder alongside the LaserWriter and/or ImageWriter drivers you already have there.

To print to the DeskJet, you must first select the utility's new DeskJet driver using the Chooser. Typically, you'll be asked at this point to choose a serial communications speed for the hookup—select 19200 by clicking on the corresponding button.

You make other printer setup choices from your application software menus. Depending on the driver you're using, you may be able to select paper size, choose between portrait and landscape orientation (remember, the DeskJet's landscape mode can only print in a few special fonts, and does not print graphics at all), and select which text printing method of those described earlier you want to use.

Speeding things up

Because of the Macintosh's heavy reliance on graphics, printing to the DeskJet can be painfully slow. I highly recommend a Mac print spooling utility such as SuperMac Software's SuperLaserSpool—it won't speed up the actual printing, but it will let you get back to your work in your application software in a fraction of the time that you'd otherwise have to wait (for more information about how print spoolers work, see Chapter 4).

Profile: MacPrint

$149/Insight Development Corp.
2200 Powell St., Suite 500
Emeryville, CA 94608
415/652-4115

If you're set on using your DeskJet with a Macintosh, do yourself a big favor and get a copy of Insight Development's MacPrint.

Like most DeskJet utilities, MacPrint works with any Hewlett-Packard PCL printer, which means all the models in the LaserJet family as well as the

DeskJet. The package consists of a driver for each of the printers it supports—to its credit, it provides separate drivers for the DeskJet and DeskJet Plus—along with a set of compressed fonts and a font generating utility.

MacPrint handles graphics from most Mac programs capably, the exception being any PostScript output. But it's in text printing that MacPrint really shines. The MacPrint driver lets you choose between printing text as graphics or with the DeskJet's own fonts, and it handles either option remarkably well.

With the graphics method, MacPrint can reproduce text characters dot-for-dot as they appear on the screen, and do so at a reasonable clip. But the program doesn't restrict you to the screen's low 72-dpi resolution. If you select Medium or High quality in the Print dialog box, MacPrint will search your system file for a larger version of the current screen font—double size for Medium quality, quadruple size for High quality. If the oversize font is available, MacPrint uses it for printing, and produces double or quadruple the resolution of the screen.

This is the same trick Apple uses to achieve high-quality output from its flagship dot matrix printer, the ImageWriter LQ. It works because each character in one of these larger fonts has many more dots than the corresponding character in the regular font. When you shrink the large character down to the size you want printed, all the extra dots are still there, just much tinier. As a result, any stair-step jaggedness in the curved outline of the character at its large size is far less apparent.

This system works well with any font for which you have the correct oversized version. Since most Mac screen fonts aren't provided in the large sizes required, however, MacPrint supplies complete screen font sets for four different typefaces, including renditions of Courier, Times, Helvetica, and Symbol. In each set you get 9, 10, 12, 14, 18, and 24 point fonts for use on the screen, and duplicates of each of these at four times the size for printing.

MacPrint's graphics method lets you print a wide variety of fonts and font sizes with excellent print quality, but it's terribly slow. Fortunately, MacPrint can also use a much faster technique, printing in text mode with the DeskJet's own fonts. The only drawback here is that the dimensions of ordinary Mac screen fonts don't match those of the DeskJet fonts. Since your program will space the characters in your text file based on whatever screen font you're using, not on the DeskJet font, spacing of the printed text will be incorrect. MacPrint overcomes this problem by supplying screen versions of all the DeskJet's internal and cartridge fonts. Actually, MacPrint doesn't come with the fonts themselves. Instead, you generate them with a program called Font Mapper—simply pick out the cartridges you own from a list, and Font Mapper generates the necessary screen fonts. Once you've installed the new screen fonts in your system file, your application programs will have the information they need to space the characters properly, and the letters themselves will look right on screen to boot.

Aside from the fact that it works so well, one of the nicest things about MacPrint is its manual. In addition to complete operating instructions, it features clear explanations of the obstacles that have to be faced in connecting a Mac to a "foreign" printer, and frank discussions of the tradeoffs to be weighed when deciding among alternative solutions. The manual also offers tips about a large number of specific applications.

22

DeskJet Programming

If you really want to make the DeskJet jump through hoops, you'll eventually have to learn to program it yourself. Given the complexities of escape sequences and control codes, the do-it-yourself approach may be more, well, challenging, than using a built-in DeskJet driver. But programming usually gives you better control of your printer, and sometimes it's the only way to get the results you want in your printouts.

Earlier chapters have introduced some of the most useful DeskJet commands, and some techniques for employing them with your application programs. In this chapter, though, we really roll up our sleeves and dive into DeskJet programming in depth. If you want the ultimate in DeskJet control from your application programs, or if you want to actually write your own DeskJet programs or drivers, this is your chapter.

We'll begin with an exploration of the PCL language in general: Then we'll look at each of the DeskJet commands in detail, in sections divided according to function: font selection, print positioning, graphics printing, and odds and ends. If you plan to use the PCL commands within application software, you'll find tips on how to do so in Section III. If you'll be incorporating the commands in programs you write yourself, you'll need to know how to send characters to the printer using your programming language.

PCL

Although versions of Hewlett-Packard's Printer Command Language, or PCL, were built into earlier printers, it was the release of the original LaserJet in 1984 that really established PCL as a major printer programming language. PCL was enlarged substantially with the LaserJet Plus, but it has been fairly stable in the subsequent members of the LaserJet family (the 500 Plus, the Series II, the 2000, the IID, and the IIP). However, with each new model, a few commands have been added that are specific to that particular printer. The two DeskJet models understand some, but not all, of the commands added to PCL with the LaserJet Plus, and have a set of ten or so commands that no other PCL printers recognize.

Thus, compatibility between PCL printers is good, but not perfect. While all printers in the extended family respond identically to a common core set of PCL commands, the original LaserJet can't carry out commands that have been added to PCL with the later models, and the DeskJet doesn't recognize some advanced commands. In addition, the commands that are unique to each printer model are ignored by all the other members of the family.

Understanding PCL levels

HP has separated PCL commands into categories called *levels,* with each level supposedly associated with a general type of function. Actually, each level includes such a hodgepodge of different kinds of commands that it's impossible to see any pattern in the groupings. There's certainly no point in memorizing which commands fit into which level, since the commands in all the levels work the same way. HP describes the DeskJet as a Level

III-compatible printer, but actually it responds to almost half of the Level IV commands as well.

Just in case you run across a reference to "Level such-and-such compatibility" in a discussion of a printer, here's a brief description of each of the levels, with its official HP designation:

PCL Level I: Print and Space PCL. Level I commands control underlining, basic graphics, and perforation skip mode, among other functions.

PCL Level II: EDP/Transaction PCL. Level II commands let you select margins, line spacing, symbols set, page length, and pitch, among other settings.

PCL Level III: Office Word Processing PCL. Some of the commands in Level III are for font selection, others for determining print position.

PCL Level IV: Page Formatting PCL. Includes commands to select font point size, page orientation, soft font ID number, and print position. In addition, there are commands that the DeskJet doesn't support, including primitive line-and rectangle-drawing commands, and macro commands.

The DeskJet and PCL

For the most part, PCL commands work the same on the DeskJet as they do on all PCL printers. However, there is one major exception, which results directly from a fundamental technological differerence between laser printers and the DeskJet.

Laser printers such as the LaserJet print an entire page at a time, after "composing" an image of the whole page as a bitmap in printer memory. For this reason, PCL lets you, the programmer, "paint" the page with the freedom that a painter would have. You can place text and graphics elements on the page in any order—if you want to, there's nothing wrong with filling in a bit-map graphic at the bottom right of the page, then jumping to the top left to start printing text.

This is a fundamentally different approach to printer control than the DeskJet demands. The DeskJet is a line printer, printing only one line of text or graphics at a time, then moving on to the next line. And, unlike many dot matrix line printers, the DeskJet can't move paper in the reverse direction because this would smear the ink of the previously printed parts of the page. Therefore, your DeskJet PCL programs must generally send each line to the printer in the order in which it will appear on the page (there is an exception to this rule, as noted in the section "Moving up on the page" later in this chapter). This is one of the most important differences between PCL for the DeskJet and PCL for the LaserJet.

In addition, a variety of special commands have been added to the DeskJet version of PCL. These control features of your printer not found on other PCL machines. For example, there are special commands for feeding envelopes, for switching back and forth between portrait and landscape orientation, for accessing the DeskJet's unique graphics compaction modes, and so forth.

Control codes and escape sequences

PCL consists of a large set of software commands, each of which consists of one or more consecutive ASCII codes. In ASCII, each code value occupies a single byte. Since an ASCII code corresponds to a printed character, the codes in a PCL command are also referred to as characters. In fact, PCL commands are usually shown as the characters that correspond to their ASCII codes, even though these characters aren't printed when they're used in a command. For example, the command that sets the right margin to the 80th column requires these code bytes:

27 38 97 56 48 77

but would normally be written as

$^{E}s_{C}$&a8ØM

The first code, 27, is represented by the abbreviation $^{E}s_{C}$ and is referred to as the *escape character*. It's one of a number of control codes, special codes that are the key to controlling the DeskJet.

Control codes

All PCL commands begin with a control code, a code value that the DeskJet recognizes as a printer command rather than printable data. The values of all the control codes are in the range of 0 to 32 (decimal notation), values which do not correspond to printable characters in the standard ASCII coding system. Nevertheless, control codes such as ᴱs_c or *Control-L* are commonly referred to as characters.

♪ ***Note:*** *Just to confuse the issue, in several DeskJet character sets, including the default PC-8 set, the control codes do correspond to printable characters. However, these characters are not part of the standard ASCII code, and you must send special commands to print them.*

DeskJet commands fall into two major categories, depending on their complexity and the control code they use: ordinary control codes and escape sequences.

- A few DeskJet commands consist solely of a single control code. When the DeskJet receives one of these one-character, single-byte commands, it takes an immediate action, and then returns directly to its regular printing mode. For example, the form feed control code, 12 decimal, ØC hexadecimal, causes the DeskJet to eject the page that is currently loaded.

- Escape sequences are commands that are two or more characters (or codes, or bytes) in length, always beginning with the control code for the escape character. Again, the escape character is code 27 in decimal notation (or 1B in hexadecimal). Escape sequences consist of at least one and usually several characters in addition to the escape character. Far more important and more numerous than the one-byte control code commands, escape sequences control DeskJet functions that have two or more possible settings. For example, escape sequences are used to select which font is active from all those available, and to fix the left margin at one of the many available columns.

Name	Abbreviation	Character	Value (dec)	Value (hex)	Function
Backspace	BS	Ctrl-H	008	008	Moves the print position one character to the left
Tab	HT	Ctrl-I	009	009	Moves the print position to the next tab stop. Tab stops are preset at every eighth column, beginning from the left margin
Line Feed	LF	Ctrl-J	010	00A	Advances the print position and the paper one line
Form Feed	FF	Ctrl-L	012	00B	Ejects the current page, loads another page, and advances the print position to the top of the new page
Carriage Return	CR	Ctrl-M	013	00C	Moves the print position to the left margin
Secondary Font (Shift Out)	SO	Ctrl-N	014	00D	Selects the current secondary font
Primary Font (Shift In)	SI	Ctrl-O	015	00F	Selects the current primary font
Escape	ESC	Ctrl-[	027	01B	Begins an escape sequence

Table 22-1: DeskJet control codes. The list does not include the rarely-used codes for serial communications.

Using control codes

Single-byte control codes are easy to understand and use: you send a single character or byte to the printer, the DeskJet reacts with a specific immediate response, and then it goes back to regular printing.

Table 22-1 lists the DeskJet's control codes and the printer functions they activate. For the most part, the control codes used by the DeskJet perform the same functions indicated by their names in the ASCII code—for example, the backspace code causes the printer to move back one character on the current line, and the tab control code makes the printer move ahead to the next tab stop, if any, on the current line. On the other hand, some control codes perform functions that are not obvious from their standard names. All the control codes are described in detail in the appropriate sections of this chapter.

Using escape sequences

Escape sequences can be considerably more complicated than control codes. A quick examination of a few representative escape sequences should give you some idea of their format:

$^{E}s_{C}$E	Resets printer
$^{E}s_{C}$&l∅O	Selects portrait orientation
$^{E}s_{C}$(1U	Selects the legal character set
$^{E}s_{C}$*t75R	Sets graphics resolution to 75 dots per inch
$^{E}s_{C}$)25∅X	Selects soft font 250 as secondary font

Hidden in the jumble of characters, there's a pattern here. Let's see if we can trace it.

The first character: $^{E}s_{C}$

Again, all escape sequences begin with the escape character, ASCII value 27 decimal, 1B hex. It's written out as $^{E}s_{C}$.

Two-character escape sequences

Six escape sequences, including the $^{E}s_{C}$E in the list above, consist of just two characters: escape followed by one other character, which may be a number or a letter. These two-byte escape sequences include commands to clear the current margins settings, advance the paper half a line, reset the printer, run a self-test, and turn display functions on and off.

Multiple-character escape sequences

In escape sequences with more than two characters, the characters following the escape character each have a different function.

The second character: &, (,), or *

After the escape character, the next character in all multiple-character escape sequences is known as the "parameterized" character, either &, (,), or *. When the DeskJet receives one of the four parameterized characters, it knows to expect several further characters in the escape sequence.

Of these four characters, the one that appears in the escape sequence gives you a general clue about the function of the sequence:

&: The ampersand character sees duty in the commands that set margins, determine print position and paper size, turn underlining off, and control other general functions.

(and **)**: Both parens are used in commands that determine font characteristics: typeface, character set, print quality, and so on. (is used in commands that alter the primary font,) in commands for the secondary font (primary and secondary fonts are discussed later in this chapter).

*: The asterisk is found in commands related to graphics and soft fonts, and in the command for obtaining the printer model number.

The third character: the group character

The third character, also called the "group" character, further narrows down the kind of function performed by the sequence. In most escape sequences, the group character is a letter. All escape sequences beginning with $^{E}s_{c}$&d, for example, are related to underlining, while all those that start with $^{E}s_{c}$*c have to do with soft fonts. As far as I can tell, the letters don't stand for anything in particular.

Escape sequences used to select character sets, such as the $^{E}s_{c}$(1U command which activates the legal character set, do not contain a parameterized character. In these escape sequences, the third character begins the value field, the topic to which we now turn.

The value field

Beginning with the fourth character comes one or more numeric characters, the *value field.* The characters in the value field specify a particular value for the DeskJet function you're controlling. (Again, the value field in the escape sequences for selecting character sets begins with the third character, and the number you enter here helps determine which character set is activated.)

Sometimes there are only a few valid numbers to pick from, when there are just a few possible options for the command. For example, in the escape sequence for setting print quality, you only have two choices for the fourth character: $^{E}s_{C}$(s2Q for high (letter) quality, and $^{E}s_{C}$(s1Q for draft quality. Notice that the only difference between the two sequences is the number in the value field.

Other commands control a wider range of settings, and their escape sequences can contain a corresponding range of numeric values. In $^{E}s_{C}$&a#L, the escape sequence used to set the left margin, for instance, you can specify any column the DeskJet can print in place of the "#" in the value field.

Tip: *To enter a numeric value in a DeskJet escape sequence, you place the ASCII codes of the number's individual digits into the sequence. Do not send the actual number to the DeskJet. For example, if you're setting the left margin to the 30th column, you would place two bytes in the value field: a 3 (ASCII code 33 decimal), then a Ø (ASCII code 30 decimal). You would not send a single byte containing the number 30—the DeskJet would interpret that as a Ø, since the ASCII code for Ø is 30, and set the left margin accordingly.*

This system makes it easy to type escape sequences within an application program when you're embedding them in a document file. It works fine in programming languages as well, as long as you remember to specify that the numeric digits comprise a character string, just like the rest of the escape sequence. See the section "Using PCL commands in your programs" for practical tips on including escape sequences with various programming languages.

The terminator—"I won't be back"

The final character in any escape sequence longer than two bytes is a letter, the terminator. The terminator indicates that you've sent all the numbers in the value field, and completes the sequence.

In some cases, this letter has an obvious relationship to the function of the command—*Q* for the print quality commands, *T* for commands that choose a typeface, and "B" for commands that turn boldfacing on and off. But often, the terminator isn't mnemonic at all—*U* is the terminator for super- and subscripting commands, while underlining commands end in *D*.

Uppercase and lowercase letters

Here are the rules for using upper- and lowercase letters in escape sequences. If the escape sequence has a group character (remember, the character set commands do not), it is a letter, and must always be entered in lowercase. The final character or terminator is normally capitalized, and causes the DeskJet to return immediately to ordinary printing. If the terminator character is entered in lowercase form, however, the DeskJet interprets the characters that follow as another escape sequence in a combined escape sequence, a topic we'll cover next.

Combining escape sequences

If you're planning to send two or more escape sequences in succession, you may be able to combine them into a single sequence, reducing the number of characters you must type by cutting out those that repeat. In order to be combined, two or more successive escape sequences must all begin with the same three characters (the escape character plus the two following characters). For example, you might combine

E_{S_C}(sØUE_{S_C}(s1PE_{S_C}(s12V

into the omnibus sequence

E_{S_C}(sØu1p12V

As you can see, all you do to combine escape sequences is:

1. Enter the first three characters shared by all of the escape sequences you're combining.

2. Enter the remaining characters from each escape sequence in succession.

3. The last character in each sequence you're combining will always be a letter. This letter should be capitalized when it falls at the very end of your combination escape sequence. Otherwise, you must enter it in lowercase form.

The capitalized letter functions as the terminator for the combined escape sequence. If you accidentally capitalize any another letter, the DeskJet will print the characters of the combined escape sequence, instead of carrying out the commands.

Tip: *While combining escapes sequences might seem a good practice, don't assume it's always the best idea. Theoretically, you'll reduce the number of characters you have to enter, and thereby save little typing time and a few bytes of memory. In practice, you'll probably waste more time making sure that you combine the sequences properly. Besides, a combined sequence can be harder to read than a succession of individual sequences.*

Combined escape sequences will help you most when you're typing in a DeskJet program written by someone else. If the author has gone to the trouble of combining escape sequences when possible for you, you'll have fewer characters to type.

PCL COMMAND REFERENCE

This section describes each PCL command individually. They're grouped by general function: font and character commands (beginning on this page); print position commands (p. 349); and graphics commands (p. 363).

FONT AND OTHER CHARACTER COMMANDS

PCL offers a wide range of commands for selecting fonts and for specifying other aspects of the appearance of printed text.

Selecting fonts

Using PCL printer commands, there are three ways to select a specific font from among any of those currently resident in the DeskJet (including internal, cartridge, and soft fonts):

1. By defining each and every characteristic of the font you want to select through a long series of escape sequences.

2. By selecting a previously defined primary or secondary font through a single simple control code.

3. By selecting the font by its temporary identification number. This method only works with soft fonts.

Defining a font in every detail

The standard and usually most accurate method for choosing a particular font is what I call the "longhand" method. In the longhand method, you specify each of its characteristics, one at a time, with the necessary escape sequences. The font characteristics you can specify include: orientation (portrait or landscape); character set; character spacing (monospacing or proportional spacing); pitch (for monospaced fonts); size; type style (upright or italic); stroke weight (regular or bold); and typeface; placement (superscript, subscript, or normal); and print quality (letter or draft).

All the escape sequences for selecting font characteristics are described in detail individually later in this chapter. By the way, HP uses the vague term "print features" for what I've called font characteristics.

♪ ***Note:*** *Selecting a new font for immediate printing also selects the same font as the new primary or secondary font, depending on which is active at the time. If the secondary font is currently active, your escape sequences must be entered in a slightly different form than is shown here when you're selecting a new font for immediate use. See the section "Primary and secondary fonts" below for details.*

To switch to a new font, you simply send the required escape sequence for each of these characteristics in turn. If you want to select a portrait-oriented, legal-character set, proportionally spaced, 14-point, italicized, normal-stroke weight TmsRmn-typeface font, you'd send the following string of commands:

$$\text{E}_{\text{S}_\text{C}}\&\text{l}\emptyset\text{O}\text{E}_{\text{S}_\text{C}}\text{ (1U}\text{E}_{\text{S}_\text{C}}\text{(s1P}\text{E}_{\text{S}_\text{C}}\text{ (s14V }\text{E}_{\text{S}_\text{C}}\text{(s}\emptyset\text{S}\text{E}_{\text{S}_\text{C}}\text{(s}\emptyset\text{B }\text{E}_{\text{S}_\text{C}}\text{(s5T}$$

Actually, you can cut down on the typing somewhat by combining related escape sequences, as you've learned earlier in this chapter. And you really only have to send commands for characteristics that will be different in the new font. If you're switching from a standard 10-point TmsRmn font to a 14-point TmsRmn that's otherwise identical, all you have to send the appropriate font size escape sequence.

But although font commands look similar to other PCL escape sequences, there's a subtle but important difference in how they work. The difference is based on the fact that every dot in every character in each font is predefined, so a font can't be changed by sending a new escape sequence. When you use an escape sequence to define, say, a new left margin, you're directly setting that new margin where you want it. In contrast, when you send a command to switch from a 10 point font to a 14 point font, you're not setting a new point size, you're asking the DeskJet to look for an entirely new font that matches your point size request.

Font characteristic priorities

What happens when it turns out that the font you've specified isn't currently available in the DeskJet? Instead of ignoring your request altogether, the printer does its best to give you what you asked for.

Whenever it receives a command that changes even a single font characteristic, the printer has to start a fresh search for a new font that best matches the characterstics that are in effect. To conduct this search, the DeskJet starts with what it considers as the most important characteristic of all, which happens to be orientation. It picks out all the available fonts that match your choice for the orientation setting, and eliminates all the other fonts. Working with the fonts that remain, the DeskJet goes on to the next most important characteristic, character set, culling out the fonts that aren't available with the required set.

This process of elimination continues down the list of font characteristics, in order of their priority. The search stops as soon as only a single font remains in the group of eligibles. At this point, the remaining font is selected, even if its characteristics don't match all those you've requested.

For better or worse, the system the DeskJet uses to decide which of your commands has the highest priority is defined for you, and can't be changed. Here's the priority list for font characteristics:

1. orientation (portrait or landscape)
2. character set
3. spacing (monospacing or proportional spacing)
4. pitch (for monospaced fonts)
5. size
6. type style (upright or italic)
7. stroke weight (regular or bold)
8. typeface

An example is clearly in order at this point. Let's say you have a DeskJet Plus with built-in Courier landscape fonts, and you've installed the "TmsRmn Collection" font cartridge, which doesn't include any landscape fonts. You send the escape sequences for a landscape 12-point proportionally-spaced TmsRmn font to the DeskJet. Examining your request, the DeskJet starts with the landscape orientation command, and immediately rejects all your TmsRmn cartridge fonts, and all the internal protrait-oriented Courier fonts. That still leaves three fonts in contention, since the DeskJet Plus has 6, 12 and 24 point landscape fonts built in. All three of these fonts have the same character sets available, and none of them will print in proportionally spaced mode.

The next eliminating point is size. Obviously, only the 12 point Courier makes the cut, and it becomes the selected font.

If you've been paying close attention, you may have noticed that two font characteristics mentioned at the beginning of this section aren't on the priority list above—even though they're included in the priority list that appears in your DeskJet *Owner's Manual*. The ones I've stricken from the list include placement (super- and subscript) and print quality.

The reason these characteristics don't belong on the priority list is that they're not actually a part of any font definition. When you give a command that alters one of them, the DeskJet doesn't look for a matching font. Instead, the printer simply modifies the way it prints, so these commands can be used with *any* font. Since no font ever gets eliminated from the match based on the placement or print quality characteristics, they don't belong in the priority list.

Primary and secondary fonts

If you'll be switching between two fonts frequently during a given print job, you can define them in advance as *primary* and *secondary* fonts, and then switch between them as often as you like with a quick and easy control code.

Actually, the primary and secondary fonts are defined for you by default when you turn on the DeskJet—at this point, both are the same font, as determined by the printer's DIP switch settings. Of course, until you redefine at least one of the primary and secondary fonts for yourself, it won't do you much good to switch between identical fonts. But whether or not you redefine them, one of the two is always the active font (the font currently in use for printing). And unless you've explicitly switched to the secondary font, the active font is the primary font.

The primary/secondary approach to selecting fonts has two disadvantages. First, you can only set up two fonts for immediate access. Second, your primary and secondary font choices get erased and returned to the default font any time the printer is reset.

Defining a primary or secondary font

To set up a primary or secondary font of your own choice, you must use the longhand method outlined above, sending the complete set of escape sequences necessary to define all of the font's characteristics. Actually, each time you select a new font "on the fly" with the longhand method, you're really designating the new primary font or secondary font, whichever of these you're currently printing with.

If you wish, however, you can set up whichever of the two that's not currently active in advance, and then switch to it with a control code whenever necessary. When you define a primary or secondary font that isn't currently active, the DeskJet still goes through the regular process of searching for a matching font based on font characteristic priorities.

⌒ *Caution:* *If you define a primary font while the secondary font is active, or vice versa, you must omit the orientation command, since you can't specify a primary or secondary font with this command, and it takes effect immediately.*

The escape sequences you use to define primary and secondary fonts are identical, except that you use a left parenthesis for primary font commands, a right parenthesis for secondary font commands. So, for example

^Es_C(1U selects the legal character set for the primary font,

while

^Es_C)1U selects the legal character set for the secondary font.

In the discussions of the individual font escape sequences in the rest of this section, only the escape sequences for defining the primary font are shown. If you're defining the secondary font, just replace the (in each escape sequence with a).

Knowing this code, you can redefine the primary or secondary font at any time, whether or not the one you're redefining is currently in use for printing. If, for example, you're currently printing with the secondary font, and you want to redefine the primary font, just make sure the escape sequences you send contain the left parenthesis. When you switch to the primary font at a later time, the new font you've defined will become active.

You can also redefine the secondary font while you're printing with it, this time by sending escape sequences with the right parenthesis. In this case, the new font you choose will be selected for printing immediately. If you switch to the primary font and then back again to the secondary, this same font will again become active.

Selecting a primary or secondary font

CTRL-O   Select primary font
(15d or ØFh)

CTRL-N   Select secondary font
(14d or ØEh)

Once your primary and secondary fonts are defined, you can select either one with a single-byte commands. To select the secondary font, send the value **14** decimal (ØE hex, Control-N) to the DeskJet (send a single byte with the value 14, not the numerals *1* and *4* separately. To select the primary font, send the value **15** decimal (ØF hex, Control-O). Your *Owner's Manual* refers to these codes with their traditional but meaningless names, Shift-Out and Shift-In. If you're going to be remembering names, I recommend memorizing them as "secondary font" and "primary font" instead.

Setting the secondary font selection mode

^{E}s$_c$&kØF   Return to primary font automatically at the end of each line

^{E}s$_c$&k1F   Continue secondary font selection across lines until explicitly turned off

Default: Continuous secondary font

Notes: Not a PCL Level III feature.

The DeskJet provides two commands for controlling the way it manages your secondary font selections. In the default mode, once you select the secondary font, it continues to be the font used for printing until you explicitly reselect the primary font. In the line-by-line mode, the primary font is automatically reselected at the end of every line.

Restoring the default primary and secondary fonts

^{E}s$_c$(3@	Restore default font as primary font
^{E}s$_c$)3@	Restore default font as secondary font

To restore the default font that was automatically selected when the DeskJet was turned on as either the primary or secondary font, just send the appropriate command from this pair.

Assigning a soft font as the default primary or secondary font

^{E}s$_c$(#@	Assign soft font # as default primary font
^{E}s$_c$)#@	Assign soft font # as default secondary font

Valid values: Any soft font temporary ID number currently in use

Use one of these escape sequences to assign a soft font as the default primary or secondary font. When the printer receives a reset command, the current primary and secondary font assignments are cancelled, and the default primary and secondary fonts you've chosen with this command are automatically reestablished. The catch with this command is that the soft fonts chosen as the defaults will themselves be erased by the reset, unless you explicitly make them "permanent" when you download them. See the next section for more on soft fonts and ID numbers.

Selecting soft fonts by ID number

^{E}s$_c$(#X	Select ID number # soft font as primary font
^{E}s$_c$)#X	Select ID number # soft font as secondary font

Valid values: Ø through 32767

The third and final method for selecting a font works only with soft fonts, the kind you download to the DeskJet from disk files. When you download a soft font, you must assign the entire font a temporary identification number. From then on, you can select the font with one simple escape sequence based on this ID number.

To use these commands, you need to know how primary and secondary fonts work, as detailed in the last section. With that background, let's examine the first of these commands, the one that lets you select a soft font as the primary font. Let's say you select soft font number 5 with this command. If you're already printing with the primary font when you give the command, the next text you print comes out in soft font 5. If you were printing with the secondary font, though, there's no immediate change in the appearance of your printed text. Soft font 5 still becomes the primary font, but you have to switch to the primary font with the control code **15** decimal before your text prints with the new font.

The second of the two commands works exactly the same way, except that it selects the chosen soft font as the secondary. If you're currently printing in the primary font, you have to switch to the secondary font to print with the new font you've just selected.

A soft reset command will erase the choices you've made for primary and secondary fonts, but not the ID numbers of your soft fonts. To restore your primary and secondary fonts, just resend the above escape sequences.

Selecting page orientation

⌒ **Caution:** *It's very easy to make mistakes in entering either of these two escape sequences. Check your work carefully!*

_Es_c&l1O	Select landscape orientation
_Es_c&lØO	Select portrait orientation
Default:	portrait orientation
Notes:	1. Both of these escape sequences contain characters that can be easily mistaken for others. In both commands, the first character after the & is a lower case "el." Then comes a numeral, either a "one" for landscape, or a "zero" for portrait. Both sequences end in the letter "oh."

2. Both commands also cause a form feed, ejecting the current sheet of paper—this last effect is not a PCL Level III feature.

3. Landscape orientation does not permit graphics printing, text scaling, or underlining via the underlining escape sequence.

4. The DeskJet automatically switches to unidirectional printing when landscape orientation is selected. This can then be overriden by the bidirectional printing command.

We've gone over the difference between portrait orientation and landscape orientation before, but it won't hurt to repeat the definitions here. In portrait orientation, the ordinary mode, the long edge of the paper runs vertically, and you have lots of lines but not so many columns. In landscape mode, the long edge is oriented horizontally, so you can fit long lines, though not as many on a single page.

The DeskJet is capable of printing text in landscape orientation, but not graphics. Even in text mode, landscape printing only works with fonts specifically designed for that purpose. That's why the orientation escape sequence is functionally a font selection command, even though it's not listed as such in the PCL "dictionary." In fact, the orientation command has the highest priority in the DeskJet's heirarchy of font characteristics. In other words, if there's only a single font available for the orientation you've chosen, your printout will still be oriented properly—even if the font doesn't look anything like the one you've requested with your other font selection commands.

Of course, the easiest way to switch between landscape and portrait orientations is by pressing the FONT button on the keypad until the landscape light glows. Still, it's easy to imagine a situation where you'd want to change page orientation under software control.

Say you're planning to print a financial report, to use the standard hackneyed business-oriented scenario. Along with lots of explanatory text, the document includes a couple of tables, one of which is a month-by-month breakdown of sunflower seed sales over the past year. This means you have 12 columns to print, and the text has to be big and bold enough to make your bleary-eyed readership around the conference table take notice. With the necessary legends and margins, twelve ½-inch columns won't fit across an 8½-inch wide piece of paper, but they'll fit just fine if you turn the page sideways.

If you plan to insert the table as page 3 of your report, you need a command to switch out of portrait mode and into landscape mode after page 2, and to switch back to portrait again before page 4.

When you're switching between landscape and portrait modes, or vice versa, one thing you don't have to worry about is where the page breaks are going to fall. As soon as the printer receives the command to change orientation, it immediately spits out the page it was printing, even if the entire piece of paper hasn't been printed on.

Other points to note about the landscape mode

Valid *margin* settings change from those available in portrait mode because of the DeskJet's unprintable area. Remember that in portrait mode, the DeskJet cannot print on the bottom ½-inch of the page. In the "sideways" landscape orientation, the bottom of the page becomes the left margin, meaning you always have at least a ½-inch left margin from the edge of the paper. On the other hand, the maximum right margin is reduced from ¼-inch in portrait mode to ⅙-inch in landscape, corresponding to the unprintable ⅙-inch at the top of a portrait-oriented page. Anyway, you end up with a maximum line length (horizontal printing distance) of 10⅓ inches on letter paper, 13⅓ inches on legal.

Similarly, there are ¼-inch unprintable strips at the right and left of a portrait page and therefore at the top and bottom of a landscape page. On letter paper, that means that your landscape mode text can extend vertically over no more than 8 inches of the page. Disable the perforation skip mode if you want to automatically use these minimum ¼-inch top and bottom margins (see the discussion of the perforation skip function later in this chapter). If you want to set your own margins, set perforation skip on instead.

The *text scale* command, described later, has no effect in the landscape mode. Although the *underline* command doesn't work either, you can still create your own underlines by printing the text first, then moving the print position back on the same line and on print position commands).

When you switch the DeskJet to landscape orientation, the printer automatically configures itself for *unidirectional* (left to right) printing to ensure the best possible print quality. You can override this setup by sending the escape sequence $^E s_c$&k1W for bidirectional printing after you've switched to landscape mode.

Although the DeskJet doesn't print *graphics* in landscape mode, that shouldn't stop you from getting a landscape-oriented graphics printout. You just have to design your program so that it rotates the graphics data "sideways" first, and then sends it to the printer in ordinary portrait mode.

Choosing a character set

^{E}s$_C$(#*x*	Select character set
Values:	# is a number and *x* is a letter which together represent the character set's designation
Notes:	The default character sets are determined by the positions of DIP switches A-1 through A-4.

A character set is the specific collection of symbols, including letters, numerals, and punctuation marks, that is available for printing at any one time. In a given character set, each available symbol is assigned its own one-byte code number; to print a character, you just send its code to the DeskJet. If you change character sets, that same code number may correspond to an entirely different character, which will be printed instead.

Character sets are classified as 7-bit or 8-bit, depending on whether the printer recognizes or ignores the most significant bit in each character code byte. 7-bit character sets can contain up to 128 characters, while 8-bit character sets can have double that amount, for a total of 256 different symbols.

The DeskJet Plus has five built-in 8-bit character sets, adding the PC-850 set to the ones in the original DeskJet. In all the built-in 8-bit character sets, the first 128 characters are the same, and follow the ASCII standard. Codes 0 to 32 are non-printing control codes (although the DeskJet doesn't respond to all of them). In the character sets intended for use with IBM-compatible PCs, this group of codes also represents a group of miscellaneous symbols such as arrows, musical notes, and happy faces, but you must send a special command to make the DeskJet interpret them as printable characters instead of control codes. Codes 33 to 127 are a standardized collection of letters, numbers, and punctuation marks. The additional 128 symbols in the 8-bit character sets vary from set to set.

In the 7-bit character sets, codes 0-32 are assigned to exactly the same control codes as in the 8-bit sets. The remaining characters, 33-128 vary from set to set. Most of the DeskJet's 14 built-in 7-bit character sets conform to definitions for various languages established by the International Standards Organization, and these are designated "ISO Germany," "ISO France," and so on.

When you turn on the DeskJet, the default character set is determined by the settings of DIP switches A-1 through A-4. As it's shipped from the factory, the US version of the DeskJet is set up with the PC-8 character set, which matches the standard IBM PC screen character set, as the default.

The character sets available in the DeskJet and on optional cartridges are listed in Table 22-2, each with the escape sequence needed to select it. Many of the character sets themselves are printed in Appendix B.

Assuming you're currently printing with the primary font, you can switch immediately to another set by sending the escape sequence for the primary font character set, ^{E}s$_c$(#xD. In this sequence, replace #x with the character set's identification number and letter. For example, to choose the ECMA-94 Latin 1 set (where do they get those names?), send the escape sequence ^{E}s$_c$(ØN.

To select a character set in advance for the secondary font, use a right parenthesis instead of a left one in the escape sequence. With the example just given, the sequence would be ^{E}s$_c$)ØN. Then, when you activate the secondary font with the appropriate command, the desired character set will already be in effect (see "Selecting primary and secondary fonts" above).

Character set	Escape sequence
Roman 8	E_{S_C}(8U
PC-8	E_{S_C}(1ØU
PC-8 Denmark/Norway	E_{S_C}(11U
PC-850	E_{S_C}(12U
ECMA-94 Latin 1	E_{S_C}(ØN
ISO United Kingdom (04)	E_{S_C}(1E
ISO Germany (21)	E_{S_C}(1G
ISO France (69)	E_{S_C}(1F
ISO Italy (15)	E_{S_C}(ØI
ISO Norway v. 1 (60)	E_{S_C}(ØD
ISO (Norway v. 2 (61)	E_{S_C}(1D
ISO Sweden: Names (11)	E_{S_C}(ØS
ISO Sweden (10)	E_{S_C}(3S
ISO Spain (17	E_{S_C}(2S
ASCIII	E_{S_C}(ØU
ISO IRV (02)	E_{S_C}(2U
ISO Portugal (16)	E_{S_C}(4S
JIS ASCII (14)	E_{S_C}(ØK
Legal	E_{S_C}(1U
Line Draw	E_{S_C}(ØL
Math7	E_{S_C}(ØM
Math8a	E_{S_C}(ØQ
Math8b	E_{S_C}(1Q
Math8	E_{S_C}(8M
Pi Font	E_{S_C}(15U
Pi Fonta	E_{S_C}(2Q

Table 22-2: *DeskJet Character Sets. Those above the heavy line are available with the internal fonts, those below on cartridges. See text regarding primary vs. secondary fonts.*

Selecting proportional or fixed spacing

E_{s_C}(s1P	Select proportional spacing
E_{s_C}(sØP	Select monospacing
Notes:	All the DeskJet's internal fonts are monospaced, since all are based on the typewriter-like Courier typeface. Proportionally spaced fonts are only available on font cartridges and as soft fonts.

In monospaced spaced fonts, each character is alloted the same width—the same amount of space horizontally along a line of text—regardless of whether the character itself is wide (*m*) or skinny (*i*). Since all the characters are the same width, the number of them that will fit in one inch is always the same. This number is referred to as the font's pitch, and can be controlled by the next escape sequence we'll discuss below.

In proportionally spaced fonts, by contrast, the width alloted to each character is proportional to the character's actual width. Thus, a line of *ms* printed in a proportionally spaced font would be considerably longer than a line containing the same number of *is*.

Even though typefaces are designed as monospaced or proportionally spaced, you must still select monospacing or proportional spacing explicitly when you choose a font.

Selecting font pitch

E_{s_C}(s#H	Set pitch to # characters per inch (cpi)
Valid values:	The pitch value may include up to two decimal places. 5, 10, 16.67, and 20 pitch fonts are available among the internal fonts on the DeskJet Plus. Fonts with other pitches are available in cartridge and soft font form.
Notes:	Pitch is the reciprocal of horizontal motion index (HMI)—setting the pitch automatically resets the HMI and vice versa. Changing the pitch changes the position of the margins, but not the margin setting. The pitch setting is not relevant to proportionally spaced fonts.
Example:	E_{s_C}(s12H sets the pitch to 12 cpi

Pitch refers to the number of characters of a monospaced font that are printed per inch along a line of text, and is given in characters per inch or cpi. You can also think of cpi as standing for columns per inch, since there's one character in a text column. By extension, pitch determines the width of each individual character or column.

In addition to helping specify the font you want to print with, the pitch setting also determines the horizontal motion index (HMI), and in turn the distance the print position moves when you set it in columns. Since the DeskJet measures margins in terms of column numbers, and not by absolute measurements, the pitch setting also affects your margins. If you change the pitch from 10 cpi to 12 cpi, a right margin set to 80 columns will change from 8" to 6½".

To select the font with the desired pitch, send the escape sequence ^{E}s$_c$(s#H, substituting the value of the desired pitch for #. If you choose a pitch value that doesn't exist among the fonts currently available in the DeskJet, the printer will select the font with the next largest pitch. Since the pitch will then be larger than what you wanted, there'll be more characters per inch, and the individual characters will be skinnier.

Because the width of each character varies in proportionally spaced fonts, the number of characters per inch depends on which characters you're talking about. For this reason, the pitch setting has no effect on proportionally spaced fonts.

Selecting font size (character height)

^{E}s$_c$(s#V   Set font size to # points

Valid values: For the internal fonts, 6 and 12 points are the only valid values. Other sizes are available in cartridge and soft fonts, with the maximum size generally considered to be 18 points for the original DeskJet and 30 points for the DeskJet Plus. The font value may include up to two decimal places.

Example: Es$_c$(s14.25V sets the font size to 14.25 points

Notes: The DeskJet *Owner's Manual* is incorrect when it defines character height as the height of an uppercase character.

As you can guess, the *font size* or character height command lets you select the height of your font based on the distance from the bottom of the descenders to the top of the ascenders (see Chapter 5 for further details on the measurement of font size). Font size is given in points, which are each equal to about ¹⁄₇₂-inch.

You can only select a given font size if it's available among the fonts that are currently resident in your DeskJet. There's one exception to this rule that works only with the DeskJet, not other PCL printers: you can request a font that's half the size of any installed font, and the DeskJet will automatically scale the existing font down to match your request.

Only 12 point (and thus half-sized 6 point) fonts are built in as internal fonts, so to use other font sizes you'll have to install cartridge or soft fonts first. If no font is available that matches the size you've requested, the DeskJet will substitute the font with the next closest size.

Printing in italics (selecting type style)

ᴱs_c(s1S	Begin italics printing
ᴱs_c(sØS	Stop italics printing, return to normal upright printing
Notes:	To print in italics in landscape orientation on either DeskJet model, you need the 22706L landscape fonts cartridge.

Italics are usually used to emphasize a word or phrase within ordinary upright text. HP uses the term *type style* to refer to the font attributes of italic versus upright text. To print a passage in italics, send the escape sequence to begin italics printing, then the text you want italicized, then the escape sequence to stop italics and return to the normal upright type style.

If it's going to honor your request to print in italics, the DeskJet must have a specific italics font to work with. In other words, the printer can't take an upright font and italicize it for you. The DeskJet Plus comes with italics versions of its Courier fonts built in internally. However, the internal italics fonts are not available in landscape orientation, and you'll need the 22706L landscape cartridge if you want to print italics in landscape.

Of course, italics fonts are available in cartridge and soft font products. If the typeface on which a font package is based is intended for use in the body of a document, the font package will probably include both upright and italics fonts from the same typeface family. On the other hand, if the typeface is a display face meant for headlines and other attention-getting short stretches of text, the package usually won't include the italics version.

Printing boldface text (selecting stroke weight)

^{E}s$_C$(s3B   Begin boldface printing

^{E}s$_C$(s0B   Stop boldface printing, return to normal stroke weight

Text printed in boldface looks darker than ordinary text, another way to add emphasis. Actually, the difference is that the strokes of the bold characters are very slightly wider than those of ordinary characters, though the shapes of the characters remain almost the same. The general term *stroke weight* refers to how heavy the characters in a font look.

In the DeskJet, any font can be made bold, with an occasional exception (see the discussion on this point in Chapter 6). Thus, this command doesn't really belong in the list of font selection priorities. However, in other PCL printers, a separate bold font must be installed to select it with this command.

To print a bold passage, send the escape sequence to begin bold printing, then the text you want printed in bold, then the escape sequence to stop bold printing and return to normal stroke weight.

Choosing a typeface

^{E}s$_C$(s#T   Select typeface number #

Valid values: The typeface identification number is assigned by the font supplier. HP typefaces are numbered as follows: Courier—3; Helv—4; TmsRmn—5; Letter Gothic—6; Prestige—8; Presentations—11; Univers Condensed—87

Typeface is the very last font characteristic on the list of print feature priorities. In other words, the DeskJet will make sure that your selections for orientation, character set, pitch, font size, style (italics or upright), and weight (bold or normal) have been met before it even looks to see whether the typeface you request is available. That way, even if the characters aren't shaped the way you hoped, your overall page format will be printed as close as possible to the way you planned it.

To request a typeface change, send the escape sequence ᴱs_c(s#T, substituting the typeface's identification number for the # in the sequence. ID numbers for the typefaces sold by HP are shown in the table above. If you're using a font package supplied by another manufacturer, you'll need to get the typeface ID numbers from the vendor.

Underlining text

ᴱs_c&dØD	Select single fixed underline (default)
ᴱs_c&d1D	Select single fixed underline
ᴱs_c&d2D	Select double fixed underline
ᴱs_c&d3D	Select single floating underline
ᴱs_c&d4D	Select double floating underline
ᴱs_c&d@	Turn underlining off
Notes:	Underlining does not work in landscape mode.

All of the underlining commands print continuous underlines below the affected text, the underline extending across the spaces between words. Two underline positioning techniques are available, and either can be used with single or double underlining, bringing the total of available underlining options to four. With the "fixed" underline position option, the vertical position of all underlines on a given line of text stays constant at five dot positions below the baseline, even if you change fonts on the line. With the "floating" option, the underline position is set to where it looks best with the current font.

In general, you should choose floating underlining if you're only using one font on a line, fixed if you're mixing fonts within the same line. Note that you cannot adjust the distance from the text baseline to the underline(s).

Selecting the underlining mode

$^{E}s_{c}$&kØE	Cancel underlining automatically at the end of each line
$^{E}s_{c}$&k1E	Continue underlining across lines until explicitly turned off
Default:	continuous underlining
Notes:	Not a PCL Level III feature.

Underlining can work in one of two ways, depending on which of these commands is in effect. In the default underlining mode, once you start underlining it continues until you turn it off. In the line-by-line mode, underlining is automatically cancelled at the end of every line. That helps prevent runaway underlines, but it means you have to resend an underlining command at the beginning of every line in a block of underlined text. For some reason, HP refers to these options as the "Print Enhancement Control."

Printing subscripts and superscripts

$^{E}s_{c}$(s1U or $^{E}s_{c}$(s+1U	Begin superscript printing
$^{E}s_{c}$(s-1U	Begin subcript printing
$^{E}s_{c}$(s0U	Discontinue super- or subscripting, resume normal print position
Example:	To print $x_n + y^2 = z$ $x^{E}s_{c}$(s-1Un $^{E}s_{c}$(sØU + y$^{E}s_{c}$(s+1U2 $^{E}s_{c}$(sØU = z
Notes:	You can use either $^{E}s_{c}$(s1U or $^{E}s_{c}$(s+1U to initiate superscript print positioning. Not a PCL Level III feature.

Superscripting simply shifts the text baseline half a line or so above the normal position, while subscripting shifts it half a line below. Since this shift of position doesn't require a change in the appearance or spacing of the super- or subscripted characters, these two commands can be used with any font—you don't need a separate font file as you would to change from upright to italics, for example.

For this reason, you can ignore super- and subscripting in the hierarchy of print feature priorities, even though HP has them the third highest on the priority list in your *Owner's Manual* (see the discussion of print feature priorities at the beginning of this section).

To use the super- or subscript escape sequence, send the one you've chosen to the DeskJet immediately before the characters whose placement you want to change. Immediately after the characters, send the escape sequence that stops super- and subscripting and returns the text baseline to its normal position.

If you want smaller characters than normal for your super- and subscripts, send the escape sequence for the size change after the one for super- or subscripting. Then, when the super- or subscripted characters have been sent, send the command to shut off super- or subscripting, then the command to return to the original point size.

Changing print quality

$^{E}s_{C}$(s1Q	Select draft quality text printing
$^{E}s_{C}$(s2Q	Select letter quality text printing
Default:	Letter quality
Notes:	Not a PCL Level III feature

The *print quality* command lets you choose the best compromise between appearance and speed for the work you're doing. In letter quality mode, the DeskJet prints approximately 120 razor-sharp characters per second; in draft mode it spits out 240 slightly rougher characters per second, and uses less ink in the process. (Those numbers are according to HP, and they'll serve for comparison, though your real-world results will usually be considerably slower in either mode.)

Generally, it's a good idea to set the printer to a lower quality mode while you're printing draft copies. Once the printout looks perfect, you can then select letter quality for your final copies. Since you want to be able to switch from one quality mode to another quickly, as circumstances dictate, don't set the print quality permanently from a program. Instead, give yourself (and the users of your program) control at print time. Of course, you can always select the print quality setting from the keypad MODE button. If you want the convenience of software selection, though, you can build a print quality option into your program.

Selecting unidirectional or bidirectional printing

^{E}s$_C$&kØW	Select left-to-right unidirectional printing
^{E}s$_C$&k1W	Select bidirectional printing
^{E}s$_C$&k2W	Select right-to-left unidirectional printing
Default:	Bidirectional printing
Notes:	Not a PCL Level III feature.

Bidirectional printing is faster than unidirectional, but print quality is slightly lower because alignment of the printhead is not as accurate. In text printing, this problem is most likely to be noticeable when you print characters larger than 50 dots (12 points) high—the top and bottom portions of the characters may be slightly offset from one another.

Using text scale mode

^{E}s$_C$&k6W	Enable text scale mode
^{E}s$_C$&k5W	Disable text scale mode
Default:	As shipped from the factory, the DeskJet has text scale mode disabled. Moving DIP switch B1 to the UP position changes the default to text scale mode enabled.
Notes:	Text scale mode is ignored with perforation skip enabled, which is the default; and when printing in the landscape orientation. Not a PCL Level III feature.

Text scale mode squeezes more lines of text onto a page, allowing you to use the same page length settings typically used for other printers, despite the DeskJet's inability to print on the bottom ½" of the paper.

The fact that the DeskJet can't print on this strip has the effect of decreasing the usable page length by ½". If you're using letter size paper, it's just as if the paper was 10½" instead of 11" long. As a result, the page length settings commonly used for printers that actually do print on the entire piece of paper won't work on the DeskJet, at least not in its ordinary printing mode.

Page length settings are defined as the number of lines that can be printed on a page. Of course, the actual number of lines that will fit depends on how far apart the lines are, as well as how long the paper is.

At any rate, there are two ways to get around the mismatch between the physical length of the paper and its effective length for DeskJet printing. The simplest alternative is to reset the page length to the value that corresponds to the effective page length you're working with. For example, if you're printing 6 lines per inch on letter paper, the correct page length setting would be 63 lines.

On the other hand, there may be situations where you want to jury-rig things so you can use a standard page length value. That's where the text scale command comes in. When you give this command, the DeskJet reduces the space between lines just enough to fit the standard number of lines on a page.

Printing control codes as characters

In some character sets, printable characters have been assigned to the lowest-numbered ASCII code values, which were previously reserved for non-printing control codes. Character sets with these extra printable characters typically duplicate the screen character sets used by IBM PCs and compatibles.

Normally, the DeskJet interprets the first 32 or 33 ASCII codes as control codes (the exact number depends on whether you view code 32 which leaves a space between characters as a control code or a "space character"). To print these codes as characters instead, you must first enable one of two special modes, the display functions mode or the transparent print mode.

Using display functions mode

$^E s_c Y$	Enable display functions mode
$^E s_c Z$	Disable display functions mode
Default:	Display functions mode disabled

In display functions mode, the DeskJet prints all control codes and escape sequences as characters, and ignores all but two of them as printer commands. The two software commands to which it continues to respond are the carriage return control code (13 decimal) and the "disable display functions mode" escape sequence, $^E s_c Z$. Upon receiving either of these two commands, the DeskJet prints the characters represented by the code or codes in the command, but then executes the command itself. In the case of a carriage return, the printer prints the associated character, and then executes both a carriage return and a line feed, regardless of the line terminator setting in effect. When it receives the "disable display functions mode" command, the DeskJet prints the command as characters, then switches back to its ordinary printing mode.

Using transparent print mode

$^{E}s_{C}$**&p#X<data>** Print # bytes of data in transparent print mode

Valid values: # may be any integer value between 0 and 32,767 inclusive. The notation "<data>" refers to the actual data bytes you wish to print. The bracket characters "<" and ">" should not be included in the data you actually send.

In transparent print mode, the DeskJet prints all control codes as characters, and completely ignores them as control codes. There are two differences between transparent print mode and display functions mode. First, transparent print mode requires you to specify exactly how many bytes of data to print "transparently," while display functions mode continues in effect until you turn it off. Second, no control codes whatsoever are executed in transparent print mode, while two are executed in display functions mode.

Resetting the printer

$^{E}s_{C}$**E**   Reset the printer

The *soft reset* command restores all the DeskJet's settings to their status as determined by the most recent choices made on the keypad. If no keypad buttons have been pressed, the settings are restored to their defaults, just as they were when the printer was first powered up. The soft reset command also ejects any paper in the printer, moving the print position to the top left margin of the next sheet. It does not erase the data in the print buffer, nor does it erase "permanent" soft fonts (see Chapter 7 for more information on permanent versus temporary soft fonts).

Performing a self test

$^{E}s_{C}$**z**   Perform self test

Notes: Unlike most escape sequences, the self test command terminates in a lowercase letter.

During the self test procedure, the DeskJet goes through a built-in diagnostics routine, checking that its microprocessor and ROM firmware are in good order. As part of the self test, it also prints two pages of sample text, one in portrait mode, the other in landscape, as shown in your *Owner's Manual.* At the conclusion of the test, the DeskJet executes a soft reset command as described above. If a problem is discovered during the test, the printer goes off line and flashes all the lights on the keypad. If this occurs, or if the test pages don't look anything like the ones shown in your manual, your printer may need service. Before you call the repairshop, consult the troubleshooting section in Chapter 23 for advice.

Moving the print position and paper feeding

PCL provides many commands with which you can set the location of the *print position,* the point on the page where the next printed characters or graphics will be placed. You're free to reset the print position at any time, as long as you follow this one set-in-stone rule: you can't move the print position upward on the page. Even though PCL permits you to send commands that would move the print position up, the DeskJet cannot move the paper backwards, and it will ignore these commands.

By the way, the DeskJet automatically advances the print position -every time it prints a character or graphic dot to the next available space to the right if there's room on the same line, or to the left margin on the following line if there isn't.

Basic print position commands

Several PCL commands move the print position to a predetermined location without giving you any further say in the matter. Most of these basic commands are control codes held over from the ASCII system: the carriage return command moves the print position to the left margin, the tab command moves the print position to the next tab stop, and so on.

While most of these basic print position commands can be vital to the programmer in certain circumstances, they don't let you move the print position freely, wherever you want it on the page— that's what the advanced print position commands are for. Note, though, that two of the basic commands, the tab and backspace control codes, have little value for programmers. Several PCL commands for ejecting and loading paper are included as print position commands, since they do establish the print position at the top of the next page.

Starting a new line: the line terminator characters

In standard ASCII files, the end of a line of text is indicated by a pair of special characters, the carriage return and line feed characters. Ordinarily, this pair of control codes combine to cause the DeskJet to start a new line at the left margin. As a programmer, you can use either of these codes separately if you wish. A third control code, the form feed character, ejects the current page and loads the next. It's also considered a line terminator, since the DeskJet stops printing the current line when it receives the form feed code.

A special PCL escape sequence lets you change how the DeskJet responds to the three line terminator characters, as described later in this chapter.

Moving down a line: the line feed control code

CTRL-J   Line feed
  (1Ød or ØAh)

Normally, the DeskJet responds to the line feed control code by executing a line feed: it moves the print position to the next line on the page, but stays in the same column (horizontal position). Just how far the print position advances is determined by the current line spacing, which you can select with the line spacing escape sequence as described on below.

If the line terminator function is changed to a value of 2 or 3, sending the line feed character produces the same results that you'd normally get by sending both a carriage return and a line feed together: the print position moves down a line and over to the left margin. See the section "Changing the line terminator function" for information on the escape sequence used to change the line terminator.

Moving down a half line: the half line feed command

> ^{E}s$_c$=   Half line feed

PCL also provides an escape sequence to advance the vertical print position half of the space of a line, as defined by the current line spacing setting. Otherwise, the ^{E}s$_c$= sequence works exactly like the regular line feed control code, moving the print position down the page without changing its horizontal location. Changing the setting of the line terminator function has no effect on the half line feed command.

Moving to the left margin: the carriage return control code

> **CTRL-M**   Carriage Return
> **(13d or Øh)**

Normally, the carriage return control code causes the DeskJet to execute a carriage return—it moves the print position horizontally to the left margin, without changing the vertical position (the print position stays on the same line).

If you change the line terminator function to a value of 3, however, a carriage return causes the same effect that you'd ordinarily get with the combination of both a line feed and carriage return: the print position advances one line, and moves over to the left margin.

Selecting a paper path

> **CTRL-L**   Form Feed
> **(12d or ØCh)**
> ^{E}s$_c$&lØH   Eject current page
> ^{E}s$_c$&l1H   Feed from tray
> ^{E}s$_c$&l2H   Feed envelope

In many situations, the DeskJet handles paper loading and ejecting automatically. If a a page is not already in the paper path when you send print data to the DeskJet, the printer loads a new sheet of paper or a new envelope, depending on which paper path is currently active. If the document being printed is longer than one page, the DeskJet automatically ejects each finished page as soon it receives print data for the next page, and then loads another one.

Still, PCL provides several explicit commands for ejecting the current page and loading the next one, and there are several reasons you might want to use them. For one thing, you may want to move on to a new page before the current page has been printed all the way down to the bottom margin—perhaps you want to start a new section or chapter on the next page, for example. Another function performed by two of these commands is to select a paper path, so that paper feeds either from the paper tray or the envelope path.

Finally, it is essential that one of the page-ejecting commands gets sent at the end of a print job. Until the DeskJet receives the command, the printer doesn't eject the last page of the file, even after you've finished sending data to the printer.

Here are the details on each of the page ejecting/loading commands:

When the DeskJet executes a *form feed*, it ejects the page that's currently being printed, if any, loads the next sheet of paper, and moves the print position to the top printing line of the new page. You can get the DeskJet to execute a form feed by pressing the FF button on the keypad, or you can send the form feed control code instead.

As alternatives to the form feed character, the DeskJet's version of PCL provides three escape sequences that also eject the current page:

E_{s_c}&lØH ejects the page but does not load a new one.

E_{s_c}&l1H ejects the page, if any, and immediately loads a new sheet of paper from the paper tray. This command also establishes the paper tray as the active paper path, so that when the DeskJet loads subsequent pages automatically during a multi-page print job, it loads them from the paper tray.

$^E s_C$&l2H ejects the current page and loads an envelope from the envelope path (you have to stuff the envelope into the path first, as detailed in chapter 19). This command also sets the envelope path as the active paper path, so that from then on the DeskJet loads envelopes when it loads "pages" automatically during multiple-page print jobs.

The difference between the form feed command and the second of these escape sequences is as follows: the DeskJet does not load the next sheet of paper immediately after receiving a form feed command, but rather waits until it begins to receive print data for the new page. This way, the paper won't get permanently curled up by sitting inside the paper path waiting to print. The $^E s_C$&l1H sequence, by contrast, does load the next page immediately.

Whether you need to send the eject page command yourself depends on a couple of factors. If you're programming the DeskJet by way of commands embedded in your document, but you're having your application program actually print the file, you probably won't need to embed a form feed character in the file, since many application software programs send will send it for you. If you're printing text files from DOS or writing your own DeskJet program, you must send an eject page command yourself, or plan on pressing the FF button a lot.

Normally, the form feed character causes the DeskJet to simply spit out the current page, without changing the horizontal print position. However, if the line terminator function is set to 2 or 3, a form feed ejects the page and moves the horizontal position over to the left margin, as if you'd sent a carriage return as well. See the following section for information on the escape sequence used to change the line terminator.

Changing the line terminator function

E_{s_C}&k#G   Set line terminator function to #

Valid values: 0—CR=CR; LF=LF; FF=FF
1—CR=CR-LF; LF=LF; FF=FF
2—CR=CR; LF=CR-LF; FF=CR-FF
3—CR=CR-LF; LF=CR-LF; FF=CR-FF

By default, the DeskJet is set to respond to the three line terminator characters, line feed, carriage return, and form feed, as follows: line feed advances the print position by one line without changing the print column, carriage return moves the print position to the left margin but doesn't change the current line, and form feed ejects the current page and loads a new sheet. If necessary, however, you can change how DeskJet responds to the line terminator control codes via an escape sequence.

The reason for changing the line terminator function is to print files that don't use the line terminator characters according to DOS conventions. In DOS's ASCII text files, each line ends in a carriage return/line feed pair. In other types of files, however, the end of a line may be marked only by a line feed character, or rarely, only by a carriage return. If you leave the DeskJet's line terminator function on its default setting, and try to print a file whose lines end with line feeds but no carriage returns, you'd get something like this on your printout:

> These lines end
> in line feed characters
> but not carriage returns.

Likewise, printing a file whose lines end only in carriage returns would produce something like this:

> but not carriage returns. end in line feed characters every print line These lines end

The escape sequence for changing the line terminator function is E_{s_C}&k#G. You can substitute one of four different values for the #:

0 (default): causes the DeskJet to execute all three line terminator characters as they are normally intended: the line feed character results in a line feed

only, a carriage return character produces a carriage return only, and a form feed character executes a form feed, pushing out the current page.

1: In this setting, a carriage return causes the DeskJet to execute both a carriage return and a form feed, moving the print position to the left margin of the next line. Line feed and form feed characters retain their normal functions.

2: Carriage return characters retain their normal function, but line feed characters casue the DeskJet to execute both a carriage return and a line feed, and form feed characters result in both a form feed and a carriage return.

3: Carriage return and line feed characters each cause the DeskJet to execute both a carriage return and a line feed. At this setting, sending both a carriage return and a line feed moves the print position to the left margin *two* lines down. This setting also makes the DeskJet execute both a carriage return and a form feed when you send a form feed character.

Selecting or disabling end-of-line wraparound

^{E}s$_c$&sØC	Enable end-of-line wraparound
^{E}s$_c$&s1C	Disable end-of-line wraparound
Default:	end-of-line wraparound disabled
Notes:	Not a PCL Level III feature.

The end-of-line wraparound setting determines how the DeskJet will respond if it is sent text to print beyond the permissible right border, which is the right margin or the right paper edge, depending on the situation. This can happen either because the current line of text is too long to print within the right margin, or because you've sent a command to move the print position past the right margin, but the print position is now beyond the right edge of the paper.

Either way, if end-of-line wraparound is disabled, the text that falls beyond the right boundary will simply be ignored, and the DeskJet will go on to print the next line. If end-of-line wraparound is enabled, the extra text will be placed on the next line starting at the left margin. As a result, you'll have more lines in your printout than you did in your file, but all the text will be printed.

Moving left one column

CTRL-H   Backspace
(Ø8d or Ø8h)

The backspace command moves the print position one column to the left. This can be useful when you want to combine two characters, such as a regular letter and an accent mark, in the same position. Interestingly, column size does not depend on the current font, but is determined by the pitch setting or the equivalent horizontal motion index, settings you can alter via escape sequence. Because column size is independent of the current font selection, sending the backspace command may not place the print position directly on top of the last character you printed. This is especially true if you're using a proportionally spaced font, since the horizontal space alloted to each letter, numeral, or punctuation mark varies from character to character. The backspace command has no effect when the cursor is at the left margin.

Moving right to the next tab stop

CTRL-I   Tab
(Ø9d or Ø9h)

The tab command is a control code that works much like the tab key in your word processor, advancing the print position to the next tab stop. Unfortunately, the DeskJet's tab stops are fixed at every eighth character position, starting at the left margin, and you can't change them. For this reason, the tab command is too inflexible for most purposes, and you'll probably want to use other position control commands in your programs. The main benefit of the DeskJet's tab command is that it lets you print ASCII files that already contain tab codes—in the printout, columns of text will be aligned properly, even if their exact position on the page isn't right.

Advanced print position commands

PCL's advanced commands for moving the print position let you specify any printable location on the page, down to the level of the individual dot, as the spot where printing should begin. In PCL, you can specify a new print position with the advanced commands using three different units: rows and columns, decipoints, and dots. Whichever unit system you're working with, you set horizontal and vertical print positions via separate commands— changing one doesn't affect the other. For example, let's say the current print position is at row 4, column 16. If you send a command to change the vertical print position to the 13th row, you'll still be in column 16.

In all three unit systems, and both vertically and horizontally, the first print position is 0. In the vertical direction, the 0 position corresponds to the top margin, while in the horizontal position it corresponds to the left edge of the maximum area on which the DeskJet can print, and not the left margin.

The highest number for print position depends on the unit system you're using. Vertically, it corresponds to the bottom of the physical sheet of paper. Horizontally, it corresponds to the right edge of the printable area, not to the right edge of the paper.

Caution: Remember that the DeskJet cannot print within a strip around all four edges of the paper. You cannot move the print position to this unprintable area horizontally, but you can do so in the vertical direction. If you send print data to the DeskJet with the vertical position outside the printable area, the DeskJet simply ignores the data.

Moving up on the page

PCL lets you move the print position with complete freedom on any one page—if you like, you can give a command to print a page number at the bottom right of the page first, then one that prints a letterhead at the top left. Unfortunately, the DeskJet isn't equally free to follow these commands. While it can move its printhead from side to side, it can only move the paper forward in the paper path, and thus you can't freely move the print position to higher locations on the page.

In general, sending the DeskJet a command to move the print position higher on the page causes problems. The new text or graphics may print on top of previously printed lines, or may print on the next page. However, you *can* back up successfully over a very short distance, one or two lines up on the page. This works because the DeskJet reads through the data in its buffer before printing, looking for such commands. If it finds them, it then prints the lines in the order indicated by the commands rather than the order in which it received the data. However, this built-in function scans only a few lines worth of data before deciding to print. Otherwise, the DeskJet would have to wait until it received all the data for an entire page before beginning to print, as it must in landscape mode.

Default print position

Whenever the DeskJet loads a new page, whether in response to a paper load command or automatically during a print job, the print position is set to the top margin vertically (the 0th position) and the left margin horizontally (which may not be the 0th position).

For each direction (horizontal and vertical) and for each set of units, you're given three escape sequences for specifying the new print position: a command to move to an absolute position on the page, and commands to move a specified number of units in either direction relative to the current position.

Positioning by rows and columns

Vertical movement:

^{E}s$_C$&a#R	Move to specified row
^{E}s$_C$&a+#R	Move # rows down from current position
^{E}s$_C$&a-#R	Move # rows up from current position

Horizontal movement:

^{E}s$_C$&a#C	Move to specified column
^{E}s$_C$&a+#C	Move # columns to the right from current position
^{E}s$_C$&a-#C	Move # columns to the left from current position

Setting the print position via rows and columns is easier than doing it with the other units, since rows and columns are larger and there are fewer of them to keep track of. On the other hand, you can't be nearly as precise, for the same reasons. Of course, moving by rows and columns makes a lot of sense when you're working with text, since rows are equivalent to lines, and columns correspond to the size of a character when you're using a monospaced font such as Courier (in proportionally spaced fonts, a column is equivalent to the width of a space character, the kind you enter by pressing the spacebar).

In the vertical direction, the first available row is numbered 0, and is located at the first line of text below the top margin of the page. This is slightly different in concept than the way the way the decipoint and dot coordinate systems work. With those units, the 0th vertical position is actually flush with the top margin itself.

By contrast, setting the print position to the 0th row locates the baseline of the first text line at a distance below the top margin equal to a line, as determined by the line spacing command or the vertical motion index. Characters extend upward from the baseline toward the top margin, but depending on the font size you're using and which characters you print, they may not actually reach the margin.

The distance from one row to the next is also equal to the height of a line, again as set by the line spacing or vertical motion index commands. The greatest row position is the one at the bottom of the physical page, or as close to it as your line spacing setting will take you. The maximum number of rows on a page depend both on your line spacing setting and the size of your paper.

Horizontally, the first column is number 0, and is located at the left boundary of the area on which the DeskJet can print, which is ¼" from the paper edge (the first or 0th column is not at the left margin). The size of a column, and thus both the distance between columns and the total number of columns on a page, is determined by the print pitch or the horizontal motion index currently in effect, if you're using a monospaced font.

With text, often your main concern is just to keep columns properly aligned, rather than to print at a specific measured distance along a line. If that's your situation, all you need to to keep track of in your program is the column number where you want to be.

On the other hand, it's easy to keep track of where you are in terms of inches if you need to for any reason. Remember that pitch is expressed as the number of characters (or columns) per inch. To move to a position that's a particular distance from the left paper edge, subtract ¼" from the desired distance, and then multiply that number by the pitch (that ¼" is for the unprintable strip at the paper edge). You can also figure out the size of a column by dividing 1" by the pitch value—if the pitch is 10, for example, each column is ¹⁄₁₀" wide.

Proportionally spaced fonts have no pitch setting, since the width of each character is different. In these fonts, a column is equal in size to a space character. But since there's no way to tell how wide the space character is in any given font, you'll have to make do with relative positioning if you want to use the column commands. If you need to move the print position a measured horizontal distance, you'll have to use the decipoint or dot commands instead.

Positioning by dot

Vertical movement:

^{E}s$_c$&a#Y	Move to specified vertical dot position
^{E}s$_c$&a+#Y	Move # dots down from current position
^{E}s$_c$&a-#Y	Move # dots up from current position
Notes:	When printing text, the baseline moves to the dot position specified by the command. In graphics mode, the first raster row prints at the specified position only if you print using the escape sequence ^{E}s$_c$*r1A.

Horizontal movement:

^{E}s$_c$&a#X	move to specified horizontal dot position
^{E}s$_c$&a+#X	move # dots to the right from current position
^{E}s$_c$&a-#X	move # dots to the left from current position
Example:	Es$_c$&a35ØY moves the print position to the 350th dot position.

Although the DeskJet can print 300 dots per linear inch, it can only print those dots at fixed locations along the page. Therefore, the most precise way to control the DeskJet's print position is to specify the actual dot location you want. There's a drawback to measuring distances on your page in dot positions, however: the units don't match up too well with any common system of measurement. Sure, there are exactly 300 dots in an inch, and 75 in a quarter inch, but ⅛" inch contains 37.5 dots. Of course, one-half dot's worth of imprecision shouldn't hurt the appearance of your document. It's just that it's a little harder to make the necessary calculations than with decipoints, which fit neatly with the typographer's point-based measuring system.

The dot coordinate system begins with position 0, 0. This corresponds to the top margin vertically and the left edge of the DeskJet's printable area horizontally. When printing text, the text baseline moves to the dot position specified by the command. In graphics mode, the first row of dots prints at the dot position selected by this command.

On a standard 8½x11-inch piece of paper with a top margin set to 0, the greatest possible dot position in the vertical direction is 3100, corresponding to the bottom edge of the DeskJet's printable area. Horizontally, the maximum dot position is 2400, corresponding to the furthest right position that the DeskJet can print.

Positioning by decipoint

Vertical movement:

^{E}s$_c$&a#V	Move to specified vertical decipoint
^{E}s$_c$&a+#V	Move # decipoints down from current position
^{E}s$_c$&a-#V	Move # decipoints up down from current position

Horizontal movement:

^{E}s$_c$&a#H	Move to specified horizontal decipoint
^{E}s$_c$&a+#H	Move # decipoints right from current position
^{E}s$_c$&a-#H	Move # decipoints left from current position

A decipoint is $\frac{1}{10}$th of a typographer's point, and is therefore equal to $\frac{1}{720}$-inch. This is the most precise positioning system available for the DeskJet. Since the printer can only print at 600 different dot positions per horizontal inch, and 300 in a vertical inch, it's obvious that you can't actually print at every decipoint location. Nevertheless, this system works well for typographic purposes, because typographers measure so many distances in points and fractions of points. Decipoint positions align exactly with the dot positions at which the DeskJet can print every $\frac{1}{10}$" vertically and $\frac{1}{20}$" vertically—when you specify a decipoint position that does not align exactly with a dot position, the DeskJet rounds off your request to the closest dot.

The 0,0 position in the decipoint coordinate system corresponds to the top margin in the vertical direction and the first dot the DeskJet can print, $\frac{1}{4}$" from the left edge of the paper, in the horizontal direction. On a standard 8½x11" piece of paper, the highest possible decipoint locations are 7440 vertically, corresponding to the bottom edge of the DeskJet's printable area, and 5760 horizontally, corresponding to the right margin of the printable area.

You can readily convert inches into decipoint measurements and vice versa. To go from inches to decipoints, just multiply the number of inches by 720; two inches equal 1440 decipoints, 5½" is 3960 decipoints, and so on. To convert a measurement in decipoints into inches, divide by 720.

Decipoint-to-inches translations work a little more smoothly than do dots-to-inches conversions. Because 720 can be divided evenly by more factors, the decipoint system lets you can work with smaller distances—even multiples of ⅟₁₆" or ⅟₂₀"—without mucking around with fractional decipoints. For this reason, it may make sense to use decipoint print position commands, even if you're not already familiar with the typographic point system. Remember, though, that because the DeskJet doesn't print 720 dots per inch, the actual print position you get will usually be a tiny bit off from the one you specify.

Specifying the print area

A number of PCL commands allow you to determine the area of the page where text will actually be printed. You can set the right, left, and top margins directly. Other commands determine how tall the print area is and thus the bottom margin.

Setting right and left margins

^{E}s$_C$&a#L	Set left margin to column #
^{E}s$_C$&a#M	Set right margin to column #
^{E}s$_C$9	Clear both left and right margins, reset both to their defaults. Does not affect top or bottom margin.
Units:	Columns. The size of a column is based on the current pitch setting.
Default:	Left margin 0, right margin 79 (based on pitch 10)
Valid values:	0 is the minimum value possible. The maximum allowable column number is determined by the pitch setting and is located at the rightmost boundary of the printable area.

Margin settings work just as they do on a typewriter or in your word processor: as soon as it finishes printing one character or graphics dot, the DeskJet automatically advances the print position to the right until the right margin is reached, whereupon it stops printing on that line. When you send the command to start a new line (ordinarily a carriage return/line feed pair) the DeskJet begins printing the new line at the left margin.

The left and right margins are defined in terms of column numbers, so it helps to know how the DeskJet counts its columns. The 0th (first) column is located flush with the leftmost position that the DeskJet can print. On a standard 8½x11" sheet of paper, the leftmost printable position is located ¼" from the paper edge (see Chapter 2 for more on the printable area).

When a monospaced font is selected, the pitch setting, expressed in characters or columns per inch, determines the width of a column—if the pitch is 12, for example, there are 12 columns per inch, and each column is ¹⁄₁₂" wide. Since column width varies with the pitch setting, the same margin settings will give you different margins if you change pitch. For example, a left margin setting of 10 places the left margin 1¼" from the left edge of the paper if the pitch is 10 cps (the extra ¼" represents the strip at the paper edge that the DeskJet can't print). If you change the pitch to 12, that same left margin setting of 10 puts the left margin a little more than 1¹⁄₁₆" from the paper edge.

Unless you set them otherwise, the DeskJet's margins are set to column 0 on the left, and column 79 on the right by default. Because the DeskJet counts columns starting with 0, that gives you a total of 80 columns in which you can print characters. The default columns are ¹⁄₁₀" wide, as if the pitch was set to 10. That puts the right margin eight inches from the left, at the boundary of the printable area on the right side, ¼" from the right edge of the paper.

Left and right margin settings do not affect the way the print position commands work—regardless of the margin settings, you can still select any column position within the printable area.

Vertical spacing commands

Together, a set of several interrelated commands determine the vertical spacing characteristics of your printouts, including the spacing between lines, the number of lines per page, and the top and bottom margins. The values of all but one of the vertical spacing settings are calculated partly from the values of other settings. For instance, since page length is measured in lines, the correct page length depends on the line spacing currently in effect. For this reason, you must give these commands in the following order:

1. Set line spacing
2. Set paper size or page length

If you want to define top and bottom margins:

3. Set perforation skip to ON
4. Set the top margin
5. Set the text length

Setting line spacing

^{E}s$_C$&l#D	Set lines per inch to #
Units:	Lines per inch.
Default:	6
Valid values:	1 - 48
Notes:	Reciprocal of verical motion index (VMI). Setting line spacing automatically resets VMI and vice versa.

The line spacing setting determines the distance the DeskJet skips down the page when starting a new line of text, from the baseline of the previous line to the new baseline. Line spacing is measured in lines per inch, so you can figure the distance between the baselines of two consecutive lines by dividing 1 by the line spacing setting.

Line spacing, or leading, Changing the line spacing setting can be useful in two common situations: when you switch to a smaller or larger font, and you need to adjust the line spacing to match; and when you want to increase the space between lines for easier reading or to make room for penciled comments on the printout.

The line spacing setting also determines the size of rows when you move the vertical print position using the vertical motion by rows command. An alternative command for setting the size of a line or row is the vertical motion index, discussed next.

Setting the vertical motion index

^{E}S$_C$&l#C	Set vertical motion index to #/48"
Units:	1/48"
Notes:	Reciprocal of line spacing. Setting line spacing automatically resets VMI and vice versa.

The vertical motion index (VMI) is an alternative to the line spacing command for setting the size of a line or row (see the previous section). It determines how far the paper moves every time the DeskJet goes to the next line while printing text. It also determines the size of rows when you move the vertical print position using the vertical motion by rows command.

Whereas the line spacing determines the number of lines the DeskJet will print in a vertical inch, the VMI sets the line size directly, in 1/48" increments. Setting either of these commands automatically resets the other to a corresponding value. For example, if you set the VMI to 6/48", line spacing becomes 8 lines per inch.

You may find the lines-per-inch units of the line spacing command more familiar than the VMI's 1/48"s, since lines per inch are also used to determine line size in many older printers and typewriters. Each of the two commands can give you line sizes the other command can't. A VMI of 5 (5/48"), for instance, translates into an invalid fractional line spacing of 9-3/5 lines per inch. By the same token, a line spacing setting of 10 lines per inch would be equivalent to a VMI of 4.8, also invalid because it's fractional.

There's a comparable command for setting the horizontal motion index, discussed in the next section.

Setting the horizontal motion index

E_s_c&l#H	Set horizontal motion index to #/120"
Units:	1/120"
Notes:	Reciprocal of pitch. Setting pitch automatically resets HMI and vice versa.

The horizontal motion index (HMI) is an alternative to the pitch command (see the previous section) when you want to specify how much space each text character or column consumes in the horizontal direction. It also determines the size of columns when you move the horizontal print position using the horizontal motion by columns command described earlier. HMI is just the reciprocal of the pitch setting—inches per character (in 1/120" increments) instead of characters per inch. Setting either of these commands automatically resets the other to a corresponding value. For example, if you set the HMI to 10 (10/120"), the pitch becomes 12 characters per inch.

Pitch is a familiar term to those who've used typewriters, so you may prefer the pitch command to setting the HMI. Each of these commands can give you character sizes the other command can't. An HMI of 16 (16/120" per character), for instance, is perfectly acceptable, but it translates into an invalid fractional pitch of 7.5 characters per inch. Likewise, a pitch of 13 is equivalent to a VMI of 9.2, also invalid because it's fractional.

There's a comparable command for setting the vertical motion index, discussed above.

Selecting paper size

^{E}s$_C$&l#A	Select paper size corresponding to #
Units:	Arbitrary (each available paper size has a unique code number)
Default:	The default paper size depends on the positions of DIP switches A5 and A6. Entering a 0 in the paper size escape sequence restores the default paper size setting.
Valid values:	See table
Notes:	Not a PCL Level III feature

Paper size	Escape sequence	Dip switch settings	
		A5	**A6**
Letter (8½" x 11")	^{E}s$_C$&l2A	Down	Down
Legal (8½" x 11")	^{E}s$_C$&l3A	Up	Down
Envelopes (9½" x 4⅛")	^{E}s$_C$&l81A	Up	Up
A4 (210 x 297 mm)	^{E}s$_C$&l26A	Down	Up
(Reselect default)	^{E}s$_C$&lØA	—	—

As you can probably figure out yourself, the *paper size* setting tells the DeskJet what size paper you're going to be feeding it. The printer uses the paper size information along with other settings to calculate where the margins are and when the current page ends.

The default *paper size* setting is determined by the positions of the A5 and A6 DIP switches. Of course, the DeskJet comes from the factory set to print on 8½x11" paper as the default. If you usually print on some other size paper, change the switch positions according to the table.

Sending a *paper size* command to the DeskJet automatically clears any margin settings you've made, restoring them to their default values.

Setting page length

^Es_c&l#P	Set page length to # lines
Units:	Lines
Notes:	The height of a line is set by the line spacing command. To determine the proper value to enter in this escape sequence, divide the desired height of the printed page in inches by the current line spacing. Sets top margin and text length to default values.
Default:	The maximum number of lines that will fit on the paper size set by functions switches A5 and A6. The default page length does not reflect changes made to the paper size setting with escape sequences.
Valid values:	0 to the maximum number of lines that will fit on the current paper size.

The *page length* command sets the number of lines the DeskJet prints before ejecting the current page and loading another. In turn, it determines the length or vertical distance of the page, based on the current line spacing setting.

✂ *Tip: It's easier to set page length automatically with the page size command discussed previously.*

Why do you need a *page length* command when you already have a command to select page size? The answer is simple—usually, you don't. Whenever you set the page size, the page length gets automatically set for you, based on the number of lines that would fit on the size of paper you've selected.

There are two situations where it might make sense to set page length explicitly. Obviously, if the paper you're feeding is of non-standard length, none of the page size commands will work. For another thing, the original LaserJet and the LaserJet Plus don't recognize the *page size* command. If you want to write programs that will work on all PCL printers, you'll have to use the page length command instead.

Setting the page length is a little tricky, since it refers to the number of lines the DeskJet could theoretically print on the paper you're feeding, not the lines the DeskJet can actually print. In other words, you have to ignore the fact that the DeskJet is incapable of printing on the top ⅙" or the bottom ½" of a portrait-oriented page. You also have to remember that the page length includes the areas above the top margin and below the bottom margin that you normally don't print on.

If you're printing on 11" paper and your line spacing is set to 6 lines per inch, you should set the page length to 66 lines. At a line spacing of 8, the page length should be 88 lines.

Setting the top margin

^{E}s$_C$&l#E	Set top margin to # lines
Units:	Lines
Notes:	The height of a line is set by the line spacing command. To determine the proper value to enter in this escape sequence, divide the desired height of the top margin in inches by the current line spacing.
Default:	½", regardless of line spacing setting
Valid values:	Ø to the value of the current page length setting
Example:	^{E}s$_C$&l9E sets top margin to 1½", assuming current line spacing is 6 lines per inch (9 lines/6 lines per inch = 1½").
Notes:	The top margin setting is ignored if perforation skip mode is ON. Sets text length to default value. Not a PCL Level III feature.

Setting the top margin determines where the DeskJet starts printing on each new page. The top margin is measured from the top edge of the paper to the line specified by the top margin setting. This command has no effect if perforation skip mode is ON.

Change the top margin before you change the text length setting, covered in the next section. Whenever you set the top margin, the text length gets reset to its default value.

Setting text length

$^E\!s_c$**&l#F**	Set text length to # lines
Units:	Lines
Valid values:	1 to page length minus the top margin
Default:	Maximum number of lines that will fit on current page size at current line spacing and with current top margin
Notes:	The text length value determines the bottom margin. The height of a line is set by the line spacing command; to determine the proper value to enter in this escape sequence, divide the desired text length in inches by the current line spacing. Has no effect when perforation skip mode is ON. Use this formula: text length = page length - (top margin+desired bottom margin)
Examples:	$^E\!s_c$&l54F sets text length to 9", when line spacing is 6 lines per inch (9 lines * 6 lines per inch = 54 lines). $^E\!s_c$&l64F sets bottom margin to 1½", when line spacing is 8 lines per inch, page length is 88 lines (11"), and top margin is 12 lines (1½") (88-(12+12)=64)

The *text length* command determines how many lines of text the DeskJet actually prints on a page, beginning with the line at the top margin. In turn, since it specifies where the DeskJet stops printing, the text length determines the bottom margin as well. In other words, you don't explicitly set a bottom margin—you just set the text length, and whatever's left over at the end of the page is the bottom margin. Since the bottom margin depends on the line spacing, page length, and top margin settings, be sure to set text length *after* you set line spacing, page length, and top margin.

Setting the perforation skip mode

^{E}s$_C$&l1L	Set perforation skip mode to ON
^{E}s$_C$&lØL	Set perforation skip mode to OFF
Default:	determined by position of DIP switch A8 (up = OFF, down = ON). Factory setting is ON, switch A8 in down position.
Notes:	With perforation skip OFF, the top margin and text length settings are ignored, and the DeskJet prints on the entire printable length of the page. Changing perforation skip setting resets top margin and text length to their defaults.

The perforation skip mode determines whether or not the DeskJet pays any attention to the top margin and text length settings. When perforation skip is ON, it does pay attention, and the printer advances to the next page as soon as it moves past the area specified by the text length. When perforation skip is OFF, the top margin and text length settings are ignored, and the DeskJet prints on as much of the page as it is physically can.

Since neither the DeskJet nor any member of the LaserJet family feeds the kind of paper with perforations between each sheet (the fan-folded, continuous feeding type of computer paper), this command seems out of place, or at least misnamed. But if you can imagine the DeskJet printing on perforated paper, you should be able to get an idea of what this command does. If perforation skip is ON, the imaginary DeskJet moves past the perforation separating the pages to the top margin of the next page before starting to print.

Switching the perforation skip mode to OFF is a quick way of squeezing the maximum amount of text on each page. The OFF setting might come in handy when you're printing draft copies of your text for editing. Otherwise, it's of no use. Remember that the top margin and text length settings are returned to their default values every time you change the perforation skip mode, so you'll have to reset them when you switch perforation skip back ON again.

When the DeskJet comes from the factory, perforation skip is set via the A8 DIP switch to ON, and you should leave that switch alone.

Graphics commands

Programming the DeskJet to print graphics images is straightforward in concept but laborious in practice.

Your most fundamental task, of course, is to form the image you want to see on the page. As you'll recall, the DeskJet only prints bit-mapped graphics, meaning that you must tell it explicitly where to print each dot. Fortunately, the encoding scheme you must use in sending this bit-mapped data is as simple as you could imagine.

Each *pixel* (picture element) on the printed page corresponds to one data bit. If the value of the bit is 1, the pixel is printed; if the bit is 0, the pixel is left unprinted. At the DeskJet's top resolution of 300 dots per inch, a pixel is a single dot, and each data bit represents a dot. At lower resolutions, the DeskJet prints more than one dot per pixel, but each pixel is still controlled by just one bit (see the section "Setting graphics resolution" later in this chapter for details on graphics resolution).

When you send a byte of graphics data, the DeskJet reads the byte's 8 binary bits just as you would—the bit at the left (in computerese, the most significant bit or bit 7) represents the pixel at the beginning print position, the next bit to the right, bit six, represents the next pixel to the right, and so on.

For instance, if you send the byte 10110011 (binary notation), the DeskJet will print the following pattern of pixels:

X O X X O O X X

In actual printing, of course, adjacent pixels touch each other. A given sequence of data bytes codes for one row of pixels at a time in an unbroken series—each successive byte in the data stream picks up where the last one left off.

There are other things to attend to besides just sending the actual data to be printed. At a minimum, you have to switch the DeskJet out of text mode and into graphics mode before you , and you must signal the DeskJet to expect more data at the beginning of each row of pixels. Then, when you're through printing graphics, you must send a command to turn graphics printing off and switch back to text mode.

If you want to get fancier, you can also set margins for your graphic, change resolution, or invoke a graphics compaction mode to cut the amount of data you have to transfer.

Graphics command order

Whenever you send graphics to the DeskJet, your commands must follow a specific sequence.

1. Set graphics resolution (optional)
2. Set graphics width (optional)
3. Set graphics compaction mode (optional)
4. Start graphics
5. Set temporary horizontal offset (optional)
6. Transfer graphics
7. End graphics

As you can see from the list, several of the commands are optional—if you're not changing the current settings for resolution, width, or mode, and if you don't want a temporary horizontal offset, you don't need to send these commands. If you do send one or more of them, though, you must send them in the order shown.

Setting graphics resolution

^{E}s$_C$*t#R	Set resolution to # dots per inch
Units:	Dots per inch
Valid values:	300, 150, 100, 75
Default:	Determined by position of DIP switch B2 (up = 300 dpi, down = 75 dpi).
Notes:	If this command is used it should be sent before the start graphics command (ignored after start graphics command). Not reset to default by end graphics command. Not a PCL Level III feature.
Example:	^{E}s$_C$*t15ØR sets graphics resolution to 150 dots per inch.

Use the *graphics resolution* command to select from the DeskJet's four available graphics resolutions: 75, 100, 150, and 300 dots per inch. Depending on the selected resolution, the DeskJet prints a different number of dots for each bit of graphic data it receives. At a resolution of 300 dpi, it prints one dot for each graphic bit. At 150 dpi, it prints a square two dots wide by two dots high for each bit; at 100 dpi, a 3 x 3 dot square; and at 75 dpi, a 4 x 4 dot square.

Following HP's lead, I use the term *pixel* to refer to the entire square printed for each data bit, no matter what the resolution. Since pixel size varies with resolution, it follows that the size of the printed image will change when you print the same graphics data at a different resolution. A square block that is 1" on all sides at 300 dpi will be 3" x 3" at 100 dpi, or 9 times larger in area. But both squares will contain the same number of pixels.

Lower resolution graphics look just as nice as the high-res kind for objects with perfectly vertical and horizontal edges, such as the bars in bar graphs. With curved objects, though, the lower the resolution, the more jagged the edges. You need less data to cover the same area of the page at lower resolutions than at higher, so low res printing takes less time to transfer the data and less time for the DeskJet to interpret it (printing the dots themselves takes just as long, however).

You don't need to reset the resolution each time you print graphics. If you do wish to change the setting, though, be sure you send the command before you send the *start graphics* command—the *resolution* command will be ignored if you send it after start graphics.

Setting graphics width

^{E}s$_c$*r#S	Set graphics width to # dots
Units:	Dots
Valid values:	0 to maximum dot position for full width of the current paper, excluding unprintable strip at each edge (2400 on legal or letter paper)
Default:	Maximum value for current paper width
Notes:	Reset to default by end graphics command. Must be send before start graphics command.
Example:	^{E}s$_c$*r1200S sets width of area to be printed to 4" (1200dots/300 dots per inch)

The graphics width is the maximum number of graphics dots that the DeskJet will print horizontally across each line, and thus limits the width of your graphics images. This command can speed graphics printing somewhat, because the DeskJet can make more efficient use of its memory when it knows how much data to expect per line.

If you wish to take advantage of this speedup, set the graphics width to the value equal to the maximum width of your graphic before you send the *start graphics* command. Assuming you don't mistakenly set the width smaller than the graphic you're printing, the image won't look any different than if you'd left the width setting alone.

The graphics width setting is automatically reset to its default value, the maximum value permitted by the current page size, as soon as the DeskJet receives the *stop graphics* command.

Starting graphics printing

$^E s_C$ *rØA	Start graphics at leftmost position
$^E s_C$ *r1A	Start graphics at current position
Notes:	This is not the standard PCL Level III function for the $^E s_C$ *r1A escape sequence. In other PCL printers, this sequence sets left margin for graphics at position 1.

Obviously, the *start graphics printing* command tells the DeskJet that it's time to begin printing graphics. But the command also sets the left margin for the graphic to be printed.

If you send the *start graphics* command with a value of 0, the left margin of your graphic will be the leftmost printable position on the paper, which is ¼" from the paper edge on legal and letter paper. Sending the command with a value of 1 sets the left margin of the graphic to the current horizontal print position.

Of course, if you use the latter option (value = 1), you should first set the horizontal print position you want using any of the commands for moving the horizontal print position. Either way, printing will begin at the current vertical print position, so you should set the desired vertical position before sending the command. After you've sent the *start graphics* command, you can't change the graphics resolution, graphics width, or left margin until you send the *stop graphics* command.

Transferring graphics data

^{E}s$_c$**b#W<data>** Transfer # bytes of graphic data. The notation <data> refers to the actual data to be sent immediately following the escape sequence.

Units: Bytes

Valid values: For # (number of bytes): 0-maximum number of data bytes that will fit within the current graphics margins. Calculate the number of bytes needed to fill between the two margins by this formula:

- at 300 dpi resolution: graphics width-graphics left margin/8 (where the graphics width and graphics left margin are specified in dots);
- at 150 dpi, divide the calculated result above by 2;
- at 100 dpi, divide the result by 3;
- at 75 dpi, divide the result by 4

For data bytes: Ø-FF hexadecimal (Ø-255 decimal)

Notes: Graphics printer data must follow this command immediately, in the format described below. Send a separate transfer graphics command for each line (dot row) of the graphic.

Example: ^{E}s$_c$**b8W<255><255>** prints a horizontal line 16 dots long at 300 dpi:

Use the *transfer graphics* command immediately before you send the graphics data for the current line. The command specifies how many bytes you want the DeskJet to print. To print the next line, move the print position to the left side of the image, send the transfer graphics command again, followed by the data for that line. When you're finished with the entire graphic, send the stop graphics command, which we'll cover in the next section.

⌒ *Caution:* *You must send the transfer graphics command at the beginning of each graphics line (row of dots) in the image you're printing.*

Each byte of the data itself must be sent as a single number— don't translate the decimal digits of the number into ASCII codes. Thus you'd send the data byte 126 as a single byte, not as separate ASCII code bytes for "1", "2", and

"6". (By contrast, you do break down the values you send *within* escape sequences into their component digits.)

To determine the correct value for each data byte, remember that each pixel in the printed image is specified by one bit of data. In a data byte, the most significant bit (bit number 7) codes for the pixel at the current print position. The next bit (bit 6) codes for the pixel at the next position to the right, and so on.

So, to send the data byte for this pattern of dots

X O X O X O X O

you'd send a byte containing the bits 10101010. If you don't think in this binary notation, you can translate the byte to decimal (170) or hexadecimal (AA), depending on which system you're comfortable with, and which system is best supported by the programming language you're using.

Caution: *This discussion assumes you're in the default graphics mode. See "Setting graphics compaction modes" later in this chapter for tips on how to send compacted graphics data.*

Here's a table you can use to make the necessary translations. Just add the values of the bits you want to print to give you the correct data byte.

	Bit							
	7	6	5	4	3	2	1	0
Decimal	128	64	32	16	8	4	2	1
Hex	80	40	20	10	8	4	2	1

For example, to calculate the value for the dot pattern **x x o o x x o o**, you'd add 128 + 64 + 8 + 4. You'd then send the result, 204, to the DeskJet as a byte of data.

Ending graphics printing

Es**c*****rB**

Notes: Returns DeskJet to text mode. Resets the left graphics margin, graphics width, and graphics mode to defaults.

When you're finished printing an entire graphics image, send the *end graphics printing* command. The DeskJet returns to text mode. In the process, the graphics width, left graphics margin, and graphics mode settings are reset to their default values. The graphics resolution setting is not reset.

Selecting graphics compaction modes

Es**c*****bØM**   Select normal graphics mode, mode 0 (no compaction)

Es**c*****b1M**   Select graphics compaction mode 1

Es**c*****b2M**   Select graphics compaction mode 2

Default: Mode 0

Notes: Reset to mode 0 by end graphics command. Not a PCL Level III feature.

You can use these escape sequences to choose between the DeskJet's three available modes for interpreting graphics data sent with the *transfer graphics* command. Modes 1 and 2 allow you to compact or compress the printer data, so that you can send fewer bytes to the printer and speed up printing to some extent.

Mode 0, called *full graphics mode*, is the default. In this mode, every pixel in the printed image is specified by a corresponding bit of data.

When you have stretches of repeating data bytes to send, you can use *compacted graphics mode 1* to reduce the amount of data you send, sometimes considerably.

In mode 1, the very first data byte you send after the transfer graphics command functions as a repeat value. This first byte specifies how many times the DeskJet prints the bytes that follow. For example, if you transfer graphics data in mode 1 with the escape sequence **E**s**c*****b2W<1Ø><255>**

the DeskJet will print the data byte 255 eleven times (once to begin with, then ten repetitions). Since the data byte 255 is the code for printing a pixel at every possible location, the result will be an unbroken line 88 pixels long (11 bytes x 8 bits/byte x 1 bit/pixel). To print the same line in mode 0, you would have had to send 11 bytes of data, not two. Note that the value for the number of data bytes in the *transfer graphics* escape sequence includes the repeat value as well as the actual graphics data.

Compacted graphics mode 2 lets you combine repeated graphics data bytes and "blocks" of individual bytes. This way you don't have to switch back and forth between modes 0 and 1 all the time if you have frequent runs of repeated data bytes in your image.

Just as in mode 1, the first byte of data after the *transfer graphics* escape sequence is a special value that tells the DeskJet about the graphics data to follow. In this case, though, this first byte can be either a repeat count or a block length. After sending the data associated with this special value, you can then send another value to set up the next repeated byte or block of data.

To specify a repeat count in mode 2, you must convert the repeat count you want into a negative number using the bytewise two's complement system (all you do is subtract the repeat count from 256.) To print the following data byte four times, for instance, the first byte should be 253, which is equal to -3, and which the DeskJet will interpret as a repeat value of 3. Again, the DeskJet prints the graphics data byte once and then repeats it the number of times specified by the repeat value.

To print a block of individual bytes in mode 2, you first send a byte value one less than the length of the block. This time you use a positive rather than a negative number—that's how the DeskJet knows you're calling for a block instead of a repeated byte. Just as with the repeat count, the DeskJet automatically expects to print at least one byte in a block. To print a four-byte block, you'd send a block length value of three, which is how many more bytes the block contains.

In mode 2, the largest permitted value for either the repeat count or the block length is 127. If you're setting a repeat count of 127, you'd send the value 81 hexadecimal, which is actually -127 in the two's complement system.

Once you've sent a repeat count and the byte to be repeated, you can follow that with another repeat count and another byte to be repeated, or a block length value followed by the block data. Likewise, you can send a repeat count and its data byte after the last byte in a block. Just remember as you mix and match that you must place the number of total bytes, including all the bytes that set repeat counts and block length, in your initial *transfer graphics* escape sequence.

Here's an example. Using mode 2, you could compress the 17 data bytes 128 124 54 54 54 54 255 255 255 255 255 255 255 255 94 12 147 to 11 bytes with this escape sequence:

$$E_{S_C}\text{*b11W<1><128><124><253><54><249><255><2><94><12><147>}$$

The first data byte, 1, is a positive number and therefore sets up a block. In this case, the value of 1 means the block will be two bytes long. This takes care of the bytes 128 and 124.

The fourth data byte starts another special sequence. It's a negative number (-3) in the two's complement system, so it sets a repeat count of 3, causing the DeskJet to print the next byte, 54, a total of 4 times. Then comes another negative number, this time -7. Again, it's a repeat count, so the DeskJet prints the following byte, 255, a total of 8 times. Finally, the positive number 2 sets up a three byte block with the values 94, 12, and 147.

Setting a temporary horizontal offset for graphics

E_{S_C}*b#X — Set temporary horizontal offset to # dots

Units: — Dots

Valid values: Multiples of 8

Default: — Ø

Notes: — Added to left graphics margin for the current line only. Reset to 0 after the current line is printed.

If portions of the graphic you're printing have lots of white space on the left side, use the *temporary offset* command. With this command, you can move the beginning printing position for the current line to the location where you want your first black dots. That way, you don't have to send long strings of 0 bytes to the DeskJet just to get past the white space.

The value you send for the temporary offset is added to the left graphics margin previously set by the *start graphics* command. The temporary offset is indeed temporary—it's only in effect for the next printed line, and you have to reset it before you send the next *transfer graphics* command. The value you enter in the escape sequence must be an even multiple of 8.

Setting graphics quality and speeding graphics printing

^{E}s$_C$***rØQ**	Select highest graphics quality
^{E}s$_C$***r1Q**	Select draft quality
^{E}s$_C$***r2Q**	Select letter quality
Default:	Highest quality
Notes:	Not a PCL Level III feature.

The *graphics quality* setting determines how much ink the DeskJet applies when printing in graphics mode, and thus how dark the blacks are. In the high quality mode, it applies the optimal amount of ink, but this takes longer than in the lower quality mode. This command lets you choose the most appropriate compromise between printed quality and speed for the work you're doing. Generally, it's a good idea to set the printer to a lower quality mode while you're printing draft copies. Once the printout looks perfect, you can then select highest quality for your final copies.

Since you want to be able to switch quickly from one quality mode to another, don't set the graphics quality permanently from your program. Instead, give yourself or your program's users control at print time. Of course, you can always select the print quality setting from the keypad blank button. If you want the convenience of software, though, you can build a print quality option into your program.

23

Troubleshooting

∾

This chapter is devoted entirely to troubleshooting—what to do if your DeskJet acts up, cuts out, or collapses in ruins. The material presented here is expanded over what you'll find in the *Owner's Manual,* and it is organized by major categories of malfunction. These are indicated by the larger-type section headings.

NOTHING AT ALL HAPPENS WHEN YOU TRY TO PRINT

1. The printer is plugged in and turned on, of course.

2. Check to make sure the ON LINE light is glowing. If not, the DeskJet is off-line and can't print. Press the ON LINE button on the keypad so that the light comes on, and try again.

3. Check the cable connection. Your cable should be securely seated into the correct port at both the printer and the computer.

4. Check to see that your computer is properly configured for the type of connection you've made. If your printer is connected to LPT1:, for example, make sure your software is set to print to LPT1:, not LPT2:, COM1:, or any other port. If you're using a serial connection, check to be sure that you've successfully executed the necessary MODE commands, as described in your *Owner's Manual* (in this book, I've assumed you have used a parallel rather than a serial connection, for the reasons laid out in Chapter 2).

5. If you're using a switching box that lets you send data from more than one computer to your DeskJet, or that lets you send data to more than one printer, make sure the switch is set properly to direct data from the active computer to the DeskJet.

6. Does the print cartridge have ink? If not, replace it.

7. Is there paper in the paper tray, and is it properly loaded?

8. Check to see if the print cartridge is seated correctly. The green arrow on the top of the cartridge should be aligned with the green dot on the cartridge cradle. The cartridge should be fully seated, so that it clicks into place.

9. Make sure that the packing tape has been removed from the "nose" of the cartridge.

LIGHTS BLINKING

All the lights on the keypad are blinking at the same time

Either you've installed the wrong font cartridge—22707K and 22707E won't work in the DeskJet Plus—or the printer may require service. Before you take your printer to the shop, though, see if you can clear the problem by turning the printer off for a few seconds, then back on.

All the lights on the keypad are blinking one at a time

1. The print cartridge may have stalled. Try turning the DeskJet off for a few seconds, then back on.

2. Open the printer's top cover and check to be sure that the packaging tape that ties down the cartridge cradle has been removed. If you've previously printed successfully, and haven't shipped the printer since, you can skip this step.

3. See if the print carriage moves properly. With the DeskJet turned off, try moving the print carriage from side to side by hand. If it doesn't move, and there's nothing obvious blocking its path, the printer needs service.

4. This pattern of blinking lights also is used to indicate a RAM or ROM failure discovered by the automatic self-testing procedure the DeskJet completes every time you turn it on. If this is the cause, the printer needs to be serviced.

BUSY and ON LINE lights are blinking

This indicates a paper jam. Instructions for clearing it are found below.

ON LINE light is blinking

This indicates that the paper isn't properly loaded.

1. Check to make sure that there's paper in the printer bin, and that it's stacked squarely and pushed all the way forward.

2. Be sure you're using the right weight of paper. Use 16 to 24 pound paper for best results.

BUSY light is blinking, with the printer in landscape orientation

This indicates that the DeskJet has received data to print, but less than a full page worth. The printer won't start printing until you press the FF key, or send a form feed control code.

PAPER FEEDING PROBLEMS

How to clear a paper jam

Paper jams are rare in the DeskJet, but when they occur you'll probably lose the data that's already been sent to the printer. Follow these steps:

1. Take out the paper tray cover and the out tray, and lift the printer's top cover.

2. Locate the jammed piece of paper. Press the UP and DOWN buttons on the keypad to move the paper out of the printer by the path of least resistance.

3. If the paper is really stuck, help it along by pulling on it with one hand while you continue to fiddle with the UP and DOWN keys with the other hand.

4. Should you tear the paper, just go after each piece separately until they're all free.

5. Press the RESET button to bring the DeskJet back on line.

Paper jams repeatedly, or

The paper comes out at an angle, or printing is slanted on the page, or

Paper doesn't load at all, or

More than one sheet gets loaded at a time

1. Be sure you've loaded the paper into the paper tray squarely, with the right edge of the paper stack flush with the right side of the tray.

2. Don't load the tray with more than ½" of paper at a time. That works out to about 100 sheets.

If you're not getting paper to load at all, you should check to make sure you've put some paper in the tray to begin with, of course, and also that the paper tray extender is positioned properly so that it pushes the paper firmly against the printer.

If more than one sheet loads at a time, the paper itself may be sticky.

Envelopes don't load

1. Make sure you're inserting the envelope under the envelope guides on the out tray. See Chapter 18 for details on envelope loading and printing.

2. The envelope should be inserted top first, flap up, with its right edge square against the right side of the out tray. The top edge of the envelope should be placed under the paper feed rollers.

3. If you're loading envelopes by hand, be sure you're pressing both the UP and DOWN buttons on the keypad at the same time.

4. If you're letting your software load the envelopes, go over the proper steps for envelope feeding in your software manual.

Last page of your document doesn't appear

This is a common event, caused when the printer doesn't receive a final form feed control code. The page has actually been printed already, and will emerge as soon as the form feed command gets there. Take matters into your own hands by pressing the FF button on the keypad.

PRINT QUALITY PROBLEMS

Print is fuzzy but dark

1. Try reactivating the print cartridge by pressing the PRIME key.

2. Some kinds of paper don't hold the DeskJet ink very well. Try a recommended type of paper.

Incomplete characters or graphics—dots or lines are missing

1. Reactivate the print cartridge by pressing the PRIME key.

2. To be sure that the print cartridge is seated properly, remove it and reinstall it. The green arrow on the top of the cartridge should be aligned with the green dot on the cartridge cradle. The cartridge should be fully seated, so that it clicks into place.

Intensity of the print varies

Reactivate the print cartridge by pressing the PRIME key.

Print appears faded

Try reactivating the print cartridge by pressing the PRIME key. If this doesn't work, the cartrdige is running out of ink and needs to be replaced.

Paper comes out wrinkled

You've probably just printed a large, very dark graphic. In quantity, the DeskJet's water-based ink causes the same effect as pouring a glass of water on the paper would. Try to use lighter and/or smaller graphics.

PRINT POSITIONING AND SPACING PROBLEMS

Graphics or text are in the wrong position on the page:

1. If you're attempting to tell the DeskJet where to position some text or graphics via escape sequences, without the aid of an applications program, you've probably miscalculated the coordinates. Remember that the 0 point of the DeskJet's coordinate system is at the top left corner of the area the DeskJet can print, not the top left of the actual paper. The printable area begins ⅙" from the top edge and ¼" from the left edge.

2. If this happens in an application program, be sure the paper size you've selected in the program matches the size of the paper you're actually using.

Too much space between lines

Assuming you've set the line spacing command properly, the problem may be that your margins are just a little too wide for the font size you're using. If the DeskJet can't fit a line of your file on a single line of paper, it may automatically wrap the remaining characters down to the next line or simply ignore them, depending on the End-of-Line Wraparound setting. If the line you're trying to print are only slightly too long, this may result only in extra space between lines, not in bad line breaks.

Only a few lines print on each page

Check the page length setting. An occasional mistake is to leave off one of the digits when you type in the page length setting—you might have accidentally entered a page length of six lines instead of 60, for instance.

UNEXPECTED RESULTS

Text prints in a font other than the one you selected (internal and cartridge fonts)

1. Be sure you've actually selected the font you want by pressing the FONT key repeatedly until the light beside the font's name glows.

2. If it's a cartridge font, be sure the cartridge is fully seated in its slot.

3. Application software often overrides the choices you make from the keypad. If this is the case, you'll have to select the desired font from within your software—consult the software manual for instructions.

Text doesn't switch to bold from italics

To switch from bold to italics, you must first send the command to switch from italics to upright type style, ESC(s0s, then the command to switch from normal stroke weight to bold, ESC(s3B. That's because style has a higher priority in the hierarchy of font attributes than does stroke weight.

Unexpected characters or wierd symbols appear on the printout

Check to make sure you're using the character set that matches the one you want to print. If you select a different character set, your software may be sending out the correct character codes to the printer, but those codes may well represent characters you don't want in the other set.

The DeskJet ignores a software command

Before you blame your printer, make sure you're sending the correct control code or escape sequence. In particular, take care that you haven't mixed up the lowercase letter *l* with the numeral 1 or the uppercase I. Likewise, check to see that you haven't substituted uppercase O for the numeral 0, or vice versa. Check too that you've entered all the uppercase letters in uppercase and the lowercase ones in lowercase.

The DeskJet ignores all your software commands

The problem: You're sending a series of escape sequences to the printer from DOS or with a setup utility, but the DeskJet switches back to its default settings when you then try to print with your application program.

The explanation: your application program is automatically sending a soft reset command to the DeskJet every time it starts to print. This command returns all printer settings to their defaults.

Solution: embed the escape sequences directly within your document as described in Chapter 8 or with BackLoader, covered in Chapter 7.

SELF TEST PROBLEMS

Self test doesn't print

1. For the self test to work, the printer must be plugged in, it must have paper in the paper tray, and there must not be a paper jam. If there's a jam, clear it following the instructions in the "Paper feed problems" section above.

2. Try the self test again—maybe you made a mistake in executing the procedure.

3. If it still doesn't work, the printer needs service.

Self test prints unexpected results

Not to worry if the character patterns look a little different from those on the sample self test pages shown in your *Owner's Manual,* but basically similar and legible. The pattern changes depending on whether you have a font cartridge installed, and which one it is. If you get strange patterns of dots or lines, or completely disorganized characters, your printer needs service.

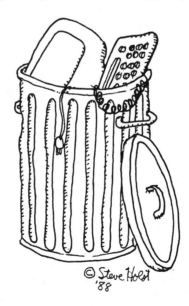

© Steve Holst
'88

Appendix A

DeskJet

Character Sets

¢

This appendix contains character set tables for 11 of the DeskJet's 19 character sets available in its internal fonts (the original DeskJet had only 18 sets, the PC-850 set being new with the Plus). In each table, the gray boxes show characters that aren't available in that set. The tiny number in each box is the ASCII code for that character. The charts were produced with MoreFonts, a font generating utility discussed in Chapter 7.

0	16	32	0 48	@ 64	P 80	` 96	p 112	128	144	160	176	192	208	224	240
1	17	! 33	1 49	A 65	Q 81	a 97	q 113	129	145	161	177	193	209	225	241
2	18	" 34	2 50	B 66	R 82	b 98	r 114	130	146	162	178	194	210	226	242
3	19	# 35	3 51	C 67	S 83	c 99	s 115	131	147	163	179	195	211	227	243
4	20	$ 36	4 52	D 68	T 84	d 100	t 116	132	148	164	180	196	212	228	244
5	21	% 37	5 53	E 69	U 85	e 101	u 117	133	149	165	181	197	213	229	245
6	22	& 38	6 54	F 70	V 86	f 102	v 118	134	150	166	182	198	214	230	246
7	23	' 39	7 55	G 71	W 87	g 103	w 119	135	151	167	183	199	215	231	247
8	24	(40	8 56	H 72	X 88	h 104	x 120	136	152	168	184	200	216	232	248
9	25	) 41	9 57	I 73	Y 89	i 105	y 121	137	153	169	185	201	217	233	249
10	26	* 42	: 58	J 74	Z 90	j 106	z 122	138	154	170	186	202	218	234	250
11	27	+ 43	; 59	K 75	[91	k 107	{ 123	139	155	171	187	203	219	235	251
12	28	, 44	< 60	L 76	\ 92	l 108	| 124	140	156	172	188	204	220	236	252
13	29	- 45	= 61	M 77	] 93	m 109	} 125	141	157	173	189	205	221	237	253
14	30	. 46	> 62	N 78	^ 94	n 110	~ 126	142	158	174	190	206	222	238	254
15	31	/ 47	? 63	O 79	_ 95	o 111	127	143	159	175	191	207	223	239	255

Symbol set code: R8   Full name: Roman-8   189 characters.
Font name: Geneva Roman

0	16	32	48	64	80	96	112	128	144	160	176	192	208	224	240
		(32)	0 (48)	@ (64)	P (80)	' (96)	p (112)			(160)	¯ (176)	â (192)	Å (208)	Á (224)	Þ (240)
		! (33)	1 (49)	A (65)	Q (81)	a (97)	q (113)			À (161)	Ý (177)	ê (193)	î (209)	Ã (225)	þ (241)
		" (34)	2 (50)	B (66)	R (82)	b (98)	r (114)			Â (162)	ý (178)	ô (194)	Ø (210)	ã (226)	· (242)
		# (35)	3 (51)	C (67)	S (83)	c (99)	s (115)			È (163)	° (179)	û (195)	Æ (211)	Ð (227)	µ (243)
		$ (36)	4 (52)	D (68)	T (84)	d (100)	t (116)			Ê (164)	Ç (180)	á (196)	å (212)	ð (228)	¶ (244)
		% (37)	5 (53)	E (69)	U (85)	e (101)	u (117)			Ë (165)	ç (181)	é (197)	í (213)	Í (229)	¾ (245)
		& (38)	6 (54)	F (70)	V (86)	f (102)	v (118)			Î (166)	Ñ (182)	ó (198)	ø (214)	Ì (230)	— (246)
		' (39)	7 (55)	G (71)	W (87)	g (103)	w (119)			Ï (167)	ñ (183)	ú (199)	æ (215)	Ó (231)	¼ (247)
		((40)	8 (56)	H (72)	X (88)	h (104)	x (120)			´ (168)	¡ (184)	à (200)	Ä (216)	Ò (232)	½ (248)
		) (41)	9 (57)	I (73)	Y (89)	i (105)	y (121)			` (169)	¿ (185)	è (201)	ì (217)	Õ (233)	ª (249)
		* (42)	: (58)	J (74)	Z (90)	j (106)	z (122)			^ (170)	¤ (186)	ò (202)	Ö (218)	õ (234)	º (250)
		+ (43)	; (59)	K (75)	[(91)	k (107)	{ (123)			¨ (171)	£ (187)	ù (203)	Ü (219)	Š (235)	« (251)
		, (44)	< (60)	L (76)	\ (92)	l (108)	| (124)			~ (172)	¥ (188)	ä (204)	É (220)	š (236)	■ (252)
		- (45)	= (61)	M (77)	] (93)	m (109)	} (125)			Ù (173)	§ (189)	ë (205)	ï (221)	Ú (237)	» (253)
		. (46)	> (62)	N (78)	^ (94)	n (110)	~ (126)			Û (174)	ƒ (190)	ö (206)	ß (222)	Ÿ (238)	± (254)
		/ (47)	? (63)	O (79)	_ (95)	o (111)	▓ (127)			£ (175)	¢ (191)	ü (207)	Ô (223)	ÿ (239)	(255)

			0	@	P	°	p	128	144	160	176	192	208	224	240
0	16	32	48	64	80	96	112	128	144	160	176	192	208	224	240
		!	1	A	Q	a	q	129	145	161	177	193	209	225	241
1	17	33	49	65	81	97	113	129	145	161	177	193	209	225	241
		'	2	B	R	b	r	130	146	162	178	194	210	226	242
2	18	34	50	66	82	98	114	130	146	162	178	194	210	226	242
		#	3	C	S	c	s	131	147	163	179	195	211	227	243
3	19	35	51	67	83	99	115	131	147	163	179	195	211	227	243
		$	4	D	T	d	t	132	148	164	180	196	212	228	244
4	20	36	52	68	84	100	116	132	148	164	180	196	212	228	244
		%	5	E	U	e	u	133	149	165	181	197	213	229	245
5	21	37	53	69	85	101	117	133	149	165	181	197	213	229	245
		&	6	F	V	f	v	134	150	166	182	198	214	230	246
6	22	38	54	70	86	102	118	134	150	166	182	198	214	230	246
		"	7	G	W	g	w	135	151	167	183	199	215	231	247
7	23	39	55	71	87	103	119	135	151	167	183	199	215	231	247
		(	8	H	X	h	x	136	152	168	184	200	216	232	248
8	24	40	56	72	88	104	120	136	152	168	184	200	216	232	248
		)	9	I	Y	i	y	137	153	169	185	201	217	233	249
9	25	41	57	73	89	105	121	137	153	169	185	201	217	233	249
		*	:	J	Z	j	z	138	154	170	186	202	218	234	250
10	26	42	58	74	90	106	122	138	154	170	186	202	218	234	250
		+	;	K	[	k	§	139	155	171	187	203	219	235	251
11	27	43	59	75	91	107	123	139	155	171	187	203	219	235	251
		,	=	L	®	l	¶	140	156	172	188	204	220	236	252
12	28	44	60	76	92	108	124	140	156	172	188	204	220	236	252
		-	=	M	]	m	†	141	157	173	189	205	221	237	253
13	29	45	61	77	93	109	125	141	157	173	189	205	221	237	253
		.	¢	N	©	n	™	142	158	174	190	206	222	238	254
14	30	46	62	78	94	110	126	142	158	174	190	206	222	238	254
		/	?	O	_	o	▓	143	159	175	191	207	223	239	255
15	31	47	63	79	95	111	127	143	159	175	191	207	223	239	255

Symbol set code: PM Full name: PC-850 Multilingual   253 characters.
Font name: Geneva Roman

(0)	► (16)	(32)	0 (48)	@ (64)	P (80)	` (96)	p (112)	Ç (128)	É (144)	á (160)	▦ (176)	└ (192)	ð (208)	Ó (224)	- (240)
☺ (1)	◄ (17)	! (33)	1 (49)	A (65)	Q (81)	a (97)	q (113)	ü (129)	æ (145)	í (161)	▦ (177)	┴ (193)	Đ (209)	ß (225)	± (241)
☻ (2)	↕ (18)	" (34)	2 (50)	B (66)	R (82)	b (98)	r (114)	é (130)	Æ (146)	ó (162)	▩ (178)	┬ (194)	Ê (210)	Ô (226)	‗ (242)
♥ (3)	‼ (19)	# (35)	3 (51)	C (67)	S (83)	c (99)	s (115)	â (131)	ô (147)	ú (163)	│ (179)	├ (195)	Ë (211)	Ó (227)	¾ (243)
♦ (4)	¶ (20)	$ (36)	4 (52)	D (68)	T (84)	d (100)	t (116)	ä (132)	ö (148)	ñ (164)	┤ (180)	─ (196)	È (212)	ō (228)	¶ (244)
♣ (5)	§ (21)	% (37)	5 (53)	E (69)	U (85)	e (101)	u (117)	à (133)	ò (149)	Ñ (165)	Á (181)	┼ (197)	ı (213)	Õ (229)	§ (245)
♠ (6)	▬ (22)	& (38)	6 (54)	F (70)	V (86)	f (102)	v (118)	å (134)	û (150)	ª (166)	Â (182)	ã (198)	Í (214)	µ (230)	÷ (246)
● (7)	↨ (23)	' (39)	7 (55)	G (71)	W (87)	g (103)	w (119)	ç (135)	ù (151)	º (167)	À (183)	Ã (199)	Î (215)	þ (231)	¸ (247)
◘ (8)	↑ (24)	((40)	8 (56)	H (72)	X (88)	h (104)	x (120)	ê (136)	ÿ (152)	¿ (168)	© (184)	╚ (200)	Ï (216)	Þ (232)	° (248)
○ (9)	↓ (25)	) (41)	9 (57)	I (73)	Y (89)	i (105)	y (121)	ë (137)	Ö (153)	® (169)	╣ (185)	╔ (201)	┘ (217)	Ú (233)	¨ (249)
◎ (10)	→ (26)	* (42)	: (58)	J (74)	Z (90)	j (106)	z (122)	è (138)	Ü (154)	¬ (170)	║ (186)	╩ (202)	┌ (218)	Û (234)	· (250)
♂ (11)	← (27)	+ (43)	; (59)	K (75)	[(91)	k (107)	{ (123)	ï (139)	ø (155)	½ (171)	╗ (187)	╦ (203)	█ (219)	Ù (235)	¹ (251)
♀ (12)	└ (28)	, (44)	< (60)	L (76)	\ (92)	l (108)		(124)	î (140)	£ (156)	¼ (172)	╝ (188)	╠ (204)	▄ (220)	ý (236)	³ (252)
♪ (13)	↔ (29)	- (45)	= (61)	M (77)	] (93)	m (109)	} (125)	ì (141)	Ø (157)	¡ (173)	¢ (189)	═ (205)	¦ (221)	Ý (237)	² (253)
♫ (14)	▲ (30)	. (46)	> (62)	N (78)	^ (94)	n (110)	~ (126)	Ä (142)	× (158)	« (174)	¥ (190)	╬ (206)	Ì (222)	¯ (238)	■ (254)
☼ (15)	▼ (31)	/ (47)	? (63)	O (79)	_ (95)	o (111)	⌂ (127)	Å (143)	ƒ (159)	» (175)	┐ (191)	¤ (207)	▀ (223)	´ (239)	(255)

Symbol set code: PC Full name: PC-8   253 characters.
Font name: Geneva Roman

(0)	▶ (16)	(32)	0 (48)	@ (64)	P (80)	` (96)	p (112)	Ç (128)	É (144)	á (160)	⠿ (176)	└ (192)	⊥ (208)	α (224)	≡ (240)
☺ (1)	◀ (17)	! (33)	1 (49)	A (65)	Q (81)	a (97)	q (113)	ü (129)	æ (145)	í (161)	▓ (177)	┴ (193)	╤ (209)	ß (225)	± (241)
☻ (2)	↕ (18)	" (34)	2 (50)	B (66)	R (82)	b (98)	r (114)	é (130)	Æ (146)	ó (162)	▦ (178)	┬ (194)	╥ (210)	Γ (226)	≥ (242)
♥ (3)	‼ (19)	# (35)	3 (51)	C (67)	S (83)	c (99)	s (115)	â (131)	ô (147)	ú (163)	│ (179)	├ (195)	╙ (211)	π (227)	≤ (243)
♦ (4)	¶ (20)	$ (36)	4 (52)	D (68)	T (84)	d (100)	t (116)	ä (132)	ö (148)	ñ (164)	┤ (180)	─ (196)	╘ (212)	Σ (228)	∫ (244)
♣ (5)	§ (21)	% (37)	5 (53)	E (69)	U (85)	e (101)	u (117)	à (133)	ò (149)	Ñ (165)	╡ (181)	┼ (197)	╒ (213)	σ (229)	⌡ (245)
♠ (6)	▬ (22)	& (38)	6 (54)	F (70)	V (86)	f (102)	v (118)	å (134)	û (150)	ª (166)	╢ (182)	╞ (198)	╓ (214)	µ (230)	÷ (246)
• (7)	↨ (23)	' (39)	7 (55)	G (71)	W (87)	g (103)	w (119)	ç (135)	ù (151)	º (167)	╖ (183)	╟ (199)	╫ (215)	τ (231)	≈ (247)
◘ (8)	↑ (24)	((40)	8 (56)	H (72)	X (88)	h (104)	x (120)	ê (136)	ÿ (152)	¿ (168)	╕ (184)	╚ (200)	╪ (216)	Φ (232)	° (248)
○ (9)	↓ (25)	) (41)	9 (57)	I (73)	Y (89)	i (105)	y (121)	ë (137)	Ö (153)	⌐ (169)	╣ (185)	╔ (201)	┘ (217)	Θ (233)	∙ (249)
◙ (10)	→ (26)	* (42)	: (58)	J (74)	Z (90)	j (106)	z (122)	è (138)	Ü (154)	¬ (170)	║ (186)	╩ (202)	┌ (218)	Ω (234)	· (250)
♂ (11)	← (27)	+ (43)	; (59)	K (75)	[(91)	k (107)	{ (123)	ï (139)	¢ (155)	½ (171)	╗ (187)	╦ (203)	█ (219)	δ (235)	√ (251)
♀ (12)	∟ (28)	, (44)	< (60)	L (76)	\ (92)	l (108)		(124)	î (140)	£ (156)	¼ (172)	╝ (188)	╠ (204)	▄ (220)	∞ (236)	ⁿ (252)
♪ (13)	↔ (29)	- (45)	= (61)	M (77)	] (93)	m (109)	} (125)	ì (141)	¥ (157)	¡ (173)	╜ (189)	═ (205)	▌ (221)	φ (237)	² (253)
♫ (14)	▲ (30)	. (46)	> (62)	N (78)	^ (94)	n (110)	~ (126)	Ä (142)	₧ (158)	« (174)	╛ (190)	╬ (206)	▐ (222)	∈ (238)	■ (254)
☼ (15)	▼ (31)	/ (47)	? (63)	O (79)	_ (95)	o (111)	⌂ (127)	Å (143)	ƒ (159)	» (175)	┐ (191)	╧ (207)	▀ (223)	∩ (239)	(255)

Symbol set code: PD   Full name: PC-8 Danish/Norwegian 253 characters.
Font name: Geneva Roman

▒ 0	► 16	▒ 32	0 48	@ 64	P 80	` 96	p 112	Ç 128	É 144	á 160	⁙ 176	└ 192	╨ 208	α 224	≡ 240
☺ 1	◄ 17	! 33	1 49	A 65	Q 81	a 97	q 113	ü 129	æ 145	í 161	▓ 177	┴ 193	╤ 209	ß 225	± 241
☻ 2	↕ 18	" 34	2 50	B 66	R 82	b 98	r 114	é 130	Æ 146	ó 162	▓ 178	┬ 194	╥ 210	Γ 226	≥ 242
♥ 3	‼ 19	# 35	3 51	C 67	S 83	c 99	s 115	â 131	ô 147	ú 163	│ 179	├ 195	╙ 211	π 227	≤ 243
♦ 4	¶ 20	$ 36	4 52	D 68	T 84	d 100	t 116	ä 132	ö 148	ñ 164	┤ 180	─ 196	╘ 212	Σ 228	⌠ 244
♣ 5	§ 21	% 37	5 53	E 69	U 85	e 101	u 117	à 133	ò 149	Ñ 165	╡ 181	┼ 197	╒ 213	σ 229	⌡ 245
♠ 6	▬ 22	& 38	6 54	F 70	V 86	f 102	v 118	å 134	û 150	õ 166	╢ 182	╞ 198	╓ 214	µ 230	÷ 246
• 7	↨ 23	' 39	7 55	G 71	W 87	g 103	w 119	ç 135	ù 151	Õ 167	╖ 183	╟ 199	╫ 215	τ 231	≈ 247
◘ 8	↑ 24	(40	8 56	H 72	X 88	h 104	x 120	ê 136	ÿ 152	¿ 168	╕ 184	╚ 200	╪ 216	Φ 232	° 248
○ 9	↓ 25	) 41	9 57	I 73	Y 89	i 105	y 121	ë 137	Ö 153	ã 169	╣ 185	╔ 201	┘ 217	Θ 233	∙ 249
◙ 10	→ 26	* 42	: 58	J 74	Z 90	j 106	z 122	è 138	Ü 154	Ã 170	║ 186	╩ 202	┌ 218	Ω 234	· 250
♂ 11	← 27	+ 43	; 59	K 75	[91	k 107	{ 123	ï 139	ø 155	ℓ 171	╗ 187	╤ 203	■ 219	δ 235	√ 251
♀ 12	└ 28	, 44	< 60	L 76	\ 92	l 108	| 124	î 140	£ 156	'n 172	╜ 188	╟ 204	■ 220	∞ 236	ⁿ 252
♪ 13	↔ 29	- 45	= 61	M 77	] 93	m 109	} 125	ì 141	Ø 157	¡ 173	╛ 189	= 205	■ 221	φ 237	^{2} 253
♫ 14	▲ 30	. 46	> 62	N 78	^ 94	n 110	~ 126	Ä 142	L· 158	^{3} 174	╝ 190	╫ 206	■ 222	ε 238	■ 254
☼ 15	▼ 31	/ 47	? 63	O 79	_ 95	o 111	⌂ 127	Å 143	I· 159	¤ 175	┐ 191	╧ 207	■ 223	∩ 239	▒ 255

			0 48	@ 64	P 80	` 96	p 112	128	144	160	° 176	À 192	Ð 208	à 224	ð 240
0	16	32	1 49	A 65	Q 81	a 97	q 113	129	145	¡ 161	± 177	Á 193	Ñ 209	á 225	ñ 241
1	17	33	! 33												
2	18	34	" 34	2 50	B 66	R 82	b 98	r 114	130	146	¢ 162	² 178	Â 194	Ò 210	â 226	ò 242
3	19	35	# 35	3 51	C 67	S 83	c 99	s 115	131	147	£ 163	³ 179	Ã 195	Ó 211	ã 227	ó 243
4	20	36	$ 36	4 52	D 68	T 84	d 100	t 116	132	148	¤ 164	´ 180	Ä 196	Ô 212	ä 228	ô 244
5	21	37	% 37	5 53	E 69	U 85	e 101	u 117	133	149	¥ 165	µ 181	Å 197	Õ 213	å 229	õ 245
6	22	38	& 38	6 54	F 70	V 86	f 102	v 118	134	150	¦ 166	¶ 182	Æ 198	Ö 214	æ 230	ö 246
7	23	39	' 39	7 55	G 71	W 87	g 103	w 119	135	151	§ 167	· 183	Ç 199	× 215	ç 231	÷ 247
8	24	40	(40	8 56	H 72	X 88	h 104	x 120	136	152	¨ 168	¸ 184	È 200	Ø 216	è 232	ø 248
9	25	41	) 41	9 57	I 73	Y 89	i 105	y 121	137	153	© 169	¹ 185	É 201	Ù 217	é 233	ù 249
10	26	42	* 42	: 58	J 74	Z 90	j 106	z 122	138	154	ª 170	º 186	Ê 202	Ú 218	ê 234	ú 250
11	27	43	+ 43	; 59	K 75	[91	k 107	{ 123	139	155	« 171	» 187	Ë 203	Û 219	ë 235	û 251
12	28	44	, 44	< 60	L 76	\ 92	l 108		124	140	156	¬ 172	¼ 188	Ì 204	Ü 220	ì 236	ü 252
13	29	45	- 45	= 61	M 77	] 93	m 109	} 125	141	157	- 173	½ 189	Í 205	Ý 221	í 237	ý 253
14	30	46	. 46	> 62	N 78	^ 94	n 110	~ 126	142	158	® 174	¾ 190	Î 206	Þ 222	î 238	þ 254
15	31	47	/ 47	? 63	O 79	_ 95	o 111	▓ 127	143	159	¯ 175	¿ 191	Ï 207	ß 223	ï 239	ÿ 255

Symbol set code: U2 Full name: ISO 2: IRV   95 characters.
Font name: Geneva Roman

0	16	32	0 48	@ 64	P 80	` 96	p 112	128	144	160	176	192	208	224	240
1	17	! 33	1 49	A 65	Q 81	a 97	q 113	129	145	161	177	193	209	225	241
2	18	" 34	2 50	B 66	R 82	b 98	r 114	130	146	162	178	194	210	226	242
3	19	# 35	3 51	C 67	S 83	c 99	s 115	131	147	163	179	195	211	227	243
4	20	¤ 36	4 52	D 68	T 84	d 100	t 116	132	148	164	180	196	212	228	244
5	21	% 37	5 53	E 69	U 85	e 101	u 117	133	149	165	181	197	213	229	245
6	22	& 38	6 54	F 70	V 86	f 102	v 118	134	150	166	182	198	214	230	246
7	23	' 39	7 55	G 71	W 87	g 103	w 119	135	151	167	183	199	215	231	247
8	24	(40	8 56	H 72	X 88	h 104	x 120	136	152	168	184	200	216	232	248
9	25	) 41	9 57	I 73	Y 89	i 105	y 121	137	153	169	185	201	217	233	249
10	26	* 42	: 58	J 74	Z 90	j 106	z 122	138	154	170	186	202	218	234	250
11	27	+ 43	; 59	K 75	[91	k 107	{ 123	139	155	171	187	203	219	235	251
12	28	, 44	< 60	L 76	\ 92	l 108	| 124	140	156	172	188	204	220	236	252
13	29	- 45	= 61	M 77	] 93	m 109	} 125	141	157	173	189	205	221	237	253
14	30	. 46	> 62	N 78	^ 94	n 110	‾ 126	142	158	174	190	206	222	238	254
15	31	/ 47	? 63	O 79	_ 95	o 111	▓ 127	143	159	175	191	207	223	239	255

0	**16**	**32**	0 48	@ 64	P 80	` 96	p 112	**128**	**144**	**160**	**176**	**192**	**208**	**224**	**240**
1	**17**	! 33	1 49	A 65	Q 81	a 97	q 113	**129**	**145**	**161**	**177**	**193**	**209**	**225**	**241**
2	**18**	" 34	2 50	B 66	R 82	b 98	r 114	**130**	**146**	**162**	**178**	**194**	**210**	**226**	**242**
3	**19**	# 35	3 51	C 67	S 83	c 99	s 115	**131**	**147**	**163**	**179**	**195**	**211**	**227**	**243**
4	**20**	¤ 36	4 52	D 68	T 84	d 100	t 116	**132**	**148**	**164**	**180**	**196**	**212**	**228**	**244**
5	**21**	% 37	5 53	E 69	U 85	e 101	u 117	**133**	**149**	**165**	**181**	**197**	**213**	**229**	**245**
6	**22**	& 38	6 54	F 70	V 86	f 102	v 118	**134**	**150**	**166**	**182**	**198**	**214**	**230**	**246**
7	**23**	' 39	7 55	G 71	W 87	g 103	w 119	**135**	**151**	**167**	**183**	**199**	**215**	**231**	**247**
8	**24**	(40	8 56	H 72	X 88	h 104	x 120	**136**	**152**	**168**	**184**	**200**	**216**	**232**	**248**
9	**25**	) 41	9 57	I 73	Y 89	i 105	y 121	**137**	**153**	**169**	**185**	**201**	**217**	**233**	**249**
10	**26**	* 42	: 58	J 74	Z 90	j 106	z 122	**138**	**154**	**170**	**186**	**202**	**218**	**234**	**250**
11	**27**	+ 43	; 59	K 75	Ä 91	k 107	ä 123	**139**	**155**	**171**	**187**	**203**	**219**	**235**	**251**
12	**28**	, 44	< 60	L 76	Ö 92	l 108	ö 124	**140**	**156**	**172**	**188**	**204**	**220**	**236**	**252**
13	**29**	- 45	= 61	M 77	Å 93	m 109	å 125	**141**	**157**	**173**	**189**	**205**	**221**	**237**	**253**
14	**30**	. 46	> 62	N 78	^ 94	n 110	‾ 126	**142**	**158**	**174**	**190**	**206**	**222**	**238**	**254**
15	**31**	/ 47	? 63	O 79	_ 95	o 111	▓ 127	**143**	**159**	**175**	**191**	**207**	**223**	**239**	**255**

Symbol set code: JS Full name: ISO 14: JIS ASCII   95 characters.
Font name: Geneva Roman

0	16	32	48	64	80	96	112	128	144	160	176	192	208	224	240
			0	@	P	`	p	128	144	160	176	192	208	224	240
0	16	32	48	64	80	96	112								
		!	1	A	Q	a	q	129	145	161	177	193	209	225	241
1	17	33	49	65	81	97	113								
		"	2	B	R	b	r	130	146	162	178	194	210	226	242
2	18	34	50	66	82	98	114								
		#	3	C	S	c	s	131	147	163	179	195	211	227	243
3	19	35	51	67	83	99	115								
		$	4	D	T	d	t	132	148	164	180	196	212	228	244
4	20	36	52	68	84	100	116								
		%	5	E	U	e	u	133	149	165	181	197	213	229	245
5	21	37	53	69	85	101	117								
		&	6	F	V	f	v	134	150	166	182	198	214	230	246
6	22	38	54	70	86	102	118								
		'	7	G	W	g	w	135	151	167	183	199	215	231	247
7	23	39	55	71	87	103	119								
		(	8	H	X	h	x	136	152	168	184	200	216	232	248
8	24	40	56	72	88	104	120								
		)	9	I	Y	i	y	137	153	169	185	201	217	233	249
9	25	41	57	73	89	105	121								
		*	:	J	Z	j	z	138	154	170	186	202	218	234	250
10	26	42	58	74	90	106	122								
		+	;	K	[	k	{	139	155	171	187	203	219	235	251
11	27	43	59	75	91	107	123								
		,	<	L	¥	l	|	140	156	172	188	204	220	236	252
12	28	44	60	76	92	108	124								
		-	=	M	]	m	}	141	157	173	189	205	221	237	253
13	29	45	61	77	93	109	125								
		.	>	N	^	n	‾	142	158	174	190	206	222	238	254
14	30	46	62	78	94	110	126								
		/	?	O	_	o	▓	143	159	175	191	207	223	239	255
15	31	47	63	79	95	111	127								

0	16	32	0 48	§ 64	P 80	` 96	p 112	128	144	160	176	192	208	224	240
1	17	! 33	1 49	A 65	Q 81	a 97	q 113	129	145	161	177	193	209	225	241
2	18	" 34	2 50	B 66	R 82	b 98	r 114	130	146	162	178	194	210	226	242
3	19	# 35	3 51	C 67	S 83	c 99	s 115	131	147	163	179	195	211	227	243
4	20	$ 36	4 52	D 68	T 84	d 100	t 116	132	148	164	180	196	212	228	244
5	21	% 37	5 53	E 69	U 85	e 101	u 117	133	149	165	181	197	213	229	245
6	22	& 38	6 54	F 70	V 86	f 102	v 118	134	150	166	182	198	214	230	246
7	23	' 39	7 55	G 71	W 87	g 103	w 119	135	151	167	183	199	215	231	247
8	24	(40	8 56	H 72	X 88	h 104	x 120	136	152	168	184	200	216	232	248
9	25	) 41	9 57	I 73	Y 89	i 105	y 121	137	153	169	185	201	217	233	249
10	26	* 42	: 58	J 74	Z 90	j 106	z 122	138	154	170	186	202	218	234	250
11	27	+ 43	; 59	K 75	Ã 91	k 107	ã 123	139	155	171	187	203	219	235	251
12	28	, 44	< 60	L 76	Ç 92	l 108	ç 124	140	156	172	188	204	220	236	252
13	29	- 45	= 61	M 77	Õ 93	m 109	õ 125	141	157	173	189	205	221	237	253
14	30	. 46	> 62	N 78	^ 94	n 110	° 126	142	158	174	190	206	222	238	254
15	31	/ 47	? 63	O 79	_ 95	o 111	▨ 127	143	159	175	191	207	223	239	255

Appendix B

Resources
¢

Hewlett-Packard Telephone Numbers

- Technical support and repairs 208/323-2551
- Hewlett-Packard DeskJet drivers 303/353-7650
- Other supplies and accessories 800/538-8787
- Information, local dealer location 800/752-0900

DeskNews

Elfring Soft Fonts publishes *DeskNews*, a DeskJet newsletter containing news, tips, and miscellany. For information, call 708/377-3520, or write Elfring Soft Fonts, P.O. Box 61, Wasco, IL 60183.

Index

M

N

O

P